Biting Off More Than I Can Chew

Biting Off More Than I Can Chew

A MAVERICK CHEF REMEMBERS

RAHUL AKERKAR

HarperCollins *Publishers* India

First published in India by HarperCollins *Publishers* 2026
HarperCollins *Publishers* India, Cyber City,
Building 10-A, Gurugram, Haryana – 122002, India
www.harpercollins.co.in

2 4 6 8 10 9 7 5 3 1

Photos courtesy of the author
Illustrations by Camila Giraldo

P-ISBN: 978-93-5629-652-7
E-ISBN: 978-93-5629-653-4

Typeset in 11.5/15.2 Arno Pro
by HarperCollins *Publishers* India Pvt. Ltd

Printed and bound at
Magic International Pvt. Ltd., Greater Noida, India

MIX
Paper from responsible sources
FSC® C120105

This book is produced from independently certified FSC® paper to ensure responsible forest management.

HarperCollins *Publishers*, Macken House, 39/40 Mayor Street Upper, Dublin 1, D01 C9W8, Ireland

CONTENTS

FOREWORD

IN 1988 WHEN I joined the staff of the then three-year-old Union Square Cafe in New York as executive chef, I knew almost nothing about Indian cuisine and could probably count on one hand the times I had dined on the food of the subcontinent. One of my earlier memories came from 1982 when I was working as chef de cuisine at the renowned Chez Max restaurant in Zurich, Switzerland. I accompanied the chef and proprietor, Max Kehl, to The Dorchester hotel in London to help prepare a gala dinner. After it was all over, the hotel manager took us all out for dinner to his 'favourite restaurant', which happened to be Indian. I recall the place offering, to put it mildly, very little in the way of decor. But the food was a marvel! It was probably the spiciest food I had tasted to date, and a true revelation.

Back in New York, I began exploring the multitude of Indian eateries right in my Murray Hill neighbourhood, an area so dense with Indian restaurants and food shops it was nicknamed Curry Hill! I was converted. So much so that these combined experiences finally led me to embark on an extensive culinary tour of India in early 1995 to deepen my understanding and appreciation of its culture and cuisines.

Upon my return to New York, at a friend's dinner, I met Avantika Akerkar or 'Tiki', as everyone called her—Rahul's extremely talented and vivacious sister. We met several times thereafter and I fondly remember her continued enthusiasm as she spoke about her brother who, she related, also had a great passion for food and cooking. She thought Rahul and I would have much to discuss if we ever met.

She wasn't wrong. Avantika informed me one day that her brother would be in NYC, and would it be okay for me to meet him and perhaps have him take a look around my kitchen? As you will discover in this wonderful book (in words I found extremely kind and flattering), Rahul came to my kitchen in the fall of 1997 and worked his way around the stations, soaking up as much knowledge as he could. But what I most vividly recall are the talks we would have about food, cooking and running restaurants. I could feel that he was driven and would not settle for less than opening and operating his own innovative, fine-quality establishments. I was impressed by the seriousness evident in him, yet I never got the sense of an overbearing ego or heard any braggadocio on his part about what he had already accomplished. There was just this intense desire to learn and absorb all he possibly could. Oh, and no lack of chutzpah either!

And that leads me to what a revelation this book has been. Rahul writes in an open, almost breezy, familiar style, which immediately brings the reader into the 'inner circle' of his life and his adventures, culinary and otherwise. The prose is joyful, intimate, at times risqué, like sitting around a food-and-wine-laden table with an old friend and listening to him recount the amazing twists and turns of his fascinating life. Having also met Rahul's parents, I was moved to learn the history of his family in greater depth, especially as it relates to the origins of his passion for food and cooking. The reader can share in Rahul's early exploration of ingredients in his grandmother's garden, and revel, as he does, in each new experience of texture, colour and taste. I found my mouth watering! His deep respect for food and tradition and his devotion to his family comes through these tales of his parents and grandparents, so lovingly related. Learning of Rahul's studies in biology and biochemical engineering and the work he accomplished before deciding to become a restaurateur made me feel like I was exploring multiple facets of his personality previously unknown to me. As I learnt here that he was so accomplished in other, quite divergent, fields, I better understood how the path Rahul eventually decided upon was definitely the result of a bold choice and not merely a necessity. Some of my favourite parts of the book relate to the story of Rahul's extremely eclectic training as a cook. He writes with great wit and humour about the various positions he undertook, the famous and infamous chefs that he worked under and the establishments in which he was employed. The richness and variety of these experiences make for truly fascinating reading and clearly helped mould the inspired chef and restaurateur Rahul has become. His story unfolds as an almost picaresque tale, written in an always heartfelt, often hilarious and extremely entertaining manner.

I also found it extremely pleasing to see the attention paid in the book to the understanding and service of wine. I have long felt that no chef's training is complete without a certain level of knowledge of wine and this is a sentiment that Rahul clearly shares. His ground-breaking work in opening the minds and palates of his guests in a country that did not have a strong tradition of wine-drinking is nothing short of awe-inspiring. You will enjoy reading how his team's wine programme, as with so many of its efforts, goes on to win a plethora of coveted awards.

As we read further, we discover that the chef's toque is not the only hat our author has worn—far from it. Rahul invites us along on a detailed, at times exuberant, at times harrowing, journey through the trials and travails of what it takes to actually open a restaurant—or two or three. I believe Rahul's writing on the subject will serve as an excellent Baedeker for any young entrepreneur who has set his or her sights on becoming a restaurateur. Being no stranger to opening restaurants myself, I marvelled at the extraordinary twists and turns that beset Rahul, his wife Malini and their team as they negotiated the rollercoaster ride that is permits, payoffs, landlords, dishonesty, even downright treachery. The book takes us up to the unprecedented challenge of a devastating pandemic, the havoc it wreaked on the restaurant world and after. But through it all, most importantly, one can sense Rahul's joy of accomplishment, how justifiably proud he is of having become an independent thinker, a standard-bearer and an industry leader.

And blended into all these fascinating ingredients are the recipes. On a personal note, it is so gratifying for me to have access not only to Rahul's entrepreneurial tales but also to his culinary creativity. It's about coming full circle: I once had Rahul in my kitchen to show him what I did and why, and now I get the opportunity to learn from his experience. I know these recipes will excite and broaden my interest in Indian cuisine, as interpreted by a highly talented, cutting-edge practitioner. As he states, Rahul is not so concerned about labelling his food Indian or Western or some fusion of the two—it is cooking from the heart, informed by all the myriad influences he has had. Having the recipes, as well as various menus, interspersed throughout the text was like taking a break in the journey and punctuating the pause with creative, delicious, approachable food. Truly a superb strategy for writing a work that is sure to stimulate the senses on so many levels.

In the end, I leave it to you, the reader, to decide whether Rahul Akerkar does indeed bite off more than he can chew, but I can assure you, you're in for an extremely satisfying and delicious adventure, no matter what.

Michael Romano
Chef and restaurateur
Union Square Hospitality Group

INTRODUCTION

The Making of a Chef: A Mother's Long View

RAHUL IS MY FIRST-BORN. I'm convinced that right from the moment of conception, he knew what he wanted and wasted no time in doing or getting it. He gave me an easy pregnancy and an express delivery: four hours from first pain to last swab. Looking at his current avatar, it is hard to imagine that he was born with a forest of dark curls on his head.

He was a friendly, smiley baby, loved people, but could also amuse himself alone for hours, sitting in his gated playpen in the middle of our living room, with any type of building or assembling toy. He had an immense curiosity about the world around him; the unending questions, most of them quite logical, drove his father and me around the bend. 'Why doesn't this caterpillar have arms and a neck? How will he walk up the stairs? Who is sitting inside the wall, putting on lightbulbs when you hit a switch? If I put my fingers into the holes of this [wall plug], will my head also light up? What makes a car start and run when all you do is turn a key?'

You get the idea. We tried to answer everything as logically as we could, which only led to more questions.

He was an early talker but a late walker. Why bother when he could crawl? And could he crawl! He was like the wind-up toys or battery-operated cars that zip off as soon as you release the brake. And he didn't just laugh while doing that; he cackled. One minute he was on the floor in front of you examining a dead moth; the next you heard his gleeful cackle at the other end of the hallway. His traditional tricycle bored him quickly, but the spiffy pedal-operated car he got for his birthday made him a danger to mankind. He turned corners deftly without hitting anything, but to see him barrelling towards you at full speed could be scary.

He took his first independent steps in my parents' home in Manhattan. We had a sunken living room with two steps and an antique wrought-iron spiral railing. One day, Rahul crawled up to the steps, tried to figure out how to get down to visit his Opa (Grandpa in German), turned himself around and slid down the two steps, got hold of the railing and stood up. I had come out of the kitchen to see where he was and watched in wonder as he attempted his first upright steps. Liking the feeling, he tottered towards Opa, who was comfortably ensconced in his favourite armchair in front of the TV, a cigar in one hand and a small post-prandial cognac in the other, his traditional digestif. Opa smiled and encouraged Rahul to come up, and so he did. Rahul put his hands on a large coffee table with a thick plate of glass in the centre, picked up a sharp-edged crystal ashtray, cackled with glee, and brought the ashtray down with a bang ... unfortunately with the sharp corner down, shattering the glass plate into a spiderweb pattern. Dead silence. Mom and I held our breaths, waiting for the explosion, but all that came out of Dad's mouth in German was, 'Claire, look at what your grandson has done. You better get it cleaned up.' We fled to the kitchen and burst out laughing. We both had the same thought: had it been me as a child, I would have had my bottom soundly spanked!

I brought little Rahul back to New York when he was three years old, as my husband Anand and I made a short trip to California, leaving him with my parents. We found a very creative summer nursery school near my parents' home, where he had a joyous time with children of different ethnic backgrounds. This gave my mother a bit of respite during the day. One day, after we'd returned to NY from California, when I was picking him up at school, the teacher asked me whether he suffered from depression. I said no and asked why. She showed me a hand painting from that morning: a sheet of paper totally covered in grey. Parents had been told never to ask their children 'What is this?' but instead, 'Tell me about your painting.' So I appropriately asked my son. He looked at me quite disdainfully, stating with authority, 'Mom, don't you know what Bombay looks like in the monsoon?'

I brought him back to New York every couple of years, either alone or along with his younger sister, Avantika. We would spend the entire summer vacation months with my parents. One year we had to spend extra time in the city, so I got him admitted into the fourth grade of a local public school across the street from my parents' home. He settled in well and used to come home for lunch. One day, he brought a young African American boy with him, and asked whether his friend could have lunch with us. When school ended around 3 p.m., he came home and told me that his buddy couldn't go home for lunch, as he had been bussed from a distant neighbourhood in Harlem, then largely African American. He just couldn't understand what bussing represented and was angry that his friend had nowhere to eat lunch but in class. This sense of equality and doing the right thing has stayed with him into his adult life, and he still gets outraged by discrimination of any kind.

Back in India, he had a happy school life at Bombay International School (BIS), made many close friends, but when he was in the sixth grade, Anand announced that Rahul would be sitting for the Doon School entrance exam. Apparently, unbeknownst to me, Anand (a Dosco himself) had put down our son's name on the waiting list the day after he was born. I was not happy, and neither was Rahul. He showed his unhappiness by purposely failing the exam. I was secretly delighted and made the mistake of telling this to my father-in-law, who proceeded to give me a severe lecture (actually a tongue-lashing) on spoiling children. I was in tears and asked Rahul to sit for the exam the following year and pass it. He did; he passed and unenthusiastically got ready to leave home, aged eleven. I made him a solemn promise, in-law lectures or not, that if after a full year he was unhappy in boarding school, I would bring him back to Bombay and BIS. But it had to be one full year. He was rather miserable the first semester, hated the food, hated the rather spartan accommodations, missed the comforts of home, his friends, the excitement of Bombay life and threatened to run away. But at the end of the first year when he came home, he had no complaints and when I gingerly asked him if he wanted to stay on in Dehradun, he gave me another of his disdainful looks. So that was that. He graduated from Doon School with high marks in the sciences and maths, with a love of the great outdoors, a body used to assorted sports and another set of friends.

Then came a period of college applications to the US. Because the Indian system had only eleven years of schooling, instead of the American twelve-year system, he started college at St. Xavier's in Bombay while waiting for replies from American colleges. With a couple of classmates, he set up a mini lab at home, and we had the 'joy' of staring at opened frogs, dissected roaches and other lab specimens. My husband was a lot more squeamish than I and stopped going into Rahul's room altogether.

College in Bombay bored Rahul as it was mostly rote learning and keeping journals, and discouraged questioning. When his acceptance into the excellent Franklin & Marshall College in Lancaster, Pennsylvania, arrived, he couldn't wait to go to the US of A. His first-year roommate Niccolo was half-American and half-Italian, and the boys became very close friends.

Rahul blossomed at F&M, did well in his major pre-med studies, and came under the wing of a wonderful professor of philosophy. For a boy who read mostly comics at school, except for prescribed class reading, he suddenly was getting top marks in philosophy and made the subject his minor. He took part in sports and cultural activities, and found his way into the kitchen of Jethro's, a well-known restaurant in Lancaster, for an exciting part-time job. He's told that story himself later in the book. I'll just say, without giving away the plot, that when his boss asked him to produce a decent Indian meal, there were a number of frantic phone calls to me in India, asking for his beloved Aji's (Marathi for grandmother) recipes. Aji was a superb instinctive cook, with no idea of measured quantities. It was a little of this, a pinch of that and a fistful of thus. I set our cook the task of following Aji around my kitchen, trying to figure out quantities in teaspoons and tablespoons, and then teletyped everything to Rahul in Pennsylvanian (this was pre-internet, pre-email, pre-fax days). He'll tell you the rest, but I just wanted to plug my own rescue mission for my first offspring. There was an encore with more of Aji's teletyped recipes, and then he graduated.

His original goal was to study medicine and become a surgeon—one of the reasons he picked F&M College, which had a highly rated pre-med programme. Unfortunately, my whole family suffers from a familial tremor of the hands, and when I asked him to hold out his hand one day, it was obvious that that annoying condition had landed on his doorstep as well. I told him bluntly that I would be afraid to trust him with a scalpel on any part of my body and he reluctantly agreed. But science was in his blood and he was very good in maths and physics, so he enrolled in Columbia University in New York City and obtained a BS in chemical engineering. That didn't satisfy him either and he went on to get an MS in biochemical engineering, also at Columbia University. Having found his direction in the sciences, he embarked upon a PhD at Columbia. He has himself narrated in the pages of this book what happened to that programme and also how he morphed into an avid participant in the food and hospitality industry.

In 1987, he announced that he wanted to return to India and open a restaurant. I pointed out that while he knew a lot about food, he didn't have much experience in running a restaurant. He agreed and joined a team of young managers in training at the very popular restaurant and bar, The Saloon, rotating into all the departments of this beautifully located eatery opposite Lincoln Center in NYC. In 1989 he felt he had learned enough and came back to India.

He had precious little to start a restaurant in Bombay. Then a friend challenged him to prepare a meal for a party. Out came the white chef's toque, the starched white coat and the magnificent set of chef knives he had brought with him, including my own butcher and meat-store-owner grandfather's full silver handled carving set, still in perfect condition.

The party food was a huge success, and there followed a period of insanely frenetic gigs catering to society homes, all prepared in our kitchen, with the assistance of fourth-year students from the IHM Catering College on Cadell Road. We occasionally were the beneficiaries of the good food, and it was GOOD and innovative.

One day in May, Rahul announced he had been asked to prepare a vegetarian continental lunch for 300 for a society wedding reception. I casually asked him about the menu and was informed even more casually that it would be lasagna and four cold salads. I even more casually told him that good lasagna pasta was not really available in Bombay (it was 1990, after all) and that our domestic refrigerator was not in a position to support four salads for 300 overnight. Ever more nonchalantly, I was informed that he had brought a non-electric manual pasta machine on which he would grind out his lasagna sheets.

Me: For 300 people?

R: No probs ...

Me: You know, of course, that the pasta has to be dried before it can be used?

R: No probs...

Me: And four salads for 300?

R: No probs. I bought four 40-litre plastic buckets, we have an empty bedroom, I'll turn the AC on full and the fan on high, and the buckets will be kept underneath overnight.

Anand and I were leaving for the US the next day and we went out on last-minute errands, dreading our return to our house. With good reason: we ran into a curtain of drying lasagna sheets strung across our large living room, with our light-blue durrie considerately rolled up in a corner. I so wish I had taken a picture. On our way to the bedroom, we passed a frigid zone in which four big plastic laundry buckets were enjoying a cool night, filled with a German potato salad, my favourite Sunshine salad, and a couple of others I can't remember. Total jugaad!

We took off the next evening and on arrival in NYC, got a jubilant phone call from Bombay's new rising chef—the food was a huge success, and he was launched. But before that, there was:

R: Oh, Mom, I need to redo the kitchen so I can cater properly.

Me: My kitchen?

R: Of course.

Me: And who will pay for that, please?

R: It's YOUR kitchen after all. (I said it earlier; he was logical!)

Me: I still have to use my kitchen and I'm shorter than you ... no counter higher than 36 inches, please.

R: Sure.

I came back to a beautifully designed kitchen (for catering) with the wooden shelves and drawers at 36 inches, BUT with a thick granite top over the whole area, which was uncomfortable for me afterwards.

Rahul always seemed happiest when 'elbow deep in the pasta bowl'. He always passionately loved—and loves—good, clean food, and imagined flavours in his head before trying new combinations in the kitchen. He set—and sets—very high standards for himself and his staff, in his search for ingredients (even if the price is on the higher side); and guest-oriented service is primary for him. This search for excellence has paid off in the success of his restaurants.

In this introduction, I merely wanted to share a mother's-eye-view of the formative years of a rambunctious Bombay boy who became an iconic chef. Consider this essay, admittedly sentimental but accurately recorded, an amuse-bouche to the feast you will devour in his autobiography, *Biting Off More Than I Can Chew*.

Jinx Akerkar
11 July 2025

1: MY COOKING SEEDS WERE PLANTED IN MY GRANDMOTHER'S GARDEN

beef
tenderloin
basil oil
cured egg
yolk
pickled shimeji
mushrooms

'De gustibus non disputandum est.'
(In matters of taste, there can be no dispute.)
—Ancient Latin adage

ALMOST EVERY GREAT CHEF'S story begins in his grandmother's kitchen—from the multi-Michelin-starred French chef Alain Ducasse to the Ethiopian-born innovative chef Marcus Samuelsson to so many others. That's not surprising, since those smells wafting from Grandma's usually small and simple kitchen are indelibly imprinted somewhere in our brains, as the olfactory nerve holds memory the longest of all our senses. And what is more comforting, more familiar and familial than Aji's homemade breads and curries?

My story is no different, but that is where all the similarities end. Because, except for my Aji, there were zero signs I would become a chef, much less a respected and successful chef, despite all odds, despite people's fickle food tastes, despite the industry itself.

So how did a nice, shy, severely stuttering Jewish Hindu boy—educated at the prestigious Doon School in Dehradun, India, and the small Franklin & Marshall College in Pennsylvania, tracked from an early age for a career in medicine (biology?), who attained a master's degree in biochemical engineering from Columbia University in New York City while working summers at restaurants there—become an innovative, award-winning, trend-breaking and trendsetting chef known for his outspokenness (not unique in India) and integrity (unique in India) at what was generally acknowledged as India's first stand-alone restaurant serving Western food of a calibre the country had not tasted?

And why?

That, my new BFF (Best Foodie Friend), is the culinary adventure you are about to embark on, page by page, app by app, entrée by entrée, dessert by dessert, hopefully glass by hand-selected glass, chosen by my personal sommelier just for you.

Along the way, I'll dish on the ups and down, ins and outs, the good, bad and ugly of the business of restaurants. My story is replete with tawdry tales, near-scandalous encounters, juicy anecdotes about the great host of celebrities and dignitaries whose bellies I have filled, magic gustatory moments that have inspired me, great food epiphanies garnered from around the world, some personal and trade secrets—and recipes to accompany them all.

You will also get a behind-the-scenes glimpse of Qualia, the restaurant I opened in 2019, as it began to take shape in my mind and on my palate. I'll share the literal soup to nuts of how one goes about opening a new restaurant in India, with all its stops and starts and hits and misses. As I am known for my brutal honesty, I will divulge details ... with some discretion.

But you know what? If you can't live in truth, on the edge, why bother at all?

And while you may have read about me in newspapers and magazines over the years, those profiles skim the surface of what really makes me tick and how that all feeds the chef I've become—not to mention the husband, the father and the planetary citizen I've become. In this book, I plumb the depths of my admittedly unusual but compelling psyche to share what informs my cooking, my personal motivations, my insights about Man and Nature ... and, ultimately, what ends up on your plate at any of my eating establishments.

But first, my grandmother.

Radha Redkar, my father's mother, was married to Krishnarao Akerkar, a civil engineer responsible for building many of Maharashtra's highways. That side of my lineage has roots in the tiny village of Akeri (thus Akerkar), in the Konkan coastal region of southern Maharashtra, some 400 km from the city of my birth, Bombay (now Mumbai). How they ended up there would require another book; they were long gone from there by the time I arrived on the scene, though it's clear Radha's taste buds remembered it well. They had retired to Nashik, a small town (at the time). In my family, it's famous for the gardens that surrounded my grandparents' house and the food that came out of my Aji's kitchen. Not surprisingly, considering the climate and the rich soil, it went on to become India's major wine capital, hosting twenty-two of our country's forty-six wineries, and several wine festivals, such as SulaFest.

As a kid, come summer I would be shipped off either to New York (where my mother's parents lived) or Nashik. It could have been for only two weeks but it felt like all summer to a little boy. One big thrill was that I got to play with a bunch of other kids, the children of our driver and gardener. It was a dream come true: like Peter Pan's Lost Boys in Neverland, we created a fantasy world of cops and robbers, high seas pirates and superheroes, building hideaways and treehouses.

The theatre for all this was the 2-acre garden surrounding my grandparents' bungalow, named after my father, 'Prayag'. That is where it all began for me as a food lover as well. It was an eater's Eden. A veritable cornucopia, this proverbial horn of plenty and plenitude served as the source of almost all my grandparents' produce. They grew guava, banana, papaya, watermelon, pumpkin, gourds and chikoo, with its mysterious big black seed hidden inside.

And mangoes. My lord, were there mangoes. There must have been half a dozen varieties that I can remember—Alphonso, Pairi, Totapuri, Langra, Mankurad, Chausa—and more I can't recall. We would find a ripe Pairi, pluck it from the tree, and massage the pulp through the outside skin until it was pulverized. Then we'd bite off the cap and suck out the sweet pulp, sitting in the tree. It may have been my first mango smoothie.

In Aja's arms with Aji, walking in the Nashik garden

We would take the leaves from the papaya tree and make flutes out of the hollow, reedy stems; from the banana tree, we would roll strips of leaves tightly and blow into them to make an annoying clarinet or shehnai sound that bugged the hell out of any adult within earshot.

Yup, you could say we were playing with our food. But what fun it was!

We did all kinds of creative and wacky boy things like that. Catch dragonflies, tie one end of a piece of string to their tails and the other around a finger and drag them around, still flying, as if they were our pet dogs. Terrible stuff—I'm afraid to even think of the karma I incurred. But we had an excuse: we were young boys with the whole otherwise boring summer to fill.

Cashew trees lined one section of the garden, and my Aji used their nuts in many dishes. I identify the taste of those milky nuts with her, so much so that she comes to mind every time I bite into one or taste it in a dish. And I use them frequently in my own recipes too.

There was every kind of flower, and beehives from which we ate honey, as sweet and fresh a nectar as I've ever had. I recall a row of Gulmohar trees forming a canopy of bright red, under which we would pretend to fight battles with the woody sword-like bean that hung from their branches.

But inside the kitchen was where the real magic took place.

How does a grandmother become a great cook? Simple: she cooks. And cooks. I highly recommend it to neophyte chefs. It seemed as if the only thing my Aji did was cook. She did so without resentment or resignation, without complaint and jealousy that everyone else was outside having fun. This was her passion, her sadhana. More than loving her food, it was this quality of hers that I respected the most. And while becoming a chef was nowhere in my consciousness at that time, I must have squirelled away that idea for some future. In truth, one of my great regrets is that by the time I had gotten serious about cooking, she was gone. I'm sure she's cooking up a storm wherever she is.

Though the undisputed master of the kitchen, she was a slight woman, petite, almost frail. She was kind and had a serenity about her presence that I think came from her spiritual devotion. When she wasn't in the kitchen, she was in what she called her God room, a traditional Indian puja space within the home where statues and photos of various deities cluttered her beautiful old sandalwood altar. There was Ganapati, Shiva, Durga, Krishna and others in various avatars, and occupying pride of place, her guru, Shri Dattatreya—an ascetic monk venerated as a God, representative of the Hindu trilogy of Shiva, Vishnu and Brahma.

I used to sit in that room with her as she meditated and prayed. Like her, I would sit on a small wooden puja chowki or paat—a stool low to the ground. With a busy mind like mine (or any nine-year-old boy's), I could not concentrate enough to attain a calm centre. Instead, my eye would focus on the columns of black ants on the walls that inevitably invaded the room, lured by the flowers, fruit and the sweet prasad she placed on the altar. I'd pass the time annihilating the invaders one by one with my pointer finger, unaware of how much bad karma I was invoking.

But my Aji knew. She'd turn to me and say, 'They have as much right to be here as you do. They are taking care of their families in the same way I am taking care of ours.' It was her simple way of explaining ahimsa, the Hindu principle of non-violence, of showing respect for all living things and avoiding doing harm towards others. She would tell me stories from the Ramayana and Mahabharata, allegorical tales of morality and courage that my little mind took in deeply. In fact, I got a good chunk of my spirituality from her, which helped me develop a sense of right practice.

She was also patient—a life lesson, on the other hand, I did not take away. She loved animals; was a sucker for any animal.

'All animals are creatures of God, all have souls,' she'd say. I am *like that only* as well. Even as I yell at people on the phone, I am petting my dear beagles Riley and Spud.

It was for her gentle style of imparting wisdom, perhaps even more than her cooking, that I felt a deep kinship with her. No matter how immature I was at that age, I got where she was coming from and these concepts, like the smells originating from her kitchen, stay with me till this day.

Gentleman Spud and young Riley

She made everything by hand. She would churn fresh white butter in a large ceramic jar with an old, well-used, four-foot-long wooden churner that was agitated by pulling back and forth on a rope wrapped several times around the centre spindle. From time to time, I would help and I got a kick out of seeing my effort of pulling the rope back and forth resulting in this edible dairy product. One time I churned a little too violently and the milk contents spewed out of the container all over the place.

'You're making butter,' she would gently remind me, 'not churning the ocean like the Devas looking for amrita,' referring to the Mahabharata.

She pickled anything and everything, made jams of the fruits and stored them all in her pantry through all the seasons, and she did it all with the most basic of kitchenware and appliances. She had an old and well-worn Primus stove, one of those kerosene contraptions used for high-pressure flame cooking that seemed to serve her just as well as the modern professional multi-burner stoves I came to know. She also used a traditional wood-burning stove seen in so many village homes across India: a longish structure made from brick and dried cow dung, with holes interspaced at regular intervals where the brass and copper cooking vessels sit above the burning wood and coal beneath.

With Aji in the Nashik house

Though she was a self-described vegetarian, that did not exclude eating fish—as would be expected from a Konkan coast native. After all, fish is often called fruit of the sea. But she cooked meat and chicken for everyone else, and with great skill, considering she probably never tasted them.

I equally loved her chuda, chaklis, karanjis, kadbole, kurmura chi ladoo, and pedhas.

Perhaps even more primal than what I learned about Western cuisine from my years in the United States, these tastes, flavours, smells and memories inform what and how I cook. And while the food pundits can dissect my dishes to discern whether I have Indianized Western cuisine or Westernized Indian cuisine, I can say for a fact that these early influences in Nashik are the baseline palette that colour my palate. I can also say that my palate, so international in experience and training, does not distinguish between East and West, as I do not distinguish people by their ethnic background or country of origin. Humans eat, is all I know, and I like to feed everyone without judgement or discrimination.

Throughout this book I will share many recipes, each connecting to a personal episode in my life, several drawn directly from my Aji's. At the end of this chapter, there's one, kairas or kairi curry, that became wildly popular at my restaurant Indigo.

For me, this dish was the perfect expression of Aji's ambat-gode—a sweet-and-sour flavour profile that underscored much of her cooking. The Konkan coastal dish called kairas harmonized the tartness of the raw, green mango (kairi) and the smoky sweetness of the jaggery (gud) with an added tropical pop from the fresh coconut.

Meanwhile, on my maternal side, the story of the Oppenheimers, German Jews, is much more dramatic (befitting my mother's outspoken personality) and reveals as much about my ability to overcome obstacles as it does my love of food.

My maternal grandfather or Opa, Siegfried 'Fritz' Oppenheimer, owned a successful hats and haberdashery manufacturing company in what became East Berlin. My mother, Jeanne Hanna 'Jinx'

Oppenheimer, was born in that same town in 1931. Though they lived in relative middle-class comfort, Germany was still in the throes of the Great Depression. Hitler's Nazi Party was making significant gains, becoming the largest party in the Reichstag, the legislative seat of the German government, for the first time. The Nazis 'bought'—meaning took without paying—my grandfather's business, though they kept him on the payroll and let him travel. Life for Jews in Europe was precarious, to say the least.

My Opa was in Switzerland on one such trip when he got wind that the situation in Berlin and all over Germany was deteriorating rapidly for Jews, and that they were being collected and shipped to parts unknown from the smaller towns.

My mother, who has an amazing memory even at ninety-four as I write this, tells the subsequent events better in her inimitable manner: 'Papa, your Opa, asked my mother to pick me up at school, pack a bag and go to visit her parents in Holland. So, aged six, I found myself on a train bound for Holland, when the Gestapo came into the compartment at the frontier. They checked everyone's documents, and questioned me very "sweetly", asking me where I was going.

'"To see my Oma [grandmother] and Opa," I said, equally sweetly.

'"Shouldn't you be in school?" I was asked.

'"I guess so, but Mama said I had a holiday."

'They let us continue our journey.'

My mom was a great actress even then. Safely in Holland for the time being, they awaited my Opa, who joined them for a bit. But my mother stayed with her grandparents until her parents came back for her and then settled in Paris, where she celebrated her seventh birthday in 1938. All was calm for a little while.

There is much of my mother's history that I really did not know. But several years ago, as I was helping her clean up some of her cupboards, we found photo albums that brought back a flood of memories, which she shared. With them I also found a German-made yellow star cloth patch with 'Jude' (German for Jew) written on it. She told me it was sewn on the outside of the coats of all Jews, who were forced to wear them to identify themselves in Nazi Germany. I'll paraphrase from her later diaries here, as it tells a lot about what's coded into my DNA with regard to my persistence and will to overcome any and all obstacles.

On 1 September 1939, when Germany invaded Poland and started the Second World War, my Opa, being a German national, was taken to a French Assembly camp (not a concentration camp) in Francillon, just outside Paris. My Oma and my mother were allowed to visit. When the war seemed to go the Allies' way, Opa was released and returned home. But when the Wehrmacht started its long march into northern Europe, wiping up Belgium, northern France and the Netherlands (Mom's grandparents were swept up in this and disappeared into a German concentration camp), Opa was again taken away by the French, only this time the rest of the family did not know where to.

Bombings started in Paris, and their apartment building was the only one hit by Stuka dive-bombers in the whole residential area where they lived, simply because it was across the street from a hospital with a very large red cross on its roof. Fortunately, my Oma, a lunch guest and Mom had gone downstairs to the shelter next door and were not hurt, but their apartment was mostly destroyed. Oma got the windows boarded up and they moved in with friends.

In 1940–41, when the German advance speeded up, another lady and her son, Oma and my mother took a taxi southwards, toward their friend's husband's Assembly camp in Angoulême. They got as far as Étampes, where the taxi driver said he could not continue as he had to get back to his family in Paris. Next morning, they got another taxi and drove to Orléans, a large railway junction. One day after they left, Étampes was flattened by German air force bombing since it was a French air force base.

They made it to Orléans and were about to board a train when there was another air raid and everyone scattered. They finally boarded the train and started a slow movement southwards, with several air-raid stops on the way. They got to the camp, met the friend's husband, who miraculously had received a postcard that morning from my Opa in another camp in Le Cheylard, near Lyon. Oma and Mom took a train to Lyon and were able to go up into the mountains to Opa's camp. That camp commander was a very kind man, my mother wrote, and he allowed my Opa to come out during the daytime to spend time with his family, but he had to return to camp at night.

One day Opa did not come, and Oma seemed nervous. She packed their bags and the next morning took the train to Lyon, where she told my mother they would meet Opa, who had managed to escape from the camp, as they were being transferred to a very bad camp in southern France. But Opa was not at the Lyon station, leaving them stranded. There was an underground organization to help uprooted Jews that got them from the station, and a few days later Opa suddenly showed up ... he had apparently come to the station but saw the camp commander get off the train between two policemen and thought they were after him when they were really arresting the commander for being too lenient. So he fled.

In late summer 1941 they were informed that US immigration visas awaited them at the American Embassy in Paris and decided to return to Paris to get them. Unfortunately, their German passports had a validity of less than the required six months, so they could not obtain their visas. Of course, there was no way they could go to the German occupying authorities to get new passports as Jews (they would probably have been deported to a concentration camp had they done so). So, with the help of another underground organization, they were smuggled out of Paris and landed in still free French Marseilles in autumn, where they stayed a few months.

Disaster struck on 7 December 1941, when the Japanese attacked Pearl Harbor. American President Theodore Roosevelt ruled that no

Germans would be admitted into the US, no matter what the reason. My Opa and a few of his fellow refugees approached the Cuban Consulate and managed to get their visas for Cuba, after obtaining fake, backdated baptismal papers. They boarded the *Eridan*, a French boat travelling from Marseilles to Casablanca, where they stayed for a week, along with many other Jewish refugees, in a maternity home just outside the city. They tried to get a berth on a neutral Portuguese ship, the *Serpa Pinto*, that sailed trans-Atlantic to Jamaica, which was controlled by the Royal British Navy. While they were being processed, an English officer, while checking my Oma's purse, found the baptismal papers and asked why they were leaving Europe, since they were not Jewish refugees. It just so happened that Oma also had a small Hebrew prayer book in her purse, and the officer asked her whether she could read it. She not only read it but recited the prayer by heart. The officer said, 'Only a Jew would know that.' As luck would have it, he turned out to be Jewish too! After a few days, everyone was sent back on board, and they sailed to Havana. My mother celebrated her eleventh birthday in a retention camp called Tiscornia, outside of Havana, while waiting for their documents to be processed.

Oma and Opa on board the Serpa Pinto *sailing to Havana*

With Opa on Fort Washington Avenue outside Fort Tryon Park, New York, 1965

They lived in Havana until 1946. For a pre- and early teenager, Havana was heavenly after all the turmoil of war-torn France. When the Second World War ended in June 1945, they finally got immigration visas for America. Mom was thrilled to take her first ever aeroplane flight from Havana to Miami, Florida, from where they took a train to New York City, where they settled down ... at long last. She celebrated her fifteenth birthday in Miami.

My mother lived with her parents in their apartment, first in the Bronx, then on the Upper West Side of Manhattan, from 1948 to 1955. She became a US citizen in 1952, after her twenty-first birthday. She attended New York University for two years, transferring to the University of Wisconsin, where she met a fellow student, Prayag aka Anand Akerkar, a Hindu Indian. He went back to India in 1953, she followed two years later and they married in Bombay in October 1955.

My parents' wedding day. 26 October 1955, at the CCI, Bombay

She ended her story with good news and bad: 'While my parents and I were blessed never to have been in a German concentration camp, about 80 per cent of my German family on both sides died in various concentration camps. This includes my maternal grandparents and most of my father's family.'

Quite the tale, eh? Unfortunately, there are millions of European Jews who also can tell some variation or another of the same. I share most of her story at length here because, as I said, it's part of my legacy, a piece of my pie and a window to my soul.

My mother's influence goes well beyond how much her life story inspired me. She was fiercely protective of our independence and respected our individuality without compromise. I remember the time I went on one of my earliest dates with a childhood sweetheart to see *To Sir, With Love*. I couldn't have been more than ten or eleven at the time. I bumped into a friend's mother at the movie and introduced her to my date. Later, when I got home, Mom asked how the movie was and I mentioned I'd met Usha Aunty at the theatre.

That evening, just as we sat down to dinner, as if on cue, the phone rang and Mom answered it.

'Hi Usha, how've you been?'

A short silence followed. Then Mom spoke: 'Thanks for calling, but I must stop you right there. I already know Rahul was at the movie today and he mentioned he met you ... and I have to say that what he does and who he's with is strictly his business. It's not mine, and it certainly is not yours!'

My mother, Jinx Akerkar

And just like that, order was restored in my universe. It left me feeling all warm and fuzzy that I'd been endorsed like that by my mother.

Mom and Dad always had this strategy whenever they got into an argument with my sister Avantika (Tiki) or me. They appeared to us as a team, always on the same page, whether they agreed with the other's decision or not. This was a brilliant parenting strategy as it prevented us from ever driving a wedge between them, playing one off the other to get what we wanted, as many kids do. This stance was non-negotiable and cast in stone.

That was until one day Dad decided to agree I was right, when we got him to referee an argument Mom and I were having. She was so pissed off with him (and me) that she threw us both out of the house.

'Akerkar Gothic' in honour of Grant Wood's 1930 painting, American Gothic. *New York, 1982*

So off Dad and I went to the Willingdon Sports Club for a swim and an early dinner. On the way back home, realizing the folly of his earlier actions, Dad decided to buy flowers for Mom as a peace offering. When we got home, Mom was in an amazing mood, flitting about the house listening to opera. We gave her the flowers and she said, 'For me? Thanks. How thoughtful, how lovely, such pretty flowers!' Something wasn't right. She was behaving oddly. Happy, but oddly.

We found out later that soon after Dad and I left the house, she'd gone to our neighbour's and gotten herself a big fat doobie from their twenty-year-old daughters, which she then smoked in her bathroom to take the edge off her ire. She soon forgot what she was angry about and chilled out, listening to music and pottering about the house till we returned.

Mom has always been a close friend to me. I talk to her about anything, which makes her more of a confidante today than a mother. We understand one another perfectly, share the same idiotic, slapstick humour and laugh together often.

One summer in the mid-1980s, she was staying with me in Oma's apartment in New York. I went out on a Saturday night and came home with an Indian woman who spent the night with me. I must have forgotten to tell the young lady that my mother was staying with me for a bit. So, in the morning, when she walked into the kitchen to make some coffee, Mom was sitting there drinking hers, doing *The New York Times* crossword puzzle.

'Good morning, Aunty!' she stuttered, caught completely off guard.

Mom looked up from her paper and said, 'Don't "Aunty" me, please. You just spent the night with my son; I'm not your aunty! Coffee's on the stove, by the way.'

Mom's *like that only*. Always has been. No filter at all, telling it like it is. It's what I love about her. She grabs life by the balls and squeezes it to the maximum.

Weekends, particularly Sundays, were always family days. Dad would play golf early and be home by elevenish, about the time that Mom and I would wake up to face the day. They invariably had several friends over for brunch and Bloody Marys, pink gins (Dad's specialty) or beer. I even recall having my own demitasse-sized University of Wisconsin (my parents' alma mater) beer mug and being included in the revelry. They started me off early—I was drinking shandy (beer mixed with sweet lemonade) from about the age of two. Initially it would be 95 per cent lemonade and 5 per cent beer; that ratio gradually changed in favour of the beer as I grew older.

A couple of months before Mom was ready to deliver Tiki in June 1964, she'd decided she didn't want me around competing for attention and packed me off to spend the summer with Oma and Opa in New York. I was all of five years old and flew unaccompanied, with an air hostess keeping an eye on me. Mom, notorious for her mad letter-writing, sent detailed albeit tongue-in-cheek 'Rahul-care' instructions for the poor flight attendant. Here's a similar travel letter she wrote when my sister Tiki and I flew together, unaccompanied, to New York in 1968, when we were four and nine respectively. You'll get the gist.

At Bombay airport being shipped off to New York before Tiki's birth in 1964

PLEASE READ THIS AND PUT IT BACK INTO ITS CASE, TO BE GIVEN TO THE NEXT HOSTESS AFTER YOUR CREW SLIP. THANK YOU.

To the kind Air Hostess (the Lucky One!!) who has been chosen to look after my children Bombay/Zurich and Zurich/New York.

Greetings (and commiserations...)

This will serve to introduce to you two angels (they really are ... once they've gone to sleep):

RAHUL ANAND AKERKAR, aged 9, and his beloved sister, Mlle. AVANTIKA NADINE AKERKAR (known as TIKI), aged 4. The children, who live in Bombay, are on their way to New York to visit their grandparents (that's what we say ... what we really mean, is that their father wants to get rid of them for a while !)

Rahul is a veteran air traveller, having made this same trip by himself at the age of 5. He therefore considers the plane (EVERY part of it, including the cockpit) his domain, and loves to visit and explore the aircraft. You may indulge him this technical curiosity as much as is convenient for you, but I would appreciate (for obvious reasons) your keeping him away from the Emergency Exit equipment! Tiki is not as keen a student of aircraft technology, but she will naturally copy anything her brother does. The children have been provided with enough toys and books to keep them busy... for about 15 minutes, at least.

Gastronomically, the children's taste runs to beer, potato chips, ice-cream and chocolates. Being an old-fashioned mother, I also like them to have a little bit of some such dull stuff as milk, meat, vegetables and fruit. But there is not much point in forcing the issue too much, and in any case, why spoil your sweet friendship with the children during the short period of your togetherness. What I'm getting at is, they'll eat what THEY want, no matter what you do about it, so relax.

Rahul is able to look after himself with his bathroom routine. Tiki requires assistance in that department, although she will most probably insist most indignantly that "I kin do it by me-shelf" ... but please DO go in with her!

Sleeping on the plane is another one of those hit'n'miss activities ... but I would like them to have a little nap, especially on the trans-Atlantic sector... Rahul needs no special preparation ... but Tiki has a definite routine to follow: in her bag you will find a white muslin cloth, with a "nippo" tied into one of the corners ... these two items, plus one of your little pillows are standard equipment for the trip to dreamland. If all else fails, try chloroform or a hammer!

The children will be carrying about $15 on them. They may do any shopping they like at Zurich airport... I would like them to be assisted in getting a nice big box of Tobler chocolates (Teresina, or a mixed box of miniatures) as a present for their grandparents, out of these funds. The rest may be splurged on any toy or game they would like ... one for each child (their sense of sharing needs to be developed!)

Special note for the Zurich/New York hostess:

In the children's cabin bag, are a set of clean clothes...to be put on 10 minutes before landing in New York. If it is not asking for the impossible, I would also be delighted if they could be made to wash their hands and faces at least once, just before landing, preferably...but I don't expect miracles!

I shall personally receive the children in New York...don't ask why they didn't travel with me, their mother...I think you know the answer by now!!!

Thank you for looking after them, or letting them look after you. And don't worry, if this experience has turned you sour on air-hostessing...there are many other interesting careers for an attractive girl like you...

J. Akerkar

When I flew back to Bombay in 1964, I was again unaccompanied. Soon after we left Rome en route to Bombay, the gentleman across the aisle from me ordered a beer with his lunch and as sure as day, I got out of my seat, walked over to him with a paper cup and asked for some. In Yiddish, this would be the very definition of chutzpah.

'Go ask your parents,' he said, amused at my request.

'I'm flying alone,' I replied with the brazen confidence only a three-foot-nothing five-year-old could muster.

'Aren't you a bit young to be drinking? Tell me, why should I give you some of my beer?'

'Because today's Sunday and my mummy says on Sundays, I must drink beer!'

He obviously couldn't argue against that logic and poured me a couple of fingers of his beer. I thanked him, returned to my seat, polished off my quaff and must have soon passed out. We became fast aeroplane buddies for the rest of the trip. When we got to Bombay and my mother received me at the bottom of the aircraft stairs on the tarmac (yes, that was allowed in the days when flying was still fun), he walked over to her.

'Is this child yours, Madam?' he enquired.

'Why, what did he do?' she asked hesitatingly, unsure whether to say yes with the eagerness of a proud parent or deny any connection to me.

'He's quite a remarkable chap,' he quipped and proceeded to tell her what had happened.

After a good laugh, and when all was explained about our Sunday brunch beer-guzzling tradition, he eventually became a good friend of the family and subsequently spent many a liquid Sunday with us at Chez Akerkar.

Speaking of my younger sister, Tiki, five years my junior, I cannot imagine my life without her in it in some form or fashion. We really grew up apart from one another, at least physically. First, I went to boarding school at the Doon School in Dehradun while she remained in Bombay; then when I returned and went to college in the US, she went off to boarding school at the Kodaikanal International School in Tamil Nadu. Later, in America, we attended different schools in different cities. And so it went—growing up as siblings but separated by geography. We were never close but in some ways we are so much alike. In others, we are opposites. We're both stubborn and outspoken, creative types through and through. She does not mince her words—whether of praise or criticism. Though I am the 'older brother', there are times when she reminds me I'm still a 'little boy'. In turn, I know she looks up to me, even as she calls me out on my shit ... and vice versa!

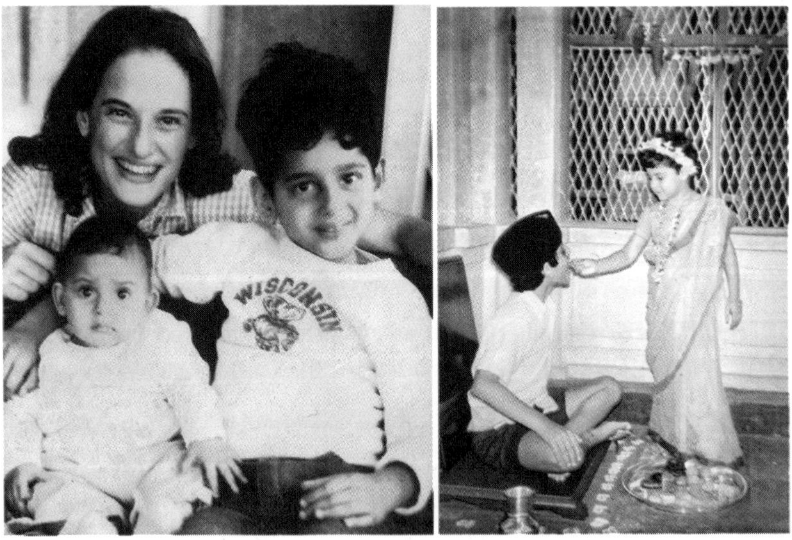

I got me a new sister in 1964; Celebrating the loving bond between brother and sister: Bhaubeej (also Bhai Dooj) in Nashik

Home from college, Bombay, January 1979

Sistuh dearest!

As she found her way into young adulthood, I was not surprised that first of all, she followed me to the US, at the more prestigious Bryn Mawr College in Pennsylvania (coincidentally 70 miles from my alma mater, F&M) before transferring to New York University to finish her bachelor's degree; nor was I completely surprised that with her flair for the dramatic, she pursued acting, in which she has carved out a very interesting career in both film and on stage. And talking about chutzpah, she was among the original India cast of the New York Off-Broadway hit *The Vagina Monologues*, a play *The New York Times* in 2006 called 'probably the most important piece of political theatre of the last decade'. In India, a country steeped in sexual repression, the show shocked the public and raised censors' ire—not surprising either. People call me a 'disruptive chef', but there's my little Tiki blowing minds and breaking barriers—live on stage—advocating for women's self-empowerment and positive attitudes about body image, rebuking gender stereotyping, discrimination and violence against women.

Over the years she has been greatly supportive of all my restaurant adventures. Drawing on her other hat, as a corporate communications consultant, she brought insight and inspiration, helping train our Indigo staff and again twenty years later with our next restaurant team at Qualia. She dived in whenever I needed help and suggestions on the social media marketing outreach at Qualia too.

We are both intensely proud of each other, though I do not tell her that enough. Tiki, if you happen to be reading this, I love you so much and am a proud big bro.

For many years Mom had a regular Thursday morning routine that made me appreciate, at an early age, the rewards of going to the market in person to buy fresh vegetables, fruit, meat, fish and other produce. You got to control exactly what your family ate. Years later I asked her why she purchased everything on a weekly basis and stocked our huge American GE fridge and freezer rather than getting items as needed, and she said it was the easiest way for her to do this herself. So off she'd go to Crawford Market (now renamed Mahatma Jyotiba Phule

Market) once a week at 6 a.m. with her weekly shopping lists, several large woven cane baskets and canvas drill shopping bags to shop for the household perishables for the week. This iconic market is the largest farmer's market in South Bombay, a Victorian Gothic structure built in the mid- to late 1800s. It sprawls over almost 23,000 square metres and is divided into distinct areas selling wholesale and retail fruit, vegetables, meat, fish, poultry and dry provisions. There's even a large but tragic pet shop that features later in this book.

Over the years of her weekly market run, Mom cultivated a group of purveyors whose produce and prices she preferred and with whom she dealt exclusively. The rapport and friendship she'd developed with these regulars was something to behold. Regardless of her clearly foreign Western appearance, she was never addressed as 'memsahib' but as 'bai' (endearment for sister). She only spoke to them in their native Marathi or Hindi, broken as it was, and always treated them with respect even while bargaining the shit out of them. They loved her for it. She even had a regular contingent of tokri-wallahs (young men who carried your cane baskets and shopping bags as you did your shopping) that schlepped all her purchases from across the market to her car over the several hours it took her to do her shopping.

I loved going to the market with her and I vividly remember these excursions, the sounds, sights and smells of a living, breathing market. Tasting and sampling the produce for freshness—the grazing we'd do as she went from stall to stall—was the best part. I can still remember shelling fresh, sweet green peas and popping handfuls of them into my mouth. Carrots were next—baby-sized, bursting with crisp freshness, eaten right off their green stalks. Some vendors only sold leafy vegetables of all colours, including herbs; some sold both dry and fresh spices, while others only roots and tubers or beans of all shapes and sizes.

The route Mom took as she navigated her 'marketing' was the same every Thursday morning. Vegetables came first. Then we'd walk outside between the rows of lemon- and coconut-sellers to the open-air wholesale fruit section, covered by a tarpaulin. Here Mom would buy in bulk the seasonal fruit we ate at home daily: mangoes, guavas, grapes, chikoos (sapotas or sapodilla plums), oranges and mosambis (local sweet limes). We would graze again. Next came the open-air butchers with carcasses of goat, lamb and water buffalo in various stages of disembowelment hanging from cast-iron hooks over well-used tree-trunk chopping blocks. All of it covered by swarms of flies as stray dogs and crows scavenged whatever scraps they could grab off the ground. Picture a medieval European market 300 to 400 years earlier. We didn't graze here!

Eventually we'd make our way to the 'fish building', a separate enclosed market. However, that did little to mask the smells and grime from the scales, fins, tails, blood and guts of all varieties and sizes of fish and seafood that were cleaned, deboned, portioned and sold right there every morning. You needed an impervious constitution, a real curiosity and sense of adventure to venture here. And you always came wearing rubber flip-flops or plastic sandals on your feet to be able to scrub the stinky fish-market juices off your legs when you went back home.

Koli fisherwomen, Crawford Market, Bombay

Mom's Koli fisherwomen, whom we affectionately addressed as maushi (aunty), always kept aside something special from their catch for her. They knew our family members were big seafood eaters. She'd always bring them fresh jasmine flower garlands for their hair in gratitude. A fine trade, I thought. I learned how to check a fish's gills, eyes and prod its mid-section to determine its freshness. One of her tokri-wallahs would stay back with several heavy-duty plastic bags (that Mom recycled every week) to collect the seafood she'd chosen and bring it directly to the car once it was cleaned.

We'd head off to our last stop to graze on and buy smaller quantities of other special fruit like berries, melons, rambutans, lychees, sitaphal (custard apples), papaya and such.

Mom was big on education and a great believer that children should develop at their own pace, unpressured to either conform or perform. Original, out-of-the-box, even wacky thinking was not only encouraged but nurtured. She and Dad always inspired us to pursue whatever intellectual or artistic ideas our little minds and hearts desired. I remember coming home from kindergarten one day with a drawing of a perfect duck. Mom's first question after the 'What a beautiful duck!' was, 'Did you draw this by yourself?' After I said I had, she pictured a young Leonardo da Vinci in the making and visited school the next morning to watch, first-hand, her young artistic prodigy at work. Instead, she saw one of the teachers hold my hand and direct another perfect drawing. I had little to do with it. Mom came over to me, collected my things, grabbed hold of my hand and walked me right out of that kindergarten. And just like that, I was enrolled in a different school.

That summer, during our annual trip to New York, she put me in a neighbourhood Jewish kindergarten for several months. Within a few weeks, she was called in for a parent-teacher meeting where she was asked whether I was a troubled or depressed child. They were asking because I'd been making paintings in various shades of grey and black when our topic for the week was 'Summers with the Family'. She quickly understood that I was painting the monsoons in Bombay—and very accurately at that. When she explained this, everyone had a good laugh.

Mom and me, 1964

When it came time for me to transition to grade school, a bunch of parents including her felt that none of the schools in Bombay provided a good enough forward-thinking, nurturing, development-driven and stimulating education. So, they got together and founded the Bombay International School (BIS), which Tiki and I attended before heading to boarding school for our final years. Both my daughters Shaan and Amalia also went to BIS for several years before transitioning to another school to finish up their International Baccalaureate (IB) boards. BIS was run by like-minded parents administratively, but the education was left entirely to professionals. One of the wonderful institutions the school created was the freshly cooked, hot vegetarian lunch that the kitchen team, comprising our mothers, prepared from scratch every day. Mom headed that for a couple of years during which her sweet corn soup became a thing of legend that alumni still talk about. None of us really understood the significance of having our own mothers cook hot lunches for us, but it really sank in many years later when I was chatting with legendary chef Alice Waters of the iconic Chez Panisse in Berkeley, California, about her Edible Schoolyard Project, a programme providing free nutritious school lunches to schoolkids, run entirely by the kids themselves. We forget just how much of one's heritage is passed down through food and the act of sharing a meal and dining together, and so, activities that embrace and promote this are vital to our human development.

Jews love food as much as Indians do. On Jewish fasting holidays my Opa used to say, 'Let's eat. God prefers a happy Jew to a hungry one!' Priorities are priorities, even for the guy who got out of Europe before Hitler's proverbial shit hit the fan full force. He became a partner in an artificial-flower manufacturing company in New York. My Oma, like any good Jewish wife of that era, would cook up a storm at home. From her I developed a taste for such delicacies as sülze, also known as head cheese, made of pork parts, aspic, pickles and some other unidentifiable mystical stuff; pickled herring in sour cream with onions; broiled flounder with sour cream, butter and paprika, which found its way to my Neel at the Tote restaurant many years later, modified with chilli powder instead of paprika and a tempering of black mustard seeds and curry leaves; and a great steak tartare that she'd make, with raw sirloin, anchovies and capers, which also turned up, slightly tweaked, on the menu at Qualia. I have given this recipe at the end of this chapter too.

I remember twice-a-week excursions to the butcher shop on 187th Street, where a man named Lester would slip me slices of salami as though they were precious contraband. Those smells of raw meat have stayed in my olfactory memory to this day. Then we'd cross the street to Gideon's, the Jewish bakery, where I was again assaulted by unforgettable smells—of fresh-baked rye bread; pumpernickel—a dense, very dark, malty, coarsely ground rye bread made from a sourdough starter; chocolate–almond Florentine cookies; Zwetschgenkuchen—a flat sheet cake made from yeast dough and Italian prune plums; flaky apfelstrudel (apple strudel); bagels and bialys—traditionally flat rolls of the Polish Ashkenazi Jews, seasoned with poppyseed and onion, which, unlike their bagel cousins, have no centre hole and aren't boiled before they're baked.

I should add that my food chops go one generation further back on my mother's side. Her grandfather, i.e., my great-grandfather, was a butcher in Schweinfurt, Bavaria. In fact, I am the inheritor of his F. Dick knives, the highest-quality cutlery for professional butchers and chefs. When my mother at last gave up the New York apartment in 2017, we went through everything and I walked off with the knives (which I still use), his two-pronged fork, some pewter cooking utensils, a soup ladle, kitchen spoons and my Oma's beautifully seasoned cast-iron skillets. Behind the fridge I even found a green bottle of the French liqueur Chartreuse, still drinkable. It must have been there for forty-odd years. So divine was it that within two days it was gone. You don't need to wonder who drank it.

When I was born ... ecstatic new grandparents and Mom.
Bombay, April 1959

My great-grandmother Babette Oppenheimer in front of their butcher shop in Schweinfurt. They lived above the shop

My great-grandfather Sigmund Oppenheimer's butcher's knife, fork and pewter utensils

INDIGO'S PAN-FRIED RAWAS, QUINOA UPMA AND KAIRI CURRY-INSPIRED SAUCE (Adapted from Radha Akerkar's Kairas)

I first tasted this delicious dish at my grandmother's Nashik house, so it's my 'comfort food'. For Indigo, we modified it to have a more sauce-like consistency to accompany the fish that we had on our first opening menu and served it with a quinoa upma. I used quinoa in place of semolina that is normally used to make upma, a South Indian breakfast dish.

INGREDIENTS FOR 4 PORTIONS

Rawas (or any other firm fish like Snapper or Grouper)

4 Rawas fillets, 125 to 150 gm each, cleaned, boned, skin on

1 tablespoon ground, roasted fennel seeds

½ teaspoon ground star anise

5 cloves garlic, crisp roasted and powdered (or ~1 teaspoon garlic powder)

1 tablespoon paprika

¼ cup freshly squeezed lemon juice

2½ tablespoons clarified butter

Salt

Freshly ground black pepper

Kairas (Kairi Curry)

½ kg raw green mango, peeled and cut into cubes (use the stone too)

125 gm jaggery (gud)

1 cup thick coconut milk

½ teaspoon red chilli powder

½ teaspoon turmeric powder (haldi)

1½ cups vegetable stock

The 'Tadka' (Infusion or Tempering) for Kairas

½ teaspoon fenugreek seeds (methi)

½ teaspoon black mustard seeds (rai)

½ teaspoon roasted cumin seeds (jeera)

¼ cup fresh green curry leaves

½ teaspoon asofoetida (hing)

1–2 tablespoons sunflower or peanut cooking oil

Quinoa Upma

150 gm quinoa—can use a mixture of red, white and black quinoa

1 cup vegetable stock

15 gm chopped onions

5 gm chopped green chillies

½ teaspoon black mustard seeds (rai)

½ teaspoon turmeric powder

1 teaspoon chopped cashew nuts

1 teaspoon golden raisins

1 teaspoon chopped parsley

1 teaspoon chopped chives

1 tablespoon olive oil

Juice from 1 lemon

Salt and pepper to taste

DIRECTIONS

Kairas (Kairi Curry):

Peel the raw mango, cut the flesh off the seed and cut into large dice. In a heavy-bottomed saucepan, heat the oil on high heat and add the 'tadka' ingredients till they splutter and pop to make an aromatic tempering. Add the raw mango and mango stones to the tempering and cook, stirring well. Add the chilli powder and turmeric and cook, mixing well. Then add enough vegetable stock to cover the ingredients and continue to simmer on low heat, cooking till the stock is incorporated and the mango disintegrates into a thick paste. If it doesn't, process the softened raw mango in a food processor to a smooth thick paste. Make sure to remove the seeds before puréeing! Add in the jaggery a little at a time to get a balanced sweet-sour taste.

Next, add the remaining vegetable stock and coconut milk to the pan and simmer the mixture on low heat for a short while. Ensure a gentle simmering on low flame, to prevent the coconut milk from splitting. Season with salt. You're done. Set aside and keep warm until ready to serve.

Quinoa Upma:

In a pan, bring the vegetable stock to a boil and once boiled, take it off the fire. Add quinoa to the hot stock, cover the pan with plastic cling wrap and set aside for 15–20 minutes till the quinoa softens. Don't let it compact or clump up; use a fork to separate and loosen the quinoa clumps if needed.

While the quinoa's resting, heat the olive oil in another heavy-bottomed pan and add the black mustard seeds to it. Once the seeds start popping add the turmeric powder, chopped onion, chillies, raisins, cashew nuts and curry leaves to the pan and sauté until the onions become translucent and the cashew nuts brown a little. Lower the flame.

Add the softened quinoa to the pan, combine well with the sautéed spice mixture, season with salt and pepper and finish with the lemon juice and chopped herbs. Set aside.

Rawas:

Make a dry spice mixture of the paprika, fennel and star anise powders with some salt and pepper and set aside.

Heat the clarified butter in a well-seasoned (much-used) skillet or non-stick sauté pan. While the pan's getting hot, rub the fish fillets in lemon juice and then rub the dry spice mixture over them to cover the outsides. When the butter and pan are hot, sear the fish skin-side down till the fish is done and the skin is nicely crisped. Remove from the pan, dab gently with a paper towel to remove any excess butter. Do not overcook the fish! Serve with the warm kairi curry and quinoa upma.

STEAK TARTARE, PICKLED MUSHROOMS, CURED EGG YOLK

If you want to include the mushrooms, remember that they require a minimum of 4–6 days of pickling before you can use them. Feel free to skip the mushrooms if you don't have the time. Their absence won't change the tartare!

INGREDIENTS FOR 4 PORTIONS

Steak Tartare

300 gm beef tenderloin cut into 5-mm dice cubes (or process to a finer, ground-beef consistency if preferred)

1 finely chopped white onion

2 teaspoons roughly chopped small capers, drained

1 tablespoon chopped gherkins, drained

1 tablespoon tinned anchovies in oil, chopped up

2 teaspoons pommery (or other whole grain) mustard

½ cup extra-virgin olive oil

Juice of 1 lemon

1 teaspoon honey

2 teaspoons chopped chives

2 teaspoons chopped parsley

Salt and pepper to taste

Cured Egg Yolks

8 eggs yolks, separated—make sure they're whole and not broken

300 gm salt

300 gm caster sugar

2 teaspoons fresh black pepper

2 teaspoons cleaned thyme leaves, chopped

Pickled Shimeji Mushrooms

250 gm shimeji mushrooms (or any other mushroom)

1 cup white wine vinegar

1 cup water

2 teaspoons salt

2 tablespoons sugar

2 teaspoons cleaned thyme leaves

12–15 whole black peppercorns

3–4 crushed garlic cloves

Basil Oil

100 gm fresh green basil leaves

4–5 cleaned spinach leaves

⅔ cup extra-virgin olive oil

DIRECTIONS

Steak Tartare:

Cut the beef tenderloin into 5-mm cubes and refrigerate in a glass or stainless-steel bowl covered in plastic wrap. If you want a smoother texture to the tartare, use ground beef tenderloin instead. Separately combine all the remaining ingredients and whisk together to form a dressing. Set aside and refrigerate. Just before serving, mix the dressing with the diced tenderloin, adjust the seasoning and serve.

Cured Egg Yolk:

In a large, non-reactive bowl, mix together the salt, sugar, thyme and crushed pepper. Set aside 200 gm or about ⅓ of the mixture. Spread out 400 gm of the mixture on the bottom of a 14 x 9-inch stainless-steel casserole pan and use the back of a spoon to make 8 evenly spaced, shallow impressions or indentations in it, about 2–3 cm apart. Separate the yolks from the whites, one egg at a time, and very carefully place the yolks in the hollowed-out wells. Repeat until all the impressions are filled separately with one egg yolk each. (Refrigerate the egg whites and use them later for anything else.) Gently cover the yolks with the remaining salt mixture, making sure to cover the yolks completely. It's best to use a spoon to carefully start filling the area immediately surrounding the yolks with the remaining salt mixture and then slowly build your way up and over the yolks. This way they're supported and contained by a thicker ring of salt mixture around their sides and covered with a thin layer of salt mixture over the top. It's important to do this to keep the yolks from bursting under the weight of excessive salt mixture over the top. Cover the pan tightly with plastic wrap and set it aside for 45 minutes to cure the yolks. They will firm up and shrivel as the moisture is sucked out of the yolk by the cure. Remove the cured yolks from the pan with a large spoon and very gently bathe each one in ice cold water to remove the excess salt. Transfer to a pan filled with refined oil, making sure the yolks don't burst. Store submerged in the oil, refrigerated. Use an oil that will not solidify or congeal in the refrigerator. To serve, gently, with a slotted spoon, remove a cured egg, and carefully pat-dry the excess oil with a paper napkin.

Pickled Shimeji Mushrooms:

Trim the 'roots' off the Shimeji mushrooms to separate them and put the mushrooms in a sterilized glass jar. Separately, in a saucepan, bring all the remaining pickling ingredients to a boil and then pour the hot pickling liquid over the mushrooms and seal the jar. Refrigerate when it cools down and only use after 4 to 5 days minimum of pickling; the longer the better.

Basil Oil:

Bring water to boil in a pot and blanch the basil and spinach leaves for under a minute or so before transferring them to an ice-water bath. Once cooled, squeeze the leaves well to remove all the excess water. In a blender, purée the blanched leaves and the olive oil till completely emulsified. Line a tea strainer with muslin and strain the oil through to remove the vegetal solids. Store in a squeeze bottle.

Assembly:

Spoon the steak tartare on to the centre of a plate and use the back of a spoon to make a shallow hollow in the meat. Carefully remove a cured egg yolk from the oil, gently pat dry and transfer to the hollow on the tartare. Garnish with pickled mushrooms, drizzle with basil oil and serve with crispy garlic sourdough.

2: IN THE BEGINNING WAS THE MARTINI

chives
blue crab

IF THERE'S ONE BEVERAGE most responsible for launching my career, it's the martini.

This needs explanation.

I love a good martini. As an undergraduate at Franklin & Marshall College in the quiet Pennsylvanian town of Lancaster in the late 1970s, there were few, if any, night spots that served the perfect mix. Now, I could go off on a long tangent about the miracle of the martini, but I will save that for a future section on drinks I have known and loved … and that nearly destroyed me. And then you will understand why people queued up six deep for the martini in all its creative varieties and formulations as the centrepiece cocktail at Indigo's extremely popular bar.

Jethro's Restaurant, Lancaster, where it all began

So there I was in the summer of my junior year at F&M, with one more year to complete my bachelor's degree in biology and too much time on my hands … always a dangerous thing for my overactive mind. The city had a restaurant called Jethro's, a tiny but excellent French bistro owned by an F&M graduate named Ed Diller. Jethro's made the best martinis in town and, trust me, I had done my research. The house martini was vodka and Lillet. My favourite was the dirty martini with olives and just the right amount of brine.

My housemate, a wacky Dutchman named Phil de Bruyn, also had too much free time when he wasn't painting houses that summer. So, two or three times a week we'd meander over to Jethro's and drown our sorrows—not that we had many, other than the frequent shortage of cash to drink. By the end of the summer, we had become familiar faces to Ed and struck up a few friendly conversations with him. We were also broke by the end of August.

'If you want me to keep spending my money here,' I explained to Ed, 'I need a job. Will you give me one?'

And, much to my surprise, he did. I started with the ignoble title of dishwasher. It was my second job in the restaurant business in the US. I am using the phrase 'restaurant business' loosely, if you count my first job: as a waiter at a hotel in the Catskills Mountains, ninety minutes north of New York City. The Catskills are called the Borscht Belt because so many Jewish people went for weekends and summer vacations to the various hotels that dotted that region. While I am half Jewish—actually fully Jewish, since among us it's the mother's religion that determines her children's—I can say the Jewish clientele are as demanding as ... well, Indian clientele. So, in retrospect, it was great training for my future as a hospitality professional in India.

The hotel was called the Edgewood Inn, in the tiny town of Livingston Manor. Waiters were assigned the same station all summer, where we would see the same guests for short stays of a week or two or even throughout the season. Somehow, possibly because I had so little experience (ya think?), I was pointed in the direction of the worst station.

Among them was one particular miser, Mrs Schwartz, who once tipped me $4 for the week—this for three meals a day for seven days. I got so pissed off with her that during lunch on the last day, as I was carrying a tray with two dozen glasses of borscht, the Jewish cold beet soup, I tripped accidentally—I swear—and spilled the entire lot all over her. She was covered in bright purple from head to toe, and jumped up screaming for me to be fired. Morris, the maître d', quite familiar with this woman, took me aside later and said, 'Good job.'

I was not born to be a waiter, especially since I had a hand tremor, a condition that runs in my family. To gain sympathy, I told everyone I was an Israeli war veteran, which I got away with since my Indian accent and the darker colour of my skin suggested to them that I might be a Mediterranean Jew. I attributed the tremors and my occasional stuttering to the post-traumatic stress—shellshock, as it used to be called—of frontline military action. When people wanted to talk with me about Israel, I would claim it brought back too many bad memories.

This all taught me that waiters can engage with guests. We were entertainers, feeding their fantasies of the best waiter in the world.

It was there that I learned how to cater to the guest, even the most difficult. I learned to pre-empt regular customers' same daily orders. 'Mr Bernstein, your three-minute egg is already on order,' I would announce with charm when Bernstein took his seat. Then I'd go into the kitchen and order it.

At Jethro's, I joined an offbeat group. I fit right in.

Ed was a damn good, if reluctant, chef. He had trained at the Restaurant School at Walnut Hill College in Philadelphia. After graduating in 1976, he'd brought ideas he learned there to Jethro's, such as tapenades and baked breads. Problem was he didn't like to cook, or at least he didn't like to work in such a tiny cramped kitchen.

Ed had a 'consulting' chef—a French character named Paul Asso who rode around town on his bicycle wearing his signature beret, because that is what Frenchmen do. Paul had highly respectable culinary credentials. A native of the hilltop village of Èze near Nice in France, he came from a family of chefs. His grandmother had worked with Escoffier, the French chef, restaurateur and writer of the late nineteenth and early twentieth centuries, and Paul regaled us with stories of how he remembered seeing the legendary chef working in his garage, standing on a box (he was very short) canning sauces and other foods. Another relative may or may not have worked in some czar's kitchen.

Regardless, Paul was a skilled technician with a knife. Even I could tell, based on the vast experience I did not have. He set the menu for each evening and it was my very good fortune that he took me under his wing. Because we were basically a two-man kitchen staff, with Ed serving as front man and maître d'hotel, I was anointed with the additional revered title of 'garde manger'. Isn't it wonderful how impressive and even sexy the French language can make a title? In English I was the salad boy, the pantry chef, prepping cold appetizers, peeling shrimp and such. In the French cook apprenticeship tradition, you'd julienne carrots for a year before being considered for the next rung up the steep foodie food chain. But this was America. Anything was possible—and in short order. It was Paul who taught me the basics: how to make stocks, tapenades, pickled eggs and a basic Caesar salad that became a regular favourite years later at Indigo. I learned to make blood jellies and amazing Hollandaise sauces. I was coached in making lumped crab in Mornay sauce and paper-thin potato slices for pommes anna.

Paul boned Shad Roe, stuffed it with spinach and Béarnaise sauce and wrapped it in lettuce. I watched in amazement as he turned food into edible art.

We did some frankly illegal things as well. He showed me how to slaughter pheasants and rabbits. That's not illegal, but doing it in the basement of the restaurant would have had the Food and Drug Administration (FDA) on our backs in a flash ... if they knew. So please help me keep the secret. Live pheasant would arrive in crates as Paul gleefully announced, 'Ees fay-san day today!' In the basement, he would bleed them, hanging them from their tongues to drain out the blood. He made peach vinegar, which he mixed with the blood, before fricasseeing them in stock with added Grand Marnier. Who needed biology and chemistry when you could marvel at this kind of culinary alchemy?

With Ed Diller in 2014 back in the Jethro's kitchen, where it all started and where nothing's changed

Jethro's had a nighttime chef de cuisine who, when the restaurant was shut on Mondays, would host barbecues with his family at home. But one Sunday night Ed found him hauling a whole side of New York strip sirloin to his car, surely dinner for twelve the next day. Ed fired him on the spot, literally catching him redhanded with the bloody meat still in his grips.

'What the hell am I going to do now?' cried Ed, still unwilling to cook.

'I'll do it,' I piped in. Ed gave me a sideways glance, like a father frowning at the son who offers to drive the treasured Mercedes without a licence or a single driving lesson.

'No way.'

I said, 'I can cook. Ask Paul.'

Paul, bless his soul and his prescience, weighed in on my behalf, 'I think the boy can handle this. And what he can't, I'll get him up to speed.'

For the rest of the week, Ed came back to the kitchen and Paul jumped in whenever he could too. I helped out.

My first night cooking professionally was a physical nightmare.

It was a Friday night, I recall very clearly. After I sent out the last order and we closed the kitchen, it fell to me to break down my hot section and clean it up. I took the heavy cast-iron grating off the stovetop, lifted it and turned to put it in the sink to scrub. The floor was wet and—I can still see this in my mind in slo-mo because that is how it felt to me then—I slipped. The grating hit my lip and chin; split wide open, they were bleeding profusely. It was midnight. The dishwasher took me to the emergency room at Lancaster General Hospital, where a doctor stitched up my face.

The next evening, at about 6 p.m., I was back in the kitchen slicing potatoes for pommes anna on the electric meat slicer. Distracted, I was talking to Ed about the night before and sliced off the top quadrant of my left hand's middle finger. Back to the emergency room, where, unbelievably, the same doc was still on duty and stitched me up again. I had brought the piece of finger in a Styrofoam cup filled with ice, thinking he could stitch it back in place. The ER doctor took one look at the shrivelled stub and immediately threw it in the garbage. However, he needed to use a bit of synthetic skin as a substrate to stop the bleeding from the finger. I still have the sliver of synthetic skin on the middle finger of my left hand. Luckily for you, I cannot show it to you in a book. Somehow I went back to Jethro's right away and resumed cooking—bandaged finger sheathed in a condom to keep it dry and my chin and lip bandaged. Hey, it was a Saturday and the show must go on.

That Sunday morning, when I came in to cook brunch, Ed asked me to bartend instead, since I was somewhat incapacitated with the bandaged finger and face that were both now really throbbing. I began making up a 5-gallon glass jar of Bloody Mary mix, a favourite brunch drink at Jethro's. As I mixed in the horseradish and continued stirring the tomato juice, the long metal spoon nicked the side of the jar and a perfectly round piece of glass about the diameter of a golf ball simply popped out. I stood there like an idiot, spoon in hand, as the entire Bloody Mary mix emptied out all along the bar like a giant bright red tsunami. Ed came out of the kitchen, laughing hysterically.

'Go home before you destroy what's left of you and Jethro's,' he ordered me. 'And take a week off to break this cycle of destruction.'

With the wisdom of 20/20 hindsight, I must admit I had an affinity for the trade, klutz that I may have been that first time out.

The other thing I had going for me was that despite my wiseass humour and my seemingly devil-may-care attitude, I took and take everything I do quite seriously. My desire for perfection makes me a bit obsessive and anal. Did I say a bit? I was later to learn this is an admirable and very recognizable quality in great chefs.

One night Ed surprised me, suggesting we do an Indian night. I was all over the idea, despite the fact that my real-time experience cooking Indian food for others at this juncture in my life was more or less nil. I had watched my grandmother cooking, so somewhere in my DNA I knew the ingredients and the technique. I had prepared meals for select dinner parties on campus, including for Professor Tom Hopkins, the chairman of the religious studies department at F&M and an India scholar. There was a night in April 1980 many still remember, in my junior year at F&M, when I can say I did my first Indian meal for the public, though without pay. It was during the Spring Arts Weekend at F&M, when the college showcased musical groups and cultural activities. My contribution to cultural enlightenment was to prepare a simple dinner of dal, rice and vegetables for seventy-five students on the second floor of the Steinman College Center building. My Indian friends would say the food was bland, but I had begun to learn the level of tolerance the Western palate had for our intense spices.

Nonetheless, when Ed suggested something Indian to celebrate the restaurant's third anniversary, I dove in. 'Yeah, let's do it,' my ears heard my mouth shout with unjustified confidence.

Yet, I took charge and took to it like a natural, as Ed recalled. I was fearless and super-organized. I printed a menu. It was a smash of a night. The resulting dinner—billed as 'Currying with the Maharaja'—included Indian specialties kali dal, dahi gosht and aloo gobhi. I even played the sitar for the guests. I'd like to say I was surrounded by gopis, but that would be a lie.

The announcement for my first professional Indian cuisine gig at Jethro's in Lancaster

Ed was such a great guy; we became fast friends and did some wild-ass stuff. One night he and I were in the back prepping for a private birthday party. While cooking up a storm, we rapidly got hammered. This also is a trait of far too many chefs. We came up with this goofy idea: we cut off our chef pants right above the knees and used the leg tubes which we stitched to the inside of our chef's aprons. We doffed the rest of our pants, stepped into each leg tube and tied the aprons around our waists. Looking at us head-on we appeared perfectly dressed in our chef whites. When it was time to walk out with the cake, candles lit, we slipped into the outfits and marched into the dining room.

As we walked by, people behind us began laughing their asses off—mainly because ours were completely bared.

On an interesting side note, in the category of Famous People You Meet in the Kitchen Before They Become Famous Outside the Kitchen, when I moved up to become the chef at night, my spot in the garde manger was filled by a local Lancaster kid named Mark Ibold. Mark later became the bass guitarist of the indie band Pavement in the 1990s. Later he played in the alternative rock band Sonic Youth from 2006 until their 2012 breakup, mainly on bass but occasionally on guitar too. But back in the summer of 1981, when he and I worked the kitchen at Jethro's, we'd catch flies, like croupiers scooping up dice off a Craps table, and throw them forcefully into a mound of flour. Then we'd crack up as our white, flour-dusted 'albino' flies took off, flying dazed all over the kitchen.

This taught me that there was great potential for amusement in the restaurant world—if not for the guest, certainly for myself. And that no matter how seriously I took my work, or any work I would undertake in the uncertain life that lay before me, I should not take myself or any of it too seriously. Those two notions of life I can say I have taken forward, to the joy of diners, friends and family.

I worked at Jethro's all through that senior year of college. And yes, I imbibed my share of martinis after work. After earning my degree in biology, I was accepted to a programme at Columbia University in Manhattan. That fall of 1981 I found myself living on New York's Upper West Side and working toward my second BS degree in chemical engineering.

I'd still need money and now, I figured, I had this little skill I could ply on nights and weekends.

JETHRO'S CRAB MORNAY

INGREDIENTS FOR 4 PORTIONS

Crab Mornay

400 gm lump crab meat carefully cleaned for pieces of shells and cartilage

120 gm unsalted butter

100 gm finely chopped onion

50 gm finely chopped celery

1 tablespoon finely chopped chives

1 tablespoon finely chopped parsley

1 teaspoon finely chopped garlic

2 egg yolks, separated

1½ cups whole milk

20 gm refined white flour

2 bay leaves

½ teaspoon grated nutmeg

½ teaspoon cayenne pepper

Juice of 2 lemons (zest the lemons before juicing them and use the zest for the breadcrumbs)

1½ teaspoon Dijon mustard

Tabasco (optional) to taste ~1 teaspoon

50 gm grated Gruyère cheese

50 gm grated Fontina cheese

Garlic-Lemon Breadcrumbs

100 gm white breadcrumbs (panko)

25 gm grated parmesan cheese

1 teaspoon chopped fresh thyme leaves

1 teaspoon finely chopped garlic

10 gm soft butter at room temperature

Zest of 2 lemons (use the zested lemons for squeezing the juice for the crab)

Salt and pepper

DIRECTIONS

Garlic-Lemon Breadcrumbs:

In a clean, dry bowl, combine all the ingredients for the garlic lemon breadcrumbs together and gently mix with your fingers, making sure the butter is well integrated throughout the breadcrumb mix and all the ingredients are blended well. Keep aside.

Mornay Sauce:

Melt the butter in a large skillet over medium-high heat. Add the onion, celery and garlic and cook, stirring, until the vegetables are softened, about 5 minutes over medium heat. While the vegetables cook, vigorously whisk the egg yolks and milk together in another bowl until well blended and set aside. Add the flour to the vegetables in the skillet, and with a flat wooden spoon, mix and combine well to create a white roux. Be sure to not brown the flour. It takes about 2 minutes. Using a whisk, add the milk-and-egg-yolk mixture, stirring constantly to blend into the roux mixture. Stir in the bay leaves, lemon juice, Tabasco (optional), salt, cayenne, black pepper, nutmeg, and Dijon mustard, and continue to stir for another 4–5 minutes. (If sauce seems too thick, add a bit of milk to thin it out; it should be the consistency of a thick creamed soup). Remove from the heat and fold in half of both cheeses; blend until totally melted and fully incorporated and then remove from the fire, letting it come to room temperature. Mix in half the chives and parsley.

To Finish the Crab Mornay:

Divide the crab meat among four ceramic oven-proof casseroles, trying not to break up the crab lumps. Alternatively, put all the crab into one large 8–9-inch baking dish for a communal serving. Pour the cheese sauce over the crab (remove the bay leaves), add in the remaining grated cheese and finish by sprinkling a thin layer of lemon garlic breadcrumb over the top.

Bake in a preheated oven at 175°C for about 15 minutes till it's bubbly. Remove from the oven and broil in a salamander (broiler), until the breadcrumbs begin to brown, about 5 minutes (keep an eye on this ... don't let it burn!). Remove from the broiler, sprinkle with the remaining chopped chives and parsley, and serve.

okra
paprika
lobster tail
chives

3: IN A NEW YORK STATE OF MIND

'New York, New York, a helluva town.
The Bronx is up, but the Battery's down.
The people ride in a hole in the groun'.'

—From the 1944 musical *On the Town*

'Everybody had to pay and pay
A hustle here and a hustle there
New York City is the place where they said:
Hey babe, take a walk on the wild side…'

—From 'Walk on the Wild Side' by Lou Reed

NEW YAWK, NEW YAWK. It was not new to me, after all those childhood summer vacations with my Oma and Opa on the Upper West Side. But it felt so to me as a freshly franchised college grad.

I maintained my academic chops, continuing at Columbia for a Bachelor of Science in chemical engineering. To be honest, those years on campus are a blur. My 'real life' was elsewhere.

What I did learn in those years about cooking and food in general, about kitchens and front-of-the-house service and management, about America's food tastes, pale in comparison to what I learnt about myself, my strengths and weaknesses, my stamina, my obsessive-compulsive disorder—all of which were, unbeknownst to me at the time, foundations for what was to come for me in India. Those lessons that I absorbed deeply, even if sometimes at the subconscious level, may well have been why my restaurant endeavours were so disruptive—and so successful—in the fairly calcified dining-out frontier back home in Bombay.

It was my typically random dumb-luck timing to stumble into this food world at just the right moment, when an incredible culinary revolution was taking place in the United States that would have a global impact. You could call it the menu heard round the world. Food writers quickly dubbed it New or Modern American or California cuisine and its forward guard were California chefs Alice Waters of Chez Panisse in Berkeley; Jeremiah Tower, first at Chez Panisse, later at his own Stars in San Francisco; Wolfgang Puck at Spago in Los Angeles; and Jonathan Waxman at Michael's, Santa Monica. The essence of this new tradition was local, fresh, seasonal, organic—all qualities in contradiction to the European approach, which had been the culinary gold standard at the time. It seems infantile to think we bowed in obeisance to this new view, since it is now the acknowledged mark of excellence at serious dining establishments.

At that point, my goal was a PhD in biochemical engineering, which at the time was at the forefront of a tiny field, mostly research-driven, called biotechnology. Even the words hooked up that way looked odd at the time; it drew blank or glazed stares when I mentioned it. Cooking and the restaurant biz were side hustles for me, means to pay off my university debts—after which I would say 'bas' to kitchen work. What would come next was slightly unclear, as I was slowly beginning to wonder if my professional goals truly aligned with my personal passions.

In the meanwhile, I could hide behind the veil of academia—the nice Jewish Hindu boy on his way with his PhD into a field, even a potentially lucrative one, in medical science. Prestige and respectability were written all over it. This would be impressive in my parents' world: I would be following an intellectual pursuit rather than joining the—*ptewie*!—workforce. I read workforce in another manner: forced to work.

My dirty little secret was that I found chemical engineering boring. Stuff like fluid dynamics left me uninspired, if not snoring. If I had had the foresight to imagine myself as a chef, you might think I'd find some molecular mystery in the alchemy each time you throw food and oils and ingredients together over heat. But for me there was no connect at the time. I feel the same now about what's been called molecular gastronomy. More about that later.

Here's the best thing I got out of Columbia and my period in academia. I had a professor in our chemical engineering department who was an advisor to Genentech, a company founded only five years earlier by a venture capitalist and biochemist, which manufactured some forty drug products available at your local pharmacy, including the flu treatment Tamiflu and the tranquilizer Valium, as well as highly profitable cancer drugs, and conducted some promising research. It is considered a pioneer in the field of recombinant DNA technology, a subject I wasn't actually studying.

Sitting outside my prof's office one day, I overheard him on the phone talking about breakthrough developments at Genentech, a conversation I probably was not supposed to hear. The next day I got a student loan of $5,000 and quickly bought stock in Genentech. (Hmmm, was this what they call insider trading?) By the time I left the US en route home to India, Genentech stock had done well enough for me to pay back some of my student loans. I thought it was a major coup on my part and an early sign that I was a born entrepreneur. Wrong. Had I any level of prescience and a sense of the long term, I would have held on to the measly number of shares for a while. In 2009 the Swiss company Roche Holding bought Genentech for $95 a share. Had I held on to them, I would have been living in a villa on the Amalfi Coast and never become a chef.

From 1981 to 1986, I lived on the Upper West Side of Manhattan either at campus housing or, as was my preference, at my maternal grandparents' apartment in Washington Heights—190th Street and

Fort Washington Avenue, to be exact. This corner of New York became my intro to New York food. It was a veritable United Nations—I discovered every four blocks of that part of Manhattan was like entering another country, with different restaurants to match. This was the melting pot I'd heard so much about.

At the old-world Hungarian Pastry Shop on the corner of 111th Street and Amsterdam, across the street from the Baroque Cathedral of Saint John the Divine, I'd order pastries—tarts, flaky cherry strudel and Viennese sacher-torte. This was the unofficial outpost of Columbia University, a de facto lounge for hyper-literate students and uptown writers since John F. Kennedy was in the White House in the early 1960s. I'd sit there and smoke Marlboro Lights, drink strong cappuccinos, stare at textbooks, looking as pseudo-intellectual as I could. I had a little Honda moped to commute between the 116th Street Columbia campus and the med school on 168th Street, where I took classes as well. I was playing the classic American student.

Nearby was Tom's Restaurant at Broadway and 112th Street, made famous in a song called 'Tom's Diner,' written in 1981–82 by frequent patron Suzanne Vega, then an unknown singer-songwriter and student at Columbia's sister school Barnard. The quintessential and ordinary Manhattan diner—the menu included approximately 8,000 omelette options (clearly an exaggeration), corned beef hash, wraps, buffalo wings, pancakes and bagels, all staples for New Yorkers—was also famous as the exterior for many scenes of the TV series *Seinfeld*.

The West End, a bar and jazz club, was right across the front entrance to the university. It had live jazz on weekend nights and cheap beer, which I loved. That's also where I learned how to play Space Invaders, Pac-Man and other essentials that served no other purpose than to help me procrastinate from the drudgery of studies and cooking.

My first restaurant job in Manhattan was at an Upper East Side eatery called Baumer & Crooks. How I ended up working there was an early lesson in how the tightly connected and protective fraternity of chefs works. How I ended up leaving taught me something more important. Maggie, a girlfriend from F&M and fellow Jethro's baker, introduced me to MaryBeth, her high school BFF, and MaryBeth's boyfriend Ned in New York. Ned just happened to be working in the city as the head chef of the newly opened Baumer & Crooks.

B&C, on Third Avenue between 92nd and 93rd, called itself 'casual American-Continental'. The decor blended romantic Art Nouveau with overtones of a plush upholstered supper club and a handsome mahogany bar. In her review in 1982, not long after it opened, Mimi Sheraton, *The Times'* powerful restaurant critic, gave it a 'meh'—some good, more bad, noting especially the bad lighting. I think the last was on purpose; it kept guests from examining the food too closely.

The fare, in my opinion, was so-so in a predictable manner. Marinated leg of lamb, broiled Norwegian salmon, cheddar cheese chicken pot pie, popovers—this was Baumer's vision of American home comfort. He was a retired Wall Street guy who'd made a pile of money and probably cooked on the weekends for his friends in Connecticut or the Hamptons. Ned and I always thought someone must have said, 'Baumer, you're such a great cook, you should open a restaurant.' So he did!

They'd cook it all in the afternoon and reheat to serve for dinner. It would have been acceptable if the food was good. It was crappy. On top of that, Mr Baumer was condescending and arrogant—the kind of arrogance that's based on no substance. He talked down to everyone.

He made me feel like a menial underling, not the best way to gain my loyalty. One time I suggested we cook meals fresh, made to order, not ahead of time.

His reaction: 'This is my restaurant; we'll do it my way.'

Mine: 'Then you can take your restaurant and lump it because, even with my limited experience, I know this is not how you cook.'

He fired me. It was okay; I'd rather be fired than burn my integrity. That was a really important learning reminder to myself.

The Monday after I was let go, I had to return to the restaurant to pick up my last pay cheque. Baumer was sitting at the bar when I walked in.

'Go stand over at the other end,' he ordered me.

'Mr Baumer, I am no longer under your employ, so where I choose to stand is my business,' I replied. 'I've come to collect my final cheque, thank you very much.'

Baumer didn't know how to respond. I left, proud that I stood up for myself. But I was jobless again.

How I landed my first real New York restaurant gig was generally how I got all my jobs in the city, an audacious way only for those with strong hearts and balls of steel. In this case it was at a restaurant called Wings, a cavernous eatery in an old warehouse on Wooster Street in the trendy SoHo neighbourhood. This would have been in early 1982, only a few months after it opened in late 1981.

I read in *The New York Times* classifieds that they were hiring cooks. I don't know what possessed me, with my limited cooking experience, to head down to SoHo and interview for the position as though I'd been cooking professionally for years. I met with Jonathan Bennett, the head chef, and told him I wanted a job and would take almost any job in the restaurant kitchen.

His first question: 'Have you gone to culinary school?'

Uh oh, I thought, *there go my chances.* I could not lie: 'Nope, sorry.'

'Great, now we can talk,' he replied, explaining that he felt culinary schools like the Culinary Institute of America (CIA) taught hopeful chefs nothing about the real restaurant world. Those students worked in kitchens the size of football fields with state-of-the-art equipment, which was far removed from the reality of most professional kitchens. He would not have to un-train then re-train me, as he did other starting chefs. So my answer was good, especially in light of the fact that I had worked at only two kitchens at that point.

Before the window of opportunity slammed on my fingers, I began: 'I'd like to work for free. After a month, if you're happy with my work, pay me for that month and hire me going forward. If not, don't pay me at all and ask me to leave.'

It was an offer few could refuse. He hired me on the spot without asking for a cooking demo. It was a great start at a restaurant that took food preparation quite seriously in a city that has an intense seriousness about its restaurants.

This experience was a huge departure from my two previous restaurant gigs. The space was gigantic, with seating for 150. The setting was grand, theatrical and romantic, designed to fulfil the diner's Art Deco dreams with pink walls, rose-velvet banquettes, streaks of blue neon across the ceiling and imaginative oversized, pink fabric calla lily sculptures, all staged with softly diffused lighting. The street-level bar overlooked the huge dining room downstairs.

The venue spoke to the new vision of American restaurants—large open spaces, high ceilings, open kitchens, plenty of ferns, long views so everyone could see each other eating and drinking and laughing and flirting—the ultimate see-and-be-seen scene.

The food was equally theatrical and fantastical. For Chef Bennett, Wings was his big moment. I have to admit that at first I recoiled at the idea of matching smoked salmon with sweet and sour pickled red cabbage and almond slices for appetizers, which I did a lot of. But dammit, it worked so well. Bennett concocted a hot custard flan burnished with mushrooms and a sauce of cream and mushroom duxelles. Very French and delicious. An escabeche of marinated cooked snapper with carrots, coriander and fennel reminded me a bit of the sweet-sour flavours and spices I grew up with. You can trace a straight line from that dish to one at Indigo that I gave my own twist to, for which I have given the recipe at the end of this chapter.

Bennett also showed off his CIA training with classic appetizers I prepared almost every night—steamed artichokes with French vinaigrette dressing; mussels in a white-wine broth, with shallots and cream; sweetbreads with a light cream sauce in puff-pastry casings. I also prepped a mountain of Caesar salads.

These were the days when vertical build became popular in food plating. While pretty and popular for a New York minute, the approach was unpractical to actually eat. I often saw attempts crumble on the fork of an unsuspecting diner. Note to self of the future: 'Not all food fads are meant to be followed. The higher the construct does not always mean the better the dish!'

Some Wings dishes reflected a crossroad, marking the end of nouvelle and the beginning of New American. Chef Bennett updated boneless braised duck with raspberry vinegar and garnished it with kumquats. Loin of pork with prunes and spinach was spiced with cumin in the sauce. *The Times'* Mimi Sheraton salivated about it all in her review of Wings.

For me, there was as much to learn about the rest of the staff and about how business was done in New York. The waiters were a particularly colourful lot. I came to understand that this was often the nature of the beast; waiters are a breed apart. Was it true only in New York? Not so.

There was Willie the Waiter—I never knew his last name. He often came to work either hungover or deep in the arms of inebriation. He was also a cokehead. This was not a good way to show up at work, but he was such a character and, even if stoned, he was talented and fearless. I will never forget the time he was serving Empress Farah Pahlavi, the wife of the Shah of Iran Mohammad Reza Pahlavi.

'Give me some mustard,' she told him, speaking in the command form as one would expect she spoke to her staff and anyone else within the range of her voice. But Willie was his own man.

'I *give* you nothing,' he said without hesitation in a deep theatrical voice, standing close to her and staring into her eyes.

To my amazement, she recanted, apologized and corrected herself. 'Please may I have some mustard?'

'Certainly, Your Highness,' he said and smiled. Just as quickly as he had put it to her, he fell right back into the role that was required of him.

By the way, in answer to your burning question, did I partake of the cocaine that was rampant in New York's professional kitchens and, frankly, lined up at almost any party or gathering of the hip and wannabe hip in the early 1980s? Well, when in Rome ... as the saying goes. Okay, I can't be coy. Ya gotta do what ya gotta do to stay awake sometimes. And, boy, did I need to. I worked a full-time, forty-hour week between Thursdays and the double shift I pulled on Sundays. On Saturday nights the last order came in at 2 a.m. and by the time the kitchen closed, it was almost 4. So, rather than schlep all the way uptown on the IRT Broadway local with the bums and subterranean dregs that made New York, The City That Never Sleeps, I'd cover myself with a couple of pink tablecloths and crash on the banquettes in the dining room. It was the only way I could make it back by 9 a.m. to prep and cook brunch. And the only way I could function on so little sleep was thanks to Willie, who'd bound in at 10 a.m. with his morning treat. 'Aarool,' he'd bellow—he could never say Rahul. 'Tudo bem? Bon dia ... time for breakfast ...' as he'd cut me a 9–10-inch line of coke on the stainless steel shelf at the pass. *Schaawiing* ... and just like that, like Gene Gene the Dancing Machine from *The Gong Show* on NBC, or the Road Runner's 'Beep beep', off I went, wired and ready to take on the day. But it never got out of hand and I was not willing to endanger my nose, a tool vital to any chef. Even if I did not have chef ambitions then, I knew I had an obsessive personality and could see myself falling too easily down that rabbit hole and never coming back. If I needed empirical evidence of what could happen from indulging too much,

I only needed to look around at the crash-and-burn characters in the kitchen and on the dining-room floor.

Then there was the Brit named Richard, another waiter. We called him Tricky Dicky. There were apocryphal stories that he had come across the Atlantic in the hold of the *Queen Elizabeth 2* and jumped ship upon arriving at the Port of New York. He too hit the bottle in a serious and dedicated manner. His bloodshot eyes and shaky hands gave him away—not that he ever pretended he did not drink. Nonetheless, even in the worst of conditions, he could balance three or four soup plates on his arms, steady as a rock. He'd arrive at the table and, as he deftly delivered each bowl from the left side of the guest, he would pleasantly say, 'Just like your ol' Mum used to make ...'

Anyone who dines at a restaurant may wonder who really runs the show, who's the money man and how much sway does he or she have. It's a question we restaurateurs ask ourselves too. Even that early stage, it was something I'd think about. At Wings I got one version of an answer.

Wings was run by a group I had never heard of—the Jewish mafia. I should have known about it; after all, there was extensive publicity about the notorious Meyer Lansky, the 'mob's accountant', who had teamed up with another Jewish American mobster named Bugsy Siegel as bootlegging partners during the Prohibition period in the US, later aligning with Italian gangster Lucky Luciano, leaving trails of blood in his wake. Lansky died in 1983, broke, in Cuba.

The landlord at Wings had a dilettante son who lived above the restaurant. The kid did all kinds of mean-ass things to annoy us. He once drilled a hole through his wooden bathroom floor and peed down upon us in the kitchen. He let his bathtub overflow and the water came through the ceiling. He was a bit cuckoo. One late Friday night when the bar was packed solid, he showed up with a baseball bat and, out of nowhere and for no reason we could perceive, yelled, 'You muddhaahfukkerz ...' as he swung his bat, shattering the lovely big frosted-glass window over the bar, and stunned revellers before walking off into the night. Pandemonium! The manager calmed everyone down with drinks on the house—something that always seems to pacify upset restaurant/bargoers anywhere in the world. The manager came down to the kitchen and told Chef Jonathan Bennett to set up the table near the kitchen for four, with a set meal. Not long thereafter, three men who looked like they had just stepped out of the film *Goodfellas*—white shoes, ill-fitting suits, rough edges—came to the restaurant, sat chatting with the manager in hushed tones, ate their meal, polished off a bottle of wine, shook hands and left. When I asked Jonathan what that was all about, he replied rather matter-of-factly, 'That kid won't be troubling us anymore.' We never saw the son again. You figure it out.

A month or two later I was in the kitchen during Sunday brunch when Chef Bennett called me over.

'The owners are out in the dining room and want to meet you.'

'Me? Why me?' I asked, picturing the police later finding my body in the swamps of New Jersey.

I walked out and saw this guy with his shirt's top buttons open, gold chains hanging around his neck, the Jewish star shimmering on his hairy chest. And the white shoes.

'Ray-ule.' He murdered my name. 'Sit down.'

He told me he'd heard I was doing a good job, that I had come from India and that I was Jewish.

'I never met an Indian Jew,' he said with sincerity. 'Tell me all about that.'

I told him what I knew, which honestly was very little. I probably mentioned the famous Jews of Cochin, which I must have read about in school at Doon. In our family we were not avid students of Judaism. But I did my best, thinking this was some test that if I failed ... well, back to those Jersey swamplands.

'And you're a student at Columbia?' he continued his interrogation. By then I had no idea where he was going with all this. 'A master's? In biochemical engineering? Really?'

'Yes, sir.'

'You all paid up with your tuition this semester?'

No, dummy, you think I'd be working here if I was paid up? I thought but did not say that.

'No, sir.'

'How short are you?'

'$5,000.'

He reached into his pocket, pulled out a thick wad of $100 bills and peeled off fifty of them. 'Go pay your tuition,' he said, as casually as though he was covering the cost of my shoeshine.

The next day I went to the Columbia bursar's office and put a stack of $100 bills—fifty to be exact—in front of the cashier.

'I've come to pay the rest of my tuition,' I said.

'How're you paying?' the cashier asked.

'Cash!' I said, like I did this every day. Neither of us had seen that much cash and rest assured, I bet no one ever had paid off a Columbia tuition with a stack of fifty $100 bills. Luckily, no one asked me any questions. And I never asked the owner why he made the gesture, though I worried that if I ever quit, I would indeed be found somewhere in New Jersey.

My next big opportunity came when I joined Vanessa's, which had opened in 1981 on Bleeker Street in the heart of Greenwich Village. A year later it had a new chef, the then relatively unknown Anne Rosenzweig, who had earned her degree in anthropology from Columbia. A protégé of the great anthropologist Margaret Mead, she had done fieldwork in Nepal and the Indian subcontinent. Somewhere in there she was drawn to food, its origins and how to prepare it. Upon returning to New York City, she got jobs as an unpaid apprentice in several restaurants.

At Vanessa's she started as a brunch and pastry chef until she became head chef. There, Mimi Sheraton 'discovered' Rosenzweig, commending her creativity. Anne would later go on to open her own Arcadia on the Upper East Side to great reviews. Later, she appeared on the *Great Chefs of the East* television series. After Arcadia, she opened the Lobster Club, another winner. She would rank among the most important and influential chefs contributing to the growing 1980s trend of New American cuisine.

This future was nowhere in sight when I found out about her and realized Anne would be the perfect target for the next level of my cooking education. Not only did we both go to Columbia, aspiring for intellectual pursuits with socially redeeming value, but I also thought my Indianness might appeal to her, considering she did her fieldwork in the Indian subcontinent. It was early September 1983 when I met her at the restaurant and she hired me right off.

Aside from her cooking, what left a lasting impression on me was her discipline, balanced with originality, and her desire to pass along her knowledge to eager cooks in her kitchen. Her recipes blended dishes familiar on European menus with the New American twist. She did a coriander linguine with chicken, broccoli and pine nuts in cilantro sauce and a saffron spaghetti with shrimp and scallops in lobster cream sauce—stuff too rich for this new emerging palate, but she lightened it all up. She sautéed snapper in a veneer of crushed macadamia nuts, and moist salmon in a sheer sorrel sauce. Medallions of veal came in a ginger, port and peppercorn sauce; calf's liver was served with onions and bacon, and rack of lamb was encrusted with garlic breadcrumbs.

Since I worked appetizers and salads, I particularly recall the flan Vanessa, a hot mousse of shrimp and scallop in lobster sauce, warm salads of wild mushrooms on greens and shrimp with slivered leeks. Her gazpacho and lobster bisque were unbelievable and unforgettable. It's no wonder that lobster bisque and lobster risotto became signature dishes and always occupied a spot on my menu at Indigo for over fifteen years.

Later I worked the pastry section, following her lead on a crème brûlée with espresso dacquoise cake, and the white and dark chocolate mousses served in a cornucopia-shaped tuille, which I also later adapted for my home catering business, Moveable Feast, and several of my future restaurants.

When Anne moved uptown and opened Arcadia, I followed her, until I had to quit to study for my final exams.

I did several short stints at other restaurants, depending on how busy I was with the semester's course-load—more for the money than for any great culinary experience. I flipped burgers at Houlihan's and waited tables at The Museum Café, both within walking distance of where I lived on Columbus Avenue. Sadly, my time at the Odeon, with Chef Patrick Clark, was too short in the summer of 1983. He, like Anne Rosenzweig and Jonathan Bennett, was in the vanguard of New York chefs marrying fine dining and French technique with casual American regional cuisine and I would have learned a lot from my time there if I hadn't been forced to give it up for my 9 a.m. chemical engineering thermodynamics course. What a waste of time that was!

It was a gruelling schedule, balancing work and school. I tried to schedule most of my classes for early afternoon, so I could wake up to get to them before running off to some restaurant by 4 or 5 p.m. I would then work oftentimes till 2 or 3 a.m. and even later on weekends. You should have seen me in this period while I was still hitting the books hard. I'd be solving (or trying to anyway) laminar fluid-flow problems with Professor Edward Leonard's chemical engineering textbook open beside me next to the stove. While stirring, I'd be memorizing Reynolds' Number and other formulae without really understanding much of anything. Sleep? What was that? I catnapped or found ways to stay awake. Caffeine was my friend. And, as I said, I had a few other powdery 'friends' too.

I did another short stint over the summer of 1985 at a typical American 100-seat restaurant across the street from where I lived, called Nikki & Kelly's. I had a defining moment there that showed how my allegiance, even at that ripe young age, was to my kitchen team of workers, not to management or the owners. I was a sous chef there. We served standard fare: angel-hair pasta, steaks and chops, etc. We did a killer, if not typical, New York Sunday brunch too. At one point on a Sunday I was heading downstairs to the prep kitchen in the basement. The manager's office was at mid-landing. As I passed, the door was ajar and I happened to catch a line or two of him on the phone with someone. All I heard was, 'I will let them know tomorrow that they are all history.'

I stood outside and listened just enough to learn what was up. The owners had hired a Chinese chef and his entire kitchen team, who had promised to save the company money on the payroll. The next day we were all going to be fired without notice. I went back to the kitchen, gathered the troops together, from dishwasher to cooks.

'Here's what I want you to do,' I explained. 'Start slowing down everything—cooking, prepping, washing, everything in the kitchen! Keep working, but really take your time.'

Of course that notion is antithetical to what every restaurant person learns and internalizes. Slowly but surely guests began complaining with increasing vociferousness: 'Where's our order?' The young college kids waiting tables for the summer were flipping out from the chaos in the dining room and bar, running into the kitchen every few minutes screaming, 'Where's my food?'

I suggested the waiters give free drinks to those waiting and start taking orders from the guests even before they were seated to placate them. The bar was full, the dining room was full, the sidewalk café was full. There must have been over twenty-five to thirty orders, or tickets as we'd call them, sitting there in the pass, waiting to be cooked. That's when I told the kitchen staff to turn off the stove, shut down, pack up and go home. As everyone went to change back to their street clothes, the manager came into the kitchen and screamed, 'What the fuck are you doing?'

I simply replied, 'Exactly what you're going to do to us tomorrow,' explaining I had overheard him on the phone.

He looked at me and smiled. 'You've got a lot of balls.'

He was just the manager so he didn't really care. He might have suspected his own neck was on the chopping block with the rest of us.

We all walked out, past the guests and right out the front door. Guests were still screaming.

The next day I went in to collect my last pay cheque. The manager was again amazed that I had the audacity to turn the tables on management and ownership. 'I've never seen anything like it,' he reiterated. 'I gotta hand it to you.'

Was it karma that the restaurant closed soon thereafter?

My feeling was that people's livelihoods depended on this employment. You don't play with people's livelihoods so cavalierly. People are hired and fired all the time in the restaurant industry, but it's important as an employer to do that with a sense of graciousness whenever possible. There are children and wives and husbands and rent and food on the table to consider. I now see that I was taught well to do things with integrity, a lesson my father demonstrated in everything he did. There is dignity in work. Have respect for workers and what they do. Treat people right. Never mind the money. Do the right thing by your employees and the profits will come. These were ideas and *ideals* I took forward when I returned to India.

As I mentioned before about the strong chef network, it often happens that someone you meet in one restaurant kitchen goes on to another, and if you get on well, you follow him or her. I had met Gary Cohen when I worked at Quo Vadis, the Upper East Side establishment often referred to as the 'fashionable Continental restaurant', a favourite of celebrities such as Princess Grace, Jacqueline Kennedy, Frank Sinatra, Truman Capote, Nat King Cole and Diana Vreeland. Aside from the Continental food, it was known for being opulently decorated with columns and red velvet, and the Italian mosaics in the entry and on the sidewalk. When I met Gary he was the pastry chef. He told me he had worked undercover for the CIA—not the culinary school—and that he carried a Magnum—not a 1.5 litre bottle of wine, but the revolver made famous in the Clint Eastwood *Dirty Harry* flicks. By this point, I took anything anyone said in the restaurant business with a grain of kosher salt ... until proven otherwise. When Gary left Quo Vadis, he invited me to follow him to a new dining experience that would feature Native American cuisine. It would be called Silverbird, after its founder, Reuben Silverbird, a Native American of Navajo and Apache heritage. I could not resist, if only to say I was an Indian American working at an American Indian restaurant in New York City. The menu consisted of possum, rattlesnake, alligator, Kodiak bear, buffalo burgers and the like. Yum?

The employees were a strange brew of folks. I recall these cute Native American twin waitresses who did not wear underwear and, just to mess with our heads, would stand at the top of the spiral staircase that led from the basement kitchen to the dining room upstairs.

One Sunday Gary checked in with me to ask if I had seen 'a black dude poking around the back alleyway entrance to the kitchen downstairs'. Sure enough, an African American gentleman walked in shortly thereafter asking, 'Is this Chang's laundry?' Right. I called upstairs to let Gary know. He said, 'Come up, you're gonna love this.' When I got upstairs I saw Gary engaging another guy at the bar. He walked over, put his arm around him and said, 'Yo, Tonto, how's it going?' Then, as if this sort of thing happened every day, Gary pulled out a Magnum revolver and put it to the man's forehead. I do not lie; I saw this happening, just like in the movies in … slow … motion. 'Get up with me now,' he said in his best gravelly *Dirty Harry* voice. 'Let's go outside.'

When we got outside there was a third guy just standing there fidgeting, waiting for his accomplice.

'If I ever see you guys here again, I will blow your brains out,' Gary told them.

Needless to say, we did not see them again. Gary had noticed the three of them scoping out the joint and coolly prevented us being hit. But perhaps karma was at work again, in the reverse.

Even though most kitchens wait for a review while they iron out the wrinkles and get their service drill down, Reuben pressed hard to get an opening review in the most influential *New York Times* food section, where a review could make or break a restaurant. Well, for better or worse, Reuben got his way. The *NYT*'s food critic Bryan Miller wrote a paragraph announcing the opening. It read:

> Navajo fry bread, buffalo burgers, roasted quail, blue corn pudding and rabbit stew—all will be served at a new American Indian restaurant called Silverbird, scheduled to open June 15 at 505 Columbus Avenue between 84th and 85th Streets. The 110-seat restaurant is owned by Reuben Silverbird, a New Mexico native of Navajo and Apache heritage. It will be open daily for lunch and dinner with complete meals costing about $20, Mr Silverbird said.[1]

That was all that was needed. The lines formed literally around the block. We got slammed and were entirely unprepared for the onslaught that followed. The whole system broke down. The kitchen, the service—all of it went to *shiite*. It was not pretty.

'Not pretty' is never a good look in restaurants—or anywhere. What I took away reminds me of the old Boy Scout motto: be prepared. In the restaurant business, we're always getting ready for service. In the kitchen, this involves doing our mise en place—a French expression for 'set in place'—to have all your ingredients ready before service and before you start cooking. It's preparedness, and it means you've thought things through beforehand. You've visualized the end goal (your dish) and therefore you've figured out the process and the journey to get there (the ingredients and recipe). You're ready to cook when the orders come in with all your ingredients and tools easily accessible and at hand. 'Mise en place is the religion of all good line cooks,' wrote Anthony Bourdain in *Kitchen Confidential*.[2] Extrapolating, don't go nuts inviting a ton of people to try your new restaurant until you are bang-on sure you can handle the onslaught of orders or reservations, especially if you blast your readiness in a major publication. Keep in mind that *The New York Times* was and is 'the newspaper of record', and that restaurants and Broadway shows can live a long time or die a quick and painful death with one 'yay' or 'nay' from it. I learned to have all my ducks lined up before asking the big guns to come in for a tasting so that in case of a good review or even a 'meh' review, when the reservations start piling up, neither the kitchen nor the service team find themselves tied up so much that they get caught unable to fulfil diners' fantasies. Start slow, grow the restaurant organically (by word-of-mouth recommendations, one hopes) and gradually build the business as the team transforms into a well-oiled machine ready to jump into high gear at a moment's notice.

Silverbird did not last long. But I had my season as an American Indian chef, now added to my résumé along with Indian American chef.

I had another 'moral of the story' experience at Silverbird in the winter of that year when my parents came to New York on a visit. I took them in one night on my day off, to eat and to see where I was working. We were a table of four. After a long-drawn-out but fun dinner, Dad asked for the bill. Our waitress disappeared and reappeared to announce, 'It's all been taken care of—it's on the house.'

'Shit, here we go,' I thought and as if on cue, Dad replied, 'Thanks, but I'd like my bill, please.'

She couldn't believe it, and reiterated that it was free, on the house, to which Dad replied, 'I reserved a table like anyone else, we were seated like anyone else, I was presented the menu like anyone else, we ordered and ate like anyone else, and now I'd like to pay my bill like anyone else too.'

She disappeared again and returned, this time with Reuben Silverbird.

'Please, Mr Akerkar,' he said, 'it's our pleasure to have you and the family dine with us today, and in appreciation of Rahul's hard work, we would like to host your dinner.'

'Then show that to him, not us,' Dad replied, 'and we'd be more than honoured and happy to come back and eat as your guests when you invite us to do so the next time.'

Reuben couldn't understand what had gone wrong and wondered what they'd done to cause my father not to take the handout. The problem was the way it played out. It was an offhandish gesture, after the fact. They knew I was coming in to eat with the family and had it really meant so much, Reuben should have come up to the table when we sat down and said the same thing at the start of the meal. Not afterwards so flippantly. Dad was very proper that way and repeated this story in several of the restaurants I worked in. It was a learning experience for me and something I'm very mindful of even today—the perception quotient in the delivery of hospitality.

All these actors in the theatrical show known as restaurants fed my personal script. Jonathan Bennett and Anne Rosenzweig were right: they fed me with information I could not have learned at any cooking school, whether the Culinary Institute of America in New York or Le Cordon Bleu in Paris. I have done every job there is in restaurants, from dishwasher to waiter to bartender, from salad boy to assistant chef to the top dog and owner. To understand any business, you need to know all the ins and outs from bottom to top. For one, you'll know who is doing it well, who is not, who is cheating you or cutting corners, who is excelling and who is faking it. Or who is slipping a bottle of wine into their gym bag, better known as the 'five-finger discount'—i.e., grab whatever you can and split without paying.

Somewhere along the way, I started to become disenchanted with the field of biochemical engineering. After attaining my second baccalaureate at Columbia, things were building up academically. The pressure was on as I developed my idea for the lofty PhD that would make my parents happy and, I could only hope, make me rich. Perhaps my waning interest was due to the daunting task of putting my nose to the grindstone to write the wretched thesis I had outlined in this abstract:

> The effect of extracellular NADH on the growth of *Methylocystis Parvus* OBBP grown on methane was determined over a range of initial NADH concentrations from 6.62 x 10-3 to 1.76 x 10-2 g-mol/l ... On the basis of the above results and the impervious nature of cell membranes to NADH, it appears that cells can take up reducing equivalents from extracellular NADH in specific concentration ranges. This could make possible the growth of these cells in the cathodic chamber of an electrolytic bioreactor to overcome their reducing power limitations.

I can translate this into English ... but why bother because, quite frankly, my thesis would not have changed the future of biochemistry, nor prevented a nuclear war. But we will never know.

The exact moment when I knew I would drop out came unexpectedly, like a 'flash bang' grenade going off. For my PhD I was working on a theory that, I felt, seemed to defy known science. When I had collected four or five months' worth of research and data, I went to my advisor and explained what I had found.

'It's impossible,' he said.

'I'm not arguing that,' I replied. 'But I'm replicating it over and over again. I don't know; maybe I am making the same mistake over and over.'

'Okay,' he said. 'Let me see.'

We repeated the study with him and kept getting similar data.

He turned to me and said, 'No one has ever reported this in the literature and people have been looking at it since the 1950s, and you're just a Master's student.'

I repeated that I was willing to accept that I was making a mistake, that there was some kind of anomaly, and asked him to suggest what that might be.

He couldn't answer. He just pooh-poohed the whole thing. A month later, a top expert in this field came over from London's Imperial College to address our department at Columbia. After the talk, he spoke to each of the postgrad students. I met with him in our lab and showed him our results. He was rapt.

'This is fascinating,' he said enthusiastically. 'Keep working on this. Please stay in touch and let me know where it goes.'

Here were two diametrically opposed reactions from leading academicians, one of pure encouragement, the other of pure disdain. In that moment I felt a total shift in my thinking. I realized academia is BS, all politically driven, all publish or perish, and I lost interest in it. Two weeks later I dropped out of Columbia.

That was when I realized that to follow my own passion, namely in the world of cooking, perhaps eventually even starting my own business, I would have to leave the path I had been on since I was a teenager.

There was one more piece I needed to collect to attain my personal degree in restauranting before I went back to India—learn how to manage the whole shebang. So I landed a job as manager at another cavernous fern-filled restaurant, the Saloon, right across Lincoln Center on Broadway at 64th Street. Once famous for its roller-skating waiters, the restaurant had brick walls painted white and old, slightly cheesy black-and-white photographs of Parisian street scenes. From some tables, you could see the Chagall paintings at Lincoln Center and stare at the iconic fountain and beautiful clock.

The menu was enormous. The food was just okay, by concession of co-owner Philip Scotti. During its closing years, he told a reporter: 'We were never known for great food. We were a neighbourhood place back when the neighbourhood really needed one. Everyone else was focusing on Lincoln Center, but we took the opposite position and saw Lincoln Center as icing.'

Co-owners Scotti and Stewart Rosen ran a disciplined ship, which I admired a great deal. On busy nights they'd leave about 25 to 30 per cent of the seating for pre- and post-show walk-ins; the rest was by reservation.

The pre-show business was crazy. Then it mellowed to just merely slammed, and again picked up after the curtains went down. It was trial by fire for me, having worked restaurant jobs focused on one plate or pot at a time. Now I would see first-hand how all the parts fit together into a working business.

Two incidents at the Saloon that were most instructive about how to run a restaurant have stuck with me. Both times Stewart's behaviour seemed kind of harsh, but years later, while running my own restaurants in India, he proved to be wise and worthy of emulation, mainly because people will try to get away with whatever they can, whether they are patrons or staff.

I worked most closely with Stewart, who sometimes came to work in shorts and a T-shirt, so guests would not really know what his status was. Sometimes he would stand next to me at the reception desk, as he did one busy night when I was at the front host stand to welcome guests. An elderly couple walked in.

'Welcome. Do you have a reservation?' I asked.

'Yes, we do.'

'Under what name would the reservation be, sir?'

'Rosen.'

I looked for their name in our reservations list but couldn't find it. 'Hmm, I am sorry, but I don't see it here.'

'You better check again,' the gentleman replied in the tone New Yorkers use when they are VIPs, even if only in their minds. (Come to think of it now, it's the same tone Indians use all the time with anyone they think is below their pay grade.) But we hospitality professionals learn to accept people at face value, assuming that even if dressed shabbily, they might own a building on Park Avenue or in Breach Candy. So I checked again.

'You're not on the list,' I politely responded, 'but if you'd like to get a drink at the bar in the meantime, I will see what I can do. I hope it will not be too long.'

'You better check again,' the guest insisted. Then he dropped his zinger: 'WE'RE STEWART ROSEN'S PARENTS. I suggest you get us a table *now* or we could get you fired.'

Stewart was standing right next to me, listening to this, and he didn't flinch or raise an eyebrow.

Diplomatically, I responded, now inferring that Stewart was testing me: 'Your getting me fired is your prerogative; I'm just doing my job.'

But this was a couple on a mission, not to be denied. 'We called several times,' the guy said. 'Find us a table now.'

I finally convinced them to have a drink at the bar, while I scrambled to clear a table myself. Stewart still said and did nothing.

Once seated, this couple had the audacity—let's call a spade a spade: they had the balls, or as we say in Yiddish, the chutzpah—to complain and complain about almost everything from the service to the heat of the soup to how underdone the steak was. It was at that point that Stewart, watching all this from the corner, walked up to the couple's table and loomed over them.

'Who are you?' the gentleman asked, almost indignantly.

'I'm Stewart Rosen.'

They turned white, with a deer in the headlights look, the face a child makes when he's caught with his hand in the cookie jar.

Stewart said: 'Get up and get out.' That was all. Needless to say, we never saw them again.

My lesson: be patient, accommodate, forgive ... until the breaking point. Then spare nothing to show them the door. The customer isn't always right. I experienced a version of this later at Indigo too.

Stewart had integrity, so much that it was his policy to pay for anything he ate or drank at the Saloon. Imagine that in India. Sure, that money would go into his coffers at the end of the day. But he was making a point to the staff, a point well taken. I hardly witnessed any five-finger thefts at the Saloon.

On another occasion, I was stationed at the reception counter during lunch. It was 3.30 p.m. and the cavernous dining room had but one table occupied, with a couple paying its bill. I saw Stewart walk in, sit at the end of the bar, grab a copy of *The New York Post* and order a burger. So I casually walked over toward him with nothing more in mind than schmoozing with the boss.

'Hey Stewart,' I started.

He barely took his eyes off the paper and said, 'I pay you to keep an eye on the floor, not to socialize with me.' Then he went back to his reading.

I was reduced to a small speck on the floor, cut off at the knees. Tail between my legs, I crawled back to the front of the restaurant, mumbling to myself, 'What an asshole.'

That was unfair of me because I quickly realized he was right, his brutal rebuke notwithstanding. Otherwise, he was a great guy, would invite staff to parties and was generally a good boss. So I had to respect his drawing a line. Work is work. Play is play. The twain should not meet while an employee is on the clock. Years later, I would be challenged to maintain that high bar with people working for me whose work ethic, shall I say, needed some realigning.

ESCABECHE OF RED SNAPPER (FROM WINGS ON WOOSTER ST)

INGREDIENTS FOR 4 PORTIONS

Escabeche

4 red snapper fillets, skin off and deboned ~125 gm each or 500 gm in total

2 red onions, sliced

2 carrots, sliced or julienned

1 fennel bulb, thinly sliced or shaved thin

2 bell peppers, julienned (red and green)

½ cup olive oil

1 tablespoon small capers

1 tablespoon green pitted olives, coarsely chopped or smashed

5 garlic cloves, coarsely chopped or smashed

1 tablespoon finely chopped parsley

2 teaspoon roasted whole coriander seeds

1 teaspoon whole black pepper corn

2 bay leaves

½ cup sherry vinegar

Flour for dredging

DIRECTIONS

Heat the olive oil in a skillet. Cut the snapper fillets into bite-sized pieces about 2–3 inches big (or leave whole if you prefer). Season with salt and pepper and lightly dust or coat the fillet pieces (or whole fillets) in the flour (make sure to remove the extra flour). Fry until lightly golden on each side and cooked through (about 1–2 minutes per side). Remove and drain on a paper towel.

In the same pan, add the garlic, sweat for a minute and then add the onions, carrots, peppers, fennel and cook until soft. Add the coriander seeds, black peppercorn and bay leaves, combine well and then add the capers and olives and sauté a minute more. Add the vinegar and bring to a simmer for 2 minutes. Adjust the seasoning (add a little sugar if it tastes too acidic or tart, to get a nice sweet–sour balance.) Remove from the heat, pour the marinade over the snapper and let it marinate refrigerated in a non-reactive dish for several hours (~3 to 5).

To serve, let the escabeche come to room temperature (about 30 minutes out of the fridge), add in the chopped parsley and carefully combine all that good oily, vinegar with everything, making sure not to break up the fish fillets in the process. Save some crusty bread to soak up the leftover juices!

INDIGO'S LOBSTER BISQUE (Adapted from Vanessa)

We used the clawless spiny lobster or langouste available in Indian ocean waters, but feel free to use the North Atlantic clawed variety too. Remove the claw meat to add to the finished bisque and use the claw shells while making the lobster reduction. We also found that making the lobster reduction in chicken stock added another dimension of richness to the soup.

INGREDIENTS FOR 4 PORTIONS

Lobster Reduction

4 lobster carapaces—heads, legs and tails after removing the meat for garnish (~250gm–350gm each)

½ kg chicken bones or 1litre of chicken stock

1 medium onion, chopped

4 cloves garlic

2 carrots, chopped

2 stalks celery, chopped

1 leek, chopped

1 fennel bulb, chopped

6 tomatoes, quartered

2 teaspoons fresh thyme leaves

1 bay leaf

1 teaspoon whole black peppercorn

100 gm unsalted butter

50 gm tomato paste

¾ cup white wine

¾ cup cognac

4 tablespoons olive oil

25 gm flour

Salt and pepper

Bisque

¾ cup heavy cream

180 gm cold unsalted butter cut into 1–2-inch cubes

2 tablespoon sherry

2 teaspoons Pernod

1 teaspoon fresh tarragon leaves

Garnish

Tail meat of 4 lobsters, poached and cut up into 1–2-inch pieces

2 cups toasted large brioche croutons

4–6 pieces of okra

5 gm chopped chives

2 tablespoons sour cream

½ teaspoon paprika

Zest of 1 lemon

½ cup white flour

DIRECTIONS

Remove and Poach the Tails:

Twist off the lobsters' heads and legs to separate from the tails. Leave the tomalley in the head cavities and save the shells. In a pot large enough to hold the 4 tails in a single layer, bring 2 inches of water to a gentle boil and poach the tails for about 4–5 minutes till the meat turns opaque white. This will just cook the tails and get them to loosen enough from the shell to remove easily. Remove the tails from the hot water and plunge them into an ice-water bath to stop them from overcooking. Don't throw away the poaching water as it's full of flavour and you'll use it when making the reduction. Using a pair of kitchen shears, cut open the thin underside of the tail from end to end along the 'belly' and carefully pry out the cooked tails, trying to keep them intact. Put the cleaned poached tails in a covered non-reactive bowl and refrigerate till ready to serve. Save the empty tail shells and any juices left behind and add to the heads and legs for the next step.

Lobster Reduction:

Dry roast the flour in a dry pan on low heat till it turns golden-brown. Remove from the pan and set aside. In a large heavy-bottomed saucepan heat the olive oil and butter together. Add the lobster carapaces and chicken bones and sauté over high heat till the lobster shells turn bright red and the chicken bones brown. Crush all the shells and bones in the pot with the back of a ladle, kitchen spoon or any other heavy cleaver or mallet. Deglaze the pot with cognac and white wine and cook till all the alcohol is either evaporated or flamed off. Next, add all the remaining vegetables and herbs and cook for 10 to 15 minutes till the vegetables soften and start caramelizing. Keep scraping the caramelized cooked solids off the bottom of the pan and combine with the pot contents. Now add the tomato paste and cook for 5 to 10 minutes. Then add the roasted flour and sauté for another minute or so to combine well. Then add enough poaching water to cover the bones and shells and simmer, covered on medium-low heat, for 2 to 2½ hours. Add salt and pepper to taste.

NOTE: If using chicken stock instead of chicken bones, cover the crushed lobster shells with the chicken stock and top up with poaching water, if needed, to just cover the shells. You may need to top up the pot with a little poaching liquid or water every now and then, to keep it from drying out too much. When you have a nice, concentrated lobster reduction, pulverize the pot's contents and then carefully double-strain several times through a colander and then a fine mesh strainer to remove all shells and other particulate matter. Try and extrude all the flavour-packed liquid out from the solids by pressing down on them against the colander with the back of a ladle. Toss out the solids and save the strained lobster reduction, letting it cool.

TIP: You can keep the lobster reduction for several weeks, well-covered and frozen. So, if you plan on making a risotto or a pasta with lobster, make this ahead of time to make the cook a whole lot easier!

The Bisque:

To finish the soup, heat the lobster reduction on low and add the heavy cream, sherry and tarragon to it. Then add the chilled butter, a cube at a time, whisking constantly, to incorporate the butter in the soup, giving it a beautiful silky rich sheen. Finish with Pernod. Adjust seasoning.

To Serve:

Cut the okra into small disks, very lightly dredge or coat in flour and deep-fry till golden brown and crispy. Remove and drain excess oil on a paper towel. In a clean bowl, just prior to serving, mix all the ingredients together to make a lobster 'salad' with the toasted brioche croutons and crispy okra. Immediately distribute the lobster salad amongst the 4 soup plates and serve with the bisque.

INDIGO'S LOBSTER RISOTTO

At Indigo, we always served variants of a lobster bisque and a lobster risotto together on our menus because it was the most efficient way to use up all the lobster shells we kept collecting. The soup was practically free to make as a by-product of our very popular lobster risotto, which was served with a whole tail. We served the risotto either with a butter-poached, de-shelled tail or a butter-poached tail, grilled in its shell.

INGREDIENTS FOR 4 PORTIONS

Option 1: Butter-Poached Lobster Tail OR Option 2: Grilled Lobster Tail in Its Shell

4 lobster tails separated from the head and legs (each lobster~250gm-350gm)

300 gm cold unsalted butter cut into 2-inch cubes

4 garlic cloves

2 sprigs of fresh thyme

Salt and pepper

Lobster Risotto

300 gm arborio rice

3–4 cups warm chicken stock

1 cup lobster reduction from the Lobster Bisque recipe earlier

6 peeled shallots, roughly cut

1 tablespoon finely chopped garlic

12 roughly chopped Kalamata olives

½ cup blanched, shelled edamame beans

¾ cup white wine

60 gm grated Parmesan cheese

100 gm cold unsalted butter cut in 2-inch cubes

½ teaspoon paprika

2 teaspoons chopped fresh chives

2 teaspoons fresh tarragon leaves

2 teaspoons finely chopped fresh parsley

¼ cup olive oil

Sea salt and pepper

DIRECTIONS

Remove and Poach the Tails:

Twist off the heads and legs to separate the tails of the lobsters. Leave the tomalley in the head cavities and save the shells to use in the lobster reduction from the Lobster Bisque recipe earlier. In a saucepan large enough to hold the 4 tails in a single layer, bring 2 inches of water to a gentle boil and poach the tails for not more than 2 minutes till the meat just begins to turn opaque. This will barely cook the tails but will firm up the meat just enough to loosen and remove them from the shell easily. Remove the tails from the hot water and plunge them into an ice-water bath to stop them cooking. (Don't throw away the poaching water as it's full of flavour and you'll use it to poach the cleaned tails a second time after removing the parboiled lobster meat.)

Option 1: Using a pair of kitchen shears, cut open the thin underside of the tail from end to end along the 'belly' and carefully pry out the cooked tails, keeping them intact. Put the cleaned poached tails in a covered non-reactive bowl and set aside or refrigerate till ready to serve. Save the empty tail shells and any juices left behind and combine with the heads and legs to use in the lobster reduction from the Bisque recipe.

Option 2: Using a pair of kitchen shears, cut open the thick top carapace of the tail from end to end, along the 'back' of the tail, splitting it open.

Do not remove the meat, but carefully spread open the shell to expose the tail meat. Set aside and refrigerate till ready to serve.

In the same saucepan used to partially poach the lobster tails in their shells earlier, add ¼ cup of the poaching water with the garlic and thyme. Bring the water to a simmer over medium heat. Put the heat on low and add one cube of cold butter to the simmering water, whisking continuously to melt the butter. DO NOT LET THE BUTTER BOIL. Before the butter cube has melted completely, add another cube and whisk it in. Keep adding cold butter cubes, whisking continuously, until all the butter has melted and emulsified in the liquid. Make sure not to let the butter boil or it will separate and you'll have to start over. Once all the butter is added and the bath is steaming, add in the lobster tails from Option 1 or Option 2. Poach the lobster meat by spooning hot liquid emulsified butter over it while gently agitating the pan, until the meat turns completely opaque white and the tails curl up. Remove the lobster tails from the pot and keep warm to serve with the risotto. For the tails in their shells, remove them before they're completely poached and transfer them to a hot grill or hot skillet, placing them cut side down to slightly char the shells and the exposed meat. It shouldn't take more than a few minutes to get a quick char on them, before serving with the risotto. Don't overcook the tails.

Lobster Risotto:

Sauté the shallots and garlic in olive oil over medium heat in a 10–12-inch pan, with a generous pinch of sea salt, and sauté until the shallots have softened. Add the risotto rice to the pan and stir continuously with a wooden spoon for about 2–3 minutes until the rice is very slightly toasted. Add white wine to the rice and stir continuously over medium heat, until the rice absorbs the liquid. Before it dries out, add in 1 cup of warm chicken stock and gently stir until the rice almost absorbs this stock as well. Continue the process of adding warm stock a cup at a time, while stirring and allowing the rice to absorb the liquid. Check the rice for doneness—it needs to be al-dente when done, cooked through but with a slight firmness when bitten. As you add in the last bit of stock also add in the edamame beans and Kalamata olives, and cook for a short while before finally adding the lobster reduction. Mix well. It can take up to 20 minutes in total to cook the rice. When the rice is ready, take the pan off the flame, immediately add the unsalted butter a cube at a time, freshly grated parmesan cheese, parsley, chives, paprika and tarragon, mix well, and serve accompanied with a poached or grilled lobster tail.

4: A CAREER AS A CHEF? FUGGEDDABOUDIT

RESTAURANTS WERE JUST A means to an end until that point. I had never for a minute considered making a life of it, much less a career. A career as a cook—only elevated to the lofty title of chef many years later—would have been an oxymoron in my family. My path was to lead towards a profession, as my parents' generation would know it: doctor, scientist, professor, even technocrat, though my parents would probably not have been so approving of that as a life's work.

Then, in that moment I saw through academia—*phoof*—gone was an entire vision of my future. So what would I do? What, as the time-honoured question is posed, do you want to be when you grow up?

Though I had dropped out of my PhD programme, I did still have my master's degree in biochemical engineering from an Ivy League school. And I loved the field of study. So, half-heartedly, until I could figure things out, I applied for some jobs, but they were all in fundamental research, where you mostly work alone. If you are a people person like me, this would feel lonely and isolating, and very quickly. I wanted a position that would allow me to interact with human beings, such as sales or marketing. But there were no such jobs. My father kept encouraging me, sending me names of friends in high places who could help me get a job, perhaps in the pharmaceutical industry. Had I done that, rest assured I would have been a man devoid of a soul, which I would have traded in for the Almighty Buck. I never followed through, never sent my résumé to any of Dad's contacts. I don't know why. Actually, I did not know why back then. Now it is crystal clear to me.

My one and only job in Corporate America, where I had to wear a tie every day to work, was for an investment bank called Dillon, Read & Company on the Upper East Side, land of Very Big Bucks. I did some computer consulting work for them—writing code for some analytical algorithms, a little skill I'd picked up from modelling chemical engineering systems and added to my toolkit. After three months, I could not take it any longer.

I took up selling Indian silver jewellery at a Sunday flea market on the Upper West Side near Columbus Avenue and 79th Street—stuff I'd imported through family in Jaipur. I made up stories to go with some pieces. After I'd sold it, I narrated the same story for the next piece. I was such a sleaze. I justified it with knowing that true sleazes would have charged much more than I did.

All my friends had already left New York and begun to fall in step with the Great American March towards a sprawling ranch house in the suburbs, 2.5 kids, a Toyota minivan (and a Porsche in the garage) and a generous 401K plan.

I did not feel their passion. I did not feel their joie de vivre. I wanted joie de vivre.

Then one day it hit me. My joie de vivre lay in cooking. I enjoyed the restaurant business and everything that went with it—the intensity, the urgency of making everything come out on time and together, the interaction with guests, the pride of work done well, the logistics of ordering ingredients, tracking sales. I decided this would be my career. It gave me what academia would not: recognition. And instant gratification. All I'd wanted from that Columbia professor was recognition. And while research may garner great acknowledgement upon the publication of one's Nobel-winning thesis, that could take twenty years or more. One of the great joys we chefs get, which most of us don't really talk about, much less acknowledge to ourselves, is the fulfilment we feel when seeing a guest take that first bite and watching their faces light up and them release a satisfied 'Mmmmmm'.

The next big hump to overcome on this new path would be telling my parents, who were more invested in my academic ascent than I was. In the summer of 1987, they came to the family apartment in Washington Heights on the way Upper West Side for a few months.

After they settled in, I let a few days pass. Then I came by and started with, 'Sit down.' Never a good way to put people at ease. I think they knew what was coming.

'I want to be a cook. I know I have these three pieces of parchment—two Bachelor's and a Master's—that say I'm a biochemical engineer, but I want you to know that your son is going to throw all that away and become a cook. I don't know if it's the right decision—only time will tell—but it's something I want to do. Something I have to do.'

This was an outrageously audacious decision at the time. I was born in 1959, making me a boomer—who, as a generation, made more traditional life choices like our parents did, but also embraced the technological jump into the twenty-first century. Today millennials, famous or infamous for job-hopping, would not blink an eye at giving up one career path and following another, no matter how off the beaten track ... such as becoming a cook, considered so much below the status of a biochemical engineer with a (almost) PhD from an American Ivy League university. My generation just didn't switch careers with the same ease.

So there were my parents, digesting my announcement. I waited for the barrage of objections and counters. But their response took me completely by surprise. I can't remember which of them actually said this, because it was probably in unison: 'You've finally made up your mind. Thank God! Now just go for it.'

I might make fun of their tendencies to keep me in line and train me, but did I mention I had the most supportive and even, from time to time, understanding parents in the world? They raised Avantika and me to pursue anything we wanted from life.

So what was I thinking and how did I come to that decision? The truth is, I wasn't thinking.

It's hard to explain my seemingly reckless decision-making process, because it defies logic. I go with my gut, or as Joseph Campbell, the

The bartender; the dishwasher; the chef

esteemed American professor and mythologist, put it, I follow my bliss. Campbell had added: 'Find where it is, and don't be afraid to follow it.'

I do dive into situations for which outwardly I might seem unprepared and inexperienced. From early childhood I was this way. One time when I could not have been older than six, my father, who'd swum for his school team, took me to a swimming pool and out of nowhere said, 'You want to learn to swim? ... Swim,' and just threw me into the water. I did not drown, though I really could not swim. But I sure learned fast. So maybe this tendency started that time, and with repeated successes at diving in and not drowning, I grew up to assume I could do anything I set my mind to.

My work choices have never been about money or other people's definition of success. What drives me is being loved and appreciated. I think a lot of people can identify with that human need, but not everyone allows it to dictate their professional moves. I got no love or appreciation as a budding biochemical engineer. And I did get love from cooking.

Another observation—I used the phrase 'I go with my gut' three paragraphs ago. Many, including me, often substitute those words with 'visceral', which the dictionary defines as 'being or arising from impulse or sudden emotion rather than from thought or deliberation'. But most interestingly, the root of that word comes from the Latin *viscera*, meaning the 'internal organs of the body, especially those contained within the abdominal and thoracic cavities'. The abdominal cavity holds the greater part of the digestive tract. So of course, it makes sense—to me at least—that my decision to cook for a living came from my gut.

I was twenty-eight, and it was time I got serious about food—not just playing with my food anymore, you could say. I approached my professional development with a whole new pair of eyes, a new nose and palate. At that point, I felt I had soaked up enough experience in New York and Pennsylvania to go to India and see what I could do in the nascent Indian restaurant world.

My initial vision was to do something out of the ordinary, befitting my upbringing and proclivities to that point. The problem was, when I landed back in India—this would have been late 1989—the dining scene in Bombay and throughout the rest of the country left a lot to be desired in the way of professionalism and creativity, compared to the levels I had begun to grow accustomed to in the US.

It was stuck in a time warp, from what I could see. To be fair to my fellows in the kitchens of India, the whole idea of dining out was a relatively new concept there, which had only emerged in the mid-twentieth century, according to Indian food authority Colleen Taylor Sen. In *Food Culture in India,* she writes:

> Eating out was tolerated as a necessity rather than valued as a luxury or a new experience. Cooking and entertaining at home were facilitated by the presence of many women in a joint family and, for the wealthy, abundant servants. For all social and religious groups, hospitality was a social and religious obligation. As a result, it was considered virtually an insult to take guests to dinner in a restaurant rather than invite them home.[1]

What I saw (and tasted) upon my return to India were basically two types of restaurants. At the high end, there were only restaurants in five-star hotels. The Taj and Oberoi hotels boasted fine dining, though 'fine' was debatable. The Taj Mahal Palace's entry in the fine-dine category was the Zodiac Grill, which had just opened the year I returned to Bombay. It had started with 300 dishes, narrowed down to 100, but quickly realized that more is not better and eventually settled on thirty-five different entrées. It was famous for such classics as the escargot de bourgogne, five varieties of caviar, and house favourites like camembert dariole, kahlua mousse and chicken zodiac. Yet, the béchamel, or white sauce, that covered some of the entrées was thick and, for lack of a more professional word, gloppy. This was the fare of old English country clubs, but people ate it up as though they had just read Julia Child.

Entering the restaurant from the hotel lobby, you felt like you had walked into a European dining establishment, maybe London, Paris or

Munich in the 1950s. Each table felt private with dim lighting, not like your typical overlit restaurant. Entrées were served with great fanfare, silver cloches lifted simultaneously for couples who'd 'ahhh' and coo like well-fed pigeons. While it was lauded as 'ahead of its time' upon its opening, it was already behind the times, in my opinion.

There was one cool and clever policy the Zodiac Grill adopted for a short period of time. Rather than include prices for every item on the menu, the restaurant suggested guests pay what they felt was appropriate. This had two effects. International visitors paid what they estimated the same meal would cost in their country, and this usually worked out to the Zodiac's benefit when converted into rupees. The Indian high-society diner, rather than be embarrassed by paying too little, always paid too much. In either case, it was win-win for the Zodiac Grill and they raked it in. Of course, there were those who took advantage of this scheme too. I told an Italian friend about it the night before he and his girlfriend returned to Italy from a two-month backpacking trip around India. They went there on their last night, pigged out Zodiac-style and left ₹10 for their dinner. My friends are *like that only*.

The Taj also boasted what is widely agreed to be India's first coffee shop, Shamiana, which opened in 1973. For many years it held a special place in the hearts and minds of Bombayites, who met for a civilized cuppa or for special occasions. It wasn't so much that the food was great—some would argue that it was good to fine. But there was something about the ambience, the big, open and clean room with a view of the Gateway of India, a perfect see-and-be-seen hangout venue for the up-and-coming generation of Indians proud of their early-stage economic growth, and the hipsters in their late twenties. In any regard, I knew from roaming the globe that Shamiana did not compare with the hip cafés I had sipped at in New York and Europe. Something was missing that I hoped to bring to India, namely the kind of cosmopolitan café scene I might want to hang out at myself.

There were others. The Oberoi at Nariman Point in Colaba had the Café Royal, the Bombay Brasserie and the Outrigger Restaurant, all okay enough but hardly groundbreaking. My wife and I had an experience at the Oberoi that typified the compartmentalizing mentality within hotel service that drove—and still drives—me nuts and that sells the customer short on true service.

On our second or third anniversary, Malu and I went to celebrate over a romantic dinner at the Rotisserie, the then fine-dining restaurant at the Oberoi. After an average but expensive meal with a bottle of wine, I asked our waiter whether she could call their stuffy French restaurant, the Café Royal downstairs, and inform them that we'd like to come in to end our dinner with Crêpes Suzette—the classic French pancakes flambéed tableside in a zesty orange sauce with Grand Marnier. I loved this dessert and the Café Royal was one of the only places in Bombay that did them, and really well at that.

'Let me check,' she said before disappearing to ask a more senior manager.

The manager came over a few minutes later and matter-of-factly said, 'I'm sorry, that won't be possible as it's not just a dessert joint.'

'Really? I've just spent a bomb on a mediocre dinner here in the Rotisserie—a restaurant in *this Oberoi hotel*—and now I want to go to another restaurant in *the same hotel* to salvage my dinner, spending more money in *the same hotel* with a dessert indulgence, and you're saying it's not possible? Why? I'm sure it is possible ... connect me with the Café Royal manager, please.'

He brought a cordless phone and dialled a number.

'Hi, my wife and I would like to come by for Crêpes Suzette right now. Would that be possible? Yes, oh, great ... see you in a few minutes ...'

I paid my bill at the Rotisserie, we walked downstairs and were seated in a totally empty Café Royal, where we had our dessert with a macchiato, and left.

When you're in the business of selling food and your restaurant has space for a customer—let alone sitting empty—you do not turn them away with some pretentious, elitist babble. You offer them the table and thank them for their business.

Aside from the hotel dining establishments, there were what I call the mom-and-pop restaurants, mostly serving Indian food. Pop sat at the cash register and Mom was the hostess; often their offspring worked the tables, and everything else. Cooks, when Pop or Mom themselves weren't at the stove, were thought of as menial labour. And they were treated that way as well, cramped into hot kitchens, unhygienic sweatboxes with less than the best cooking utensils. Underpaid and way under-respected.

However, while family-owned (the Bahls), Khyber, located in the Kala Ghoda district of Bombay, was unlike the other mom-and-pop eateries. In business since the late 1950s, then reopened in 1988 after the original restaurant was destroyed in a fire, it served traditional Mughal cuisine from the North West Frontier Province—tender kebabs, rich curries and lots of tandoori favourites roasted in its famous red masala sauce. Its signature dish was a paneer korma. The design was meant to place you in a palace, with murals depicting turbaned Mughal royalty, lots of exposed brickwork, oil lanterns, ornate arches, ceilings adorned with sleeper wood and oversized earthenware urns. This was considered high-end dining for many years. It became an institution so popular that its clientele included Brad Pitt, Sir Paul McCartney, Amitabh Bachchan, the prince of Luxembourg, the Kuwait royal family, Sir Richard Branson, Aamir Khan, Goldie Hawn, Richard Gere and Demi Moore. Despite the changing landscape and tastes of restaurants in Mumbai, Sudheer Bahl, who owns it now, has stayed true to the same menu for decades.

Another niche was picking up steam by the time I came home: the chain restaurant. United Coffee House was opened in New Delhi in 1942 by the entrepreneurial magnate, late Hans Raj Kalra. He was a suave liquor baron and a passionate hotelier with the experience of running a restaurant and bar called Esplanade in the famous Chandni Chowk area of Old Delhi. UCH has grown to many locations across India. When it opened, the cuisine was a cross between 'Conti and Indian' and appealed more to the palate of Westerners than Indians. For locals, it represented the first baby steps to real cafés, of the sort we developed in 1992 with Under the Over.

Copper Chimney, which also specializes in the cuisine of India's North West Frontier Province, opened its first outlet in Worli, Bombay, in 1972 under the auspices of Jagdish Kapur, a prominent Bollywood filmmaker and food aficionado. Today there are about ten branches in India and some in the Gulf. This popular chain won Best Indian Cuisine for a National Restaurant Chain at the Indian Restaurant Awards 2013. The signature dishes include chelo kebab, jinga nisha, vegetable kheema, Benarasi pulao prepared with its own reshmi kabab and murg makhani, the immensely popular version of butter chicken.

Wedged in between these niches, so-called Chinese restaurants also found a place among Indian diners. I say so-called because this is a cuisine unto itself. I'm even at a loss about how to describe it. Chinese is subtle; Indian is more of more and more. Not really Chinese, not really Indian, in this Sino-Punjabi amalgam, spices, herbs and other ingredients (other than maybe ginger, garlic and soy) form a disparate yet comforting mix that's so bad it's good! There they are, serving sweet-corn-and-chicken soup and chopsuey to legions of Indians who actually think this is Chinese food. To be fair, the Chinese food I ate in New York, which has the largest population of Chinese in the world outside of China, is not really the intensely spicy Szechuan food nor the mellow Cantonese food they serve in China, but a clichéd, bland, oversized Sino-American fusion cuisine.

The most famous of the Chinese restaurants had to be China Garden, a fine-dining establishment back in the day. It was near our family's house in Kemps Corner, and where Nelson Wang gave birth to chicken manchurian and changed Indians' idea of Chinese food. His hot-and-sour soup is unlike the original you'd get in China and Vietnam. He also 'invented' chicken lollipop and fried corn cream.

Now for service, extremely important because a patron's overall experience of a restaurant depends more on the service and ambience than on the quality of food, according to a 2017 study from the University of Denver's Daniel College of Business.

I could write a book on this subject. Oh, I am writing a book on it right now. Upon my arrival, I witnessed a style of service that would never fly anywhere else in the world. There were inefficiencies, disrespect and plain old misunderstanding of what it means to 'serve'. Well, I must retract that last comment about misunderstanding, because in India the service style merely reflected an age-old culture. It was my mission, starting from my first restaurant, to introduce more efficiencies and more respect for each other, both in the kitchen and between wait staff and guest. It was ... and is ... an uphill ambition, but one worth striving for.

We come from a feudal system and a deeply rooted hierarchical caste system. There is always someone above you and someone below you, and the twain are not supposed to meet, speak or even look into each other's eyes. Perhaps I exaggerate, but I have seen it too many times in workplaces, in the hospitality business and many other fields.

The key to the origins of poor service in India may be in the very word 'service'. In our culture, anyone who 'serves' must by definition be of the lower class, in service to someone from a higher class. This despite the Sanskrit phrase that became a countrywide slogan and, honestly, not much more than lip service to the Great God of Tourism. I refer to the Sanskrit phrase अतिथि देवो भव (Atithi devo bhava), or in English, 'Treat the guest as a god'.

This engrained sense that to give service is subservient leads waiters and all other service providers in India to grovel, to bow way too low, even if only figuratively speaking. While Indians may find this acceptable, even preferable, it leaves many visitors from the West uncomfortable. Even I want to strangle the server under such circumstances.

And because of this 'who's on top, who's on bottom' attitude, which is rampant throughout Indian society, people get quite hung up about their titles. I see this in my entire restaurant staff. Young cooks want to be called chef de partie, a fancy French word which simply means the man or woman in charge of a certain area of production.

This is my usual response to applicants and staff who ask about their precious title: 'In my kitchen there is the main chef (me), the chef de cuisine (the senior-most chef who actually runs the entire kitchen operation for the restaurant), and the sous chef(s) (second in charge). The rest of you are cooks. Whatever you want to call yourself, your salary is based on your skills, not your titles.'

I did not want to replicate this Indian atmosphere of workplace inefficiency and what I saw as the devaluation of human effort—nor their impact on the guest and particularly how this 'dis-service' could negatively affect the bottom line—when I owned my own restaurants. Later in this book I'll share in great detail my strategies and tactics for achieving a kind of oasis of service respect in the Indian desert. For now, I just offer this exemplary story of my approach towards modelling the behaviours I hoped my staff would emulate.

One day, a few years after my arrival in India, when I opened Under the Over, my first dining establishment, a dishwasher did not show up. I asked a junior cook to fill in, as guests were already dining and the dirty dishes and silverware were piling up. He said, 'That's not my job.' I literally rolled up my sleeves and attacked the stack of dishes with a passion. At that, several staff, most probably embarrassed and awkward seeing 'the boss' doing such a 'demeaning' job, said they would do it.

'No,' I replied. 'It's not your job, so go do your job.' I am sure there was a lot of sarcastic 'tude in my tone.

That was the last time anyone turned down a request to do something they thought was below their pay (and ego) grade. Lesson learned.

One of my former Under the Over employees, Vikrant Bhasin, later went on to get a catering degree in the US at the famous hospitality school, Johnson & Wales University in Providence, Rhode Island. He wrote to me several years after undergoing my seemingly radical approach (at least in India): 'Thank you for opening my eyes. I now understand what it means to really work and carry one's own weight, and the ethos that no work is beneath you. And I apologize if I originally recoiled at your ideas about how to work with staff and guests.'

Since then he has gone on to big things, working for acclaimed American chef Michael Mina at his eponymously named San Francisco restaurant as a sous chef, later heading an Indian concept pop-up eatery in San Francisco under the Mina umbrella and then distinguishing himself as a caterer to A-list clients based in Hawaii and as Kaiser Permanente's Moanalua Medical Center as chef-manager of the food and nutrition services department.

What I had been subjected to in New York was a culture much less concerned with who was supposed to do what, and more focused on getting the best job done in the fastest time possible, regardless of so-called job title or (and I gag on this word, because it has been so abused) deliverables.

candied
orange peel
shrikand
silver
leaf
fresh
berries

5: AN ITALIAN INTERMEZZO

I AM OFTEN ASKED what is the Best Meal I Ever Had (not cooked by me, I add without humility). People assume I will mention the feast I had at Daniel Boulud's Daniel in Manhattan or Alice Waters's Chez Panisse in Berkeley, California, or Alain Passard's L'Arpège in Paris.

None of the above. It was in the middle of nowhere during a trip to Italy.

I'm also asked why Italian cuisine seems to have a strong influence on much of what I cook.

As with any red-blooded male who may also happen to love food and have a growing love for cooking, the backstory to my affair with Italian food began with a woman. Of course. She and her family introduced me to the secrets of what really makes Italian food work so well in almost every country where it is served; and it's not just about the fresh basil.

Her name was Daniela. (And yes, my beloved wife Malini knows this whole story.) We met in New York in the period when I was still a student at Columbia. She was the girlfriend of my F&M roommate's brother. But she and I hit it off from the start—there was that natural click, a connection you hope for. Not too long after we met, she had trouble with the boyfriend and I, ever the good listener with a strong shoulder to lean on, became her confidante, the guy she talked to about the flailing relationship with 'the other guy'. Eventually she dumped the BF and there we were, New York love, '80s-style. Was it true love? Probably not, but we became very close. The heart is a lonely hunter, so we both fell in love with each other and I loved having her as my SO during those years.

It must have been the summer of 1983 when she invited me to join her and her family at their gorgeous house in the tiny fishing town of Scilla (population around 5,000, not counting the livestock), facing the Strait of Messina near the tip of Italy's boot, right across from the island of Sicily. I jumped at the chance, the eternal romantic, hoping the sparks might lead to something even more meaningful.

Almost as soon as I got there, I felt at home ... that is, my India home. Her family, and many other southern Italian families, cohabitate in joint family environments, so there were aunts and uncles and cousins and second cousins all living together under one roof. The pandemonium alone made me miss my meshugana Indian family. That also meant they ate together; so the kitchen was open and in use 24/7. And another connect to India: the southern Italians like a little fire in their recipes. Italians also like to fry and bread everything, from eggplant to tomatoes to fish and chicken. Sounds familiar, fellow Indophiles?

A typical day for me was to get up and, with her childhood sweetheart Antonio (whom she later married), take scuba equipment and spear-fishing gear down to the water's edge, dive in and spear octopus and whatever other fish we could score, and bring it up to the house to cook for fabulous lunches. Daniela's mother was a great cook and she taught me the real way (i.e., the Italian way) to make gnocchi, ravioli, lasagne and Parmigiana di melanzane (aubergine), among a bunch of other southern Italian specialities, such as biscotto a caponata (antipasti of caponata on rusk-like toast) and pesce spada (swordfish), in various ways.

Lunches were a thing to behold, and also chew. There would be many courses, interspersed with refills of wine. Out would come course after course, salads, pastas cold and hot, entrées of fish and chicken and pig and beef. And flatbreads of every variety. The meals would often end with ripe apricot, peaches, plums—the so-called summer stone fruits—picked minutes earlier from the trees that surrounded us.

But it was more than simply good honest food. The setting added to the savour. The house, like many on the Mediterranean coast, was tiered, one level stacked on top of the next, with better and better views at each tier, threatening nosebleeds at every ascent. Long wooden tables

Lunch in Scilla with Daniela, her father and Malini

on the terraces, shaded under trellises laced with ivy, were the stages for the noontime gatherings. The backdrop would be the sea itself, a canvas of changing shades of blue with touches of green.

Many summers spent at Daniela's family home in Scilla, Calabria, Italy

Even more impressive to this foreigner was how the food was prepared and presented, namely with great forethought and care, a kind of correctness to it all. For Italians, dining is almost a religious ritual. No detail is missed. The food would be laid out and no one ate until all were seated. There was no standing in the kitchen, grabbing a sandwich and coffee on the run. This was theatre, better yet, like an Italian opera. This was a way of life, not just something to fill your stomach and your time.

The entrées came in handmade bowls and other colourful serving dishes. Fruit came plated over grape leaves. People peeled the peaches carefully with sharp knives made for just that purpose. This would be followed by strong espresso and stronger cigars—those dark little Italian Toscanos that Daniela's papa smoked.

All through the meal the chatter, the gossip, the laughter, the political debates, the shared joy of a baby announcement, the sad condolence of another death—these would be the accompaniments, rather than, say, the drone of the football game in the background or people sneaking peeks into their mobile devices. And yet, even with so much to discuss about life and living, the conversations habitually wound up touching upon and describing the very food we ate. Eating while talking about food or talking about food while eating, it was always the perfect occasion to compare different versions of a dish, exchange recipes, recollect the origins of a dish, make comments, and pile up all the 'that's how my mama makes it ...'

During those several summers I spent at her family house, I developed a deep understanding of what Italian recipes contain. I delved a lot deeper into the culture of dining and serving an unforgettable meal than how many tablespoons of EVOO (extra-virgin olive oil) and how much dried red pepper you pinch into your sauce and how expensive and modern your silverware service is.

I was drawn to the kitchen, where I watched the women cut and dice and slice. Their movements were so well-practised from years of the same motion, part of the muscle memory in their DNA, passed down from hundreds of generations—many, many centuries—of women doing the same thing. It reminded me of sitting beside my grandmother in her Nashik kitchen. There was an elegance to their motions, an economy of movement, so that each act would provide the best outcome in the shortest amount of time, because, as sure as the sun would set and rise again, there was another meal to prepare just after the one they were cooking. So they needed to conserve energy.

I felt and tasted love and grace in this rustic elegance of preparation and presentation. The food seemed so directly connected to the earth and the sea and the sun and it all came together in my mouth, blending seamlessly with the ambience of the scenery and the convivial conversation. It also connected one to history—to the history of Italy, of this particular family, of the origins of these ingredients, to farmers and fishermen, to eating itself.

I also felt a passion and commitment to this way of life that I hadn't felt heretofore and thereafter for years to come, until I opened restaurants and vowed to bring this ethos to my establishments.

One weekend, instead of our usual sailing or powerboat excursions to the Aeolian Islands off Sicily, I was arm-twisted into cooking up a beach barbeque for fifty to sixty of Daniela's friends and family on the cobbled beach near Favazzina. The cookout was to help Peppe, their fisherman friend from Scilla, promote a tiny strip of the coast, his 'Lido California,' licenced to him to provide sun chairs and parasols for people to hang out during the summer. His grand plan was to also offer for sale a different 'Piatto della Mamma', a dish of the day that his mother would bring there at high noon to sell.

I drenched chicken and pork in buckets of my Texas-barbeque marinade made with, amongst other ingredients, coffee and bourbon—with a spicy kick I knew they would love. I made cornbread and salads and we washed it all down with tons of cheap, robust red wine and beer. A friend at the party told someone who either managed or owned the Hotel Raya on the island of Panarea how good the meal was; the hotel guy actually wound up offering me a job as the chef. I turned it down; I told everyone that I would be stupid to ruin my Italian summer by actually working. But the truth is I was scared and didn't have what the Italians call *coglioni quadrati* (cubic balls) to do it; I knew I was not ready to take on that responsibility, nor did I have the professional chops to pull it off.

That was just the prelude to The Best Meal I've Ever Had.

One afternoon, after spending the morning frying on a beach on the southern tip of Calabria, Daniela, some others and I drove up to the ghost town of Pentedattilo for a look-see. On the way back, we decided to visit an abandoned tuberculosis sanatorium in Contrada Zervò, and then, with the shadows growing longer as we winded home at about 5.30 p.m., we stopped at a small stone hut nestled among the pines.

The five of us occupied one of two wooden bench tables and before we knew it, pizzas started flying out from a small kitchen where a husband-and-wife team were throwing rectangular flatbreads topped with simple ingredients into their wood-burning oven and churning them out lickety-split. They made only pizzas using fresh tomatoes, their own cheese, nondescript olive oil made from their own trees and served with equally nondescript wine from their own groves. Most were margheritas, the classic recipe of tomatoes, mozzarella and basil. Others included, separately and in various combinations, anchovies, capers, salame, eggplant, mushrooms, garlic and peppers—one yummier than the other.

The sun began to set and as twilight enveloped us, from seemingly out of nowhere, a few young and old men appeared with mandolins, guitars, an accordion and tambourines. Women and girls danced the tarantella, the Calabrian traditional folk dance, with the music wafting through the now-crisp evening air.

Did I say nondescript? Hardly. In fact, it was extraordinary, though to them it was probably just another great evening. But to me, all of it melded together and turned each bite of pizza into more than the sum of its so-called nondescript parts. These were bites of perfection. Anthony Bourdain was so spot-on when he wrote in *Kitchen Confidential*, 'The perfect meal, or the best meals, occur in a context that frequently has very little to do with the food itself.[1]' The moment was perfect, the Mediterranean light and weather were perfect, the music was perfect, the company was perfect, the wine was perfect, my heart was in a perfectly romantic place. I honestly could not distinguish between how much I loved Daniela and how much I loved the whole scene, by which I felt embraced and loved right back. So yes, this was The Best Meal I've Ever Had.

As for Daniela and me, reality set in after some time. We did live in different parts of the world; hers called to her, mine to me. But a bond had been made and we stayed friends and still are. She, Antonio and their kids have come to visit us in India, and I've taken Malini and our two daughters to visit them.

On the food side, though, I'm quite sure a little fire was lit that night and by the subsequent summers I spent in Italy, fuelling my passion for the right way to eat and taste. My Italian summers were formative to a philosophy of food that was set in my soul.

Food, well served in the perfect environment, with the cook's heart and soul in that place of giving for giving's sake—really for no sake at all, just because that is and should be the natural gift from one being to another—is what makes a great meal, more than the individual ingredients or the chef's skill and talent. We forget this. I myself forgot it until years later when I took up cooking in earnest, especially when I took it upon myself to feed the world from my own kitchens.

The four basic tastes are sweet, sour, salty and bitter. In 1908, a Japanese scientist identified a fifth taste, which we call savoury and the Japanese dubbed umami. It's not easy to explain or describe it. And even when tasted, it's hidden within the complexity of our taste buds. In fact, when the Japanese discuss it, it begins to sound like another sect of Buddhism. In a *New Yorker* article, asked to describe what umami tastes like, Kazu Katoh, the president of the Organization to Promote Japanese Restaurants Abroad (which sponsored the sixth annual Umami Recipe Competition in New York in 2015), grew philosophical:

> It's something that's kind to the body. It's mild and, after eating, it's not heavy on your stomach. It helps you wake up better in the morning. That's what deliciousness is about. It's about feeling good after eating... In Japan, we talk about it as tasting good, sleeping well, and clean bowel movements. It has to do with the entire digestive process.[2]

The founder of an American hamburger chain called Umami Burger said the Japanese define umami as 'an overall harmonious state of perfection where the ingredients come together, a really rounded and harmonious dish. They have a sort of Zen way of looking at it'.

I bring all this up in the context of my summers in Italy because this, above all, was the most important thing I learned for my future career. I intuitively 'got' what umami means from the Eastern perspective even before I had ever heard of the word in the early 2000s. The Italians also 'got' umami without reading a cookbook, without eating sushi in Japan. It's not about the food alone. It's about how all the elements hang together. The sounds, smells, the conversation, the lighting, the plates and the plating, the service—all make food taste better. Or worse, depending on how conscientiously they are matched to produce the result ... which always must be deliciousness. That applies not just to the taste but also to all the senses, adding up to more than the sum of their parts.

So I end this section with a huge 'grazie mille, Italia'. Whether they know it or not, my many thousands of guests should also join me in bowing in gratitude towards the Mediterranean Sea and the Italian culture of food, family and faith. On second thought, that's the culture I grew up with, so our worlds all come together—or should—in the Kitchen of Mankind.

I couldn't decide what recipes I should include with this chapter; there were just so many dishes that meant a lot to me during the summers I spent in Italy. Pasta, albeit clichéd, would've been the obvious choice. I'd learnt many ways of cooking it and they continue to form a big part of what I love cooking. But for now I must describe a dessert that somehow connected me with joyous remembrances from my Indian childhood. I've always maintained that food, to really be enjoyed, must take you somewhere. Either it must evoke a memory connecting you with your past, or it must stir you enough in the present to be the kernel of a memory for tomorrow. That happened when I was with Daniela and Antonio in September 1990 when they tied the knot in a wonderfully elegant, intimate and joyous wedding in Scilla. The reception cocktail and dinner was spread out across all levels of Daniela's terraced home and the celebration was capped with a glorious, truck-wheel-sized wedding cake, a speciality of their local pasticceria, a torta millefoglie alla crema pasticcera e fragoline di bosco that was as simply elegant as it was delicious. Much like the French mille feuille pastry (Napoleon Cake), it was an airy construct of alternating layers of delicate, flaky puff pastry and rich pastry cream custard, dusted in icing sugar and smothered with tart, wild strawberries. Sheer perfection! Washed down with much Dom Perignon, I must have had four helpings that night.

So, where's the India connect, you're wondering? The flavours and textures of that pastry reminded me of one of my favourite childhood indulgences—Aji's shrikand. A traditional Maharashtrian dessert she made from whipped hung curd, sweetened and heady with saffron, cardamon and pistachios, always eaten with crispy fried, flaky puris. How and why these two desserts connected and harmonized together in my gustatory mind is beyond me, but they did. In fact, so much so that I eventually created a Shrikand Phyllo Napoleon dessert that I served with berries and silver leaf during a visiting chef stint I did at the Hassler Hotel in Rome, and then later put on one of my menus at Indigo.

TORTA MILLEFOGLIE ALLA CREMA PASTICCERA

INGREDIENTS FOR 4–6 PORTIONS

Pastry Cream/Custard

2 cups of fresh whole milk

1 vanilla bean, split and scraped (or 1 tablespoon of vanilla extract)

½ cup granulated sugar

6 very fresh, cold medium egg yolks

3 tablespoons cornflour

30 gm cold butter cut into 1-inch cubes (add a pinch of salt if using unsalted butter)

Puff Pastry (Millefoglie)

1 roll of readymade puff pastry or follow any easy puff pastry recipe

Egg wash made by mixing 1 egg yolk in 1 teaspoon of milk

4–5 tablespoons of powdered sugar

DIRECTIONS

Pastry Cream/Custard:

Heat the milk with the scraped vanilla and seeds/vanilla extract in a non-reactive saucepan over medium heat and bring to a simmer. Remove from the heat and let it steep, covered for about 30 minutes.

Combine and mix the sugar and cornflour in a non-reactive mixing bowl and whisk in the egg yolks until the mixture is pale yellow, smooth and fluffy. Remove the vanilla bean from the warm milk and discard the bean. While whisking continuously, slowly pour all the milk into the egg yolk mixture in a thin stream. Transfer the bowl contents to the same saucepan in which the milk was heated and cook over medium heat, whisking constantly for about 5 minutes, until the custard begins to thicken. Once it thickens, continue whisking and just when it starts bubbling, whisk for one more minute. Remove from the heat.

While it's still hot, whisk in the butter until melted and thoroughly combined. Next, strain the custard through a fine-mesh sieve into a non-reactive bowl. Immediately, spread plastic wrap directly in contact with the pastry cream surface to prevent a skin from forming as it cools. Place the bowl in an ice-and-water bath to chill the custard for 30 minutes, then refrigerate for about 2 hours before use. When ready to use the pastry cream custard, whisk until smooth.

Millefoglie:

Unroll the rectangular puff pastry and lay flat on parchment paper after letting it thaw enough to manipulate. Cut it into 3 equal parts along the length and place them on an oven tray lined with parchment paper or an ovenproof silicone mat. Brush the pastry rectangles with egg wash and prick lightly with the tines of a fork. Place the tray in a fridge to cool the pastry for 15 minutes, and while it's cooling, preheat your oven to

185°C. When it reaches this temperature, remove the tray of chilled puff pastry, dust lightly with icing sugar using a tea strainer and bake the pastry till just caramelized, crispy, flaky and well cooked (about 15 minutes). Keep an eye on the pastry so it doesn't burn. Remove and let cool for about 1 hour. This will soften the sheets just enough to allow you to cut a few millimetres off the edges to expose the pastry layers within, without cracking them. This is not a critical step, it's just to make the millefoglie layers look sexy once the cake is assembled, and can be omitted if you want. Store them in an airtight container till ready to use.

Assembly:

When you're ready to assemble the cake, remove the chilled pastry cream from the fridge and whip it again ... whip it good ... whip it real good! It should be light and creamy but not runny. Transfer the pastry cream to a piping bag with a wide nozzle and put a few dabs of custard on the serving dish. Place a baked sheet of puff pastry on the custard and press down to keep it from sliding around the plate as you construct the cake. Cover the entire surface of the rectangular puff pastry with a layer of piped, 1-inch blobs of custard arranged in a matrix. Now gently sandwich a second layer of baked pastry on the custard blobs, without pressing down too much, which might cause them to ooze out. Cover the second layer of pastry with another layer of custard blobs as you did for the first layer, and then place the third layer of baked pastry on that. You should have a rectangular cake of alternating layers of baked puff pastry and custard. Cover with a healthy dusting of icing sugar using a tea strainer. The millefoglie is ready! Refrigerate before serving with fresh, macerated berries.

SHRIKAND PHYLLO NAPOLEON WITH BERRIES (From Indigo)

This dessert requires you to hang plain yoghurt in several layers of muslin cloth overnight in a refrigerator, so start a day before. Hang it over a bowl in the fridge to collect the dripping whey.

INGREDIENTS FOR 4–6 PORTIONS

Phyllo Pastry

12–15 sheets frozen commercial phyllo pastry or 1 roll of puff pastry if you prefer

If using phyllo pastry, ½ cup clarified butter

If using puff pastry, egg wash made by mixing 1 egg yolk in 1 teaspoon of milk

4–5 tablespoons of powdered sugar

Shrikand

1 kg plain yoghurt

¼ kg castor sugar

1 teaspoon powdered green cardamom

1 teaspoon saffron infused in 1 tablespoon of milk

½ teaspoon grated nutmeg

1 tablespoon shelled, unsalted pistachios

1 tablespoon cut, blanched almonds

1 tablespoon whole milk

Berries to Accompany

(Use any mix of 3–4 different berries)

2 cups fresh or frozen blackberries

2 cups fresh or frozen raspberries

2 cups fresh or frozen strawberries

1 cup fresh red currants (optional)

½ cup castor sugar

¼ cup freshly squeezed lemon juice

1 cup candied orange peel

8–10 sheets of silver leaf

Powdered sugar for dusting

DIRECTIONS

Shrikand (start a day before serving):

Hang the yoghurt in 2–3 layers of muslin cloth, suspended over a bowl, in a refrigerator overnight. Discard the whey. Half an hour before you're ready to make the shrikand, soak the saffron in milk to extract its colour and flavour. In a large mixing bowl, combine the castor sugar, the hung yoghurt curd, the saffron and milk, powdered cardamom and nutmeg, and whisk well to a very thick, smooth, creamy consistency. Add the pistachios and almonds and mix well. Put in a glass bowl and refrigerate till you're ready to construct the dish. (The shrikand will keep refrigerated for a few days and is also delicious on its own or eaten with dry rotis or crispy pooris.)

Phyllo:*

Preheat oven to 180°C.
Line baking sheets with baking/parchment paper or use a silicone ovenproof baking mat. Layer the phyllo sheets on a damp towel, brushing each sheet with clarified butter, and sprinkle each with some castor sugar. Cut the pastry layer stack with a 3-inch cookie cutter into discs (or using a knife into 3–4-inch squares) and place the discs on the baking trays. You should have about 24–28 discs of stacked/layered pastry. Bake in the oven at 185°C for about 10 to 15 minutes or until golden and crispy. Remove and cool. Store in an airtight container till ready to use.

Berry Sauces:

For each of the berries, take 1 cup of berries separately and press them through a strainer over a bowl with a wooden spoon to extract as much of the juice and pulp as possible. Stir in about 1 tablespoon of lemon juice to each bowl and add just enough castor sugar as needed to sweeten the sauces. Don't over-sweeten. Set aside and add the remaining 1 cup of the respective berries to their respective sauces. Refrigerate the 3 berries in their sauces till ready to eat.

Assembly:

Put a small dab of shrikand in the centre of a plate and place a layer of phyllo discs on it. Spoon a tablespoon of shrikand on to the phyllo disc layer and sandwich this with another layer of phyllo discs. Alternatively, use a piping bag to pipe a layer of shrikand on the phyllo. Press down very gently on the phyllo to spread the shrikand evenly between the

---

* If using puff pastry, follow the directions for baking it in the 'Torta Millefoglie Alla Crema Pasticcera' recipe on page 121.

phyllo layers but not so much that it oozes out. Repeat the sandwiching process to construct alternating layers of phyllo and shrikand, ending with a finished stack of 4–5 layers. Top with a small dollop of shrikand and cover with candied orange peel and a generous dusting of powdered sugar using a tea strainer. Drizzle a tablespoon or more of each of the three berries in their purées around the shrikand phyllo napoleon. Decorate with silver leaf (optional).

6: BREAKING INTO BOMBAY WITH A MOVEABLE FEAST

fresh fettuccine
lamb leg
Kalamata olives

YOU WOULD THINK THAT upon landing back in Bombay and seeing the star chefs proudly showcasing their talents at high-end hotels, I'd have wanted to jumpstart my career in India at one of them.

Wrong. I never, ever, wanted to go down that route. Why? For one, I did not think that even with the formidable financial resources hotels must have had, hotel-based chefs were doing anything noteworthy. Also, I worried that working for 'The Man' could feel claustrophobic for me. I'd have to answer to and satisfy the palates of some 'suits', corporate hoteliers, boards of directors and property owners. Too many layers of approval for me, especially coming from academia. I need freedom to be inventive and that environment did not seem conducive.

I think it was then that I realized I was meant to be a chef–owner. I have too much entrepreneurial blood running through my veins ... and perhaps too much vanity to let others take the profits from my sweat and tears.

So what other path was available for a young man with big dreams of becoming a renowned chef—hell, of just becoming a chef with his own little bistro and a small profit margin? It was the classic case of the old aphorism: 'Those with vision have no means and those with means have no vision.'

While I was contemplating that ... and my navel ... and staying with my parents till I got a clue, my friends Sunil and Nikki Vijayakar, who ran a fairly successful home catering business with high-end clients, called me in a panic. They had a small catering gig they could not handle and asked me to fill in. Sure, I quickly replied—never having really done professional catering—with the courage of King Kong and balls about his size.

It was easy-peasy—canapés, a couple of main dishes and desserts for a group of twenty to thirty in a private home. I guess it went off well. People said, 'We didn't know you catered. How delicious. Give us your number.' Not long thereafter, I started getting calls and bookings and that was the birth of Moveable Feast, my catering business and my first professional cooking gig in India.

My niche then, as now, was Western cuisine and 'true to taste', which means Italian without Indian spices, French without Indian spices, American without Indian spices ... I think you get the picture. I wanted to let the true flavours and authentic origins of that particular cuisine stand out.

My catering company's name ripped off the title of Ernest Hemingway's 1964 memoir of living in Paris in the 1920s, *A Moveable Feast*. A line from his book reads: 'If you are lucky enough to have lived in Paris as a young man, then wherever you go for the rest of your life, it stays with you, for Paris is a moveable feast.' I wanted someone to say the same of me—that the memory of the tastes I served would always stay with them.

My first real executive decision after work started flowing in was where I would cook and where I would find the ingredients I knew I'd need, that were not readily available in India.

The answer to the first came from my tried-and-true parents—especially my mom, the quintessential Jewish mother: 'No, you eat, honey, I'll just starve myself'—who donated their kitchen and other spaces in their flat so I could cook up a storm. But they made me an offer I literally could not refuse. I would have to cook for them and my sister as well. I replaced some of the appliances in the kitchen, bought a professional oven, a bigger freezer and refrigerator, a KitchenAid mixer, a small Carpigiani ice-cream machine, a Cuisinart food processor shipped from the US that ran on a step-down transformer converting our 240V electricity into the 110V on which it ran, and the like. I even poached their full-time cook, Philip, who was quite a special and talented guy. I offered him a second salary to work for me, an offer he also could not refuse. I taught him to make a chocolate mousse that became a staple everywhere I cooked thereafter (thank you, Anne Rosenzweig and Vanessa), and always thought of him when I saw it leave one of my kitchens.

Everyone was happy, until I started stringing ropes across the living room and elsewhere to hang homemade pasta to dry. Still, there were not many complaints once my family sunk their teeth into my raviolis and lasagnes. The deal was simple; I could cook as much as I wanted for others from the house, but whenever that happened, I had to make a little extra to feed the family, since the kitchen and Philip were otherwise occupied through the day.

One of the dishes I made often was something that Marika, Daniela's sister, taught me; La Genovese or pasta alla Genovese, a comforting, delicious Neapolitan dish made from cooking beef for hours in nothing but onions till they caramelized and the meat fell apart. Normally served with a short, tube-shaped pasta like ziti or paccheri, she often made it with fettucine too. Because of the poor quality of beef available, I generally made the dish with a leg of baby lamb or mutton instead; it tasted better too.

Some fresh herbs and spices integral to Western cuisine were difficult to expensive to impossible to secure in India. So I made another deal with the gardener and commandeered the garden behind Chitrakoot, my parents' apartment building, converting one entire flowerbed into a herb garden. Luckily, I'd snuck a bunch of Burpee Seeds packets into my suitcase when I came home from the US. I was particularly eager to plant sage and basil since Indian basil, known as tulsi or holy basil, is bitter, while the sweet and Genovese varieties are excellent with tomato sauces and other Mediterranean dishes.

These herbs were like gold. No one was cooking this kind of stuff and using fresh herbs to boot. People would ask me where I got the basil. I was always coy in my response, partly to be as mysterious as chefs can be, partly because I was slightly embarrassed to share where exactly it came from and partly because I feared they would raid my garden.

Soon, business was booming and we had to have a name. I cannot remember how Moveable Feast came into my mind. But it was a natural. So thank you, Papa Hemingway. My Moveable Feast had a run of four years, which is long in the fickle catering business. I even continued it after I opened my first two restaurants, Just Desserts and Under the Over, selling items from my catering menu to myself at both places. You gotta do what you gotta do.

Those early years were invaluable to me. I was able to test-kitchen the Indian palate, weighing what it would appreciate from my growing repertoire of Western foods. 'Appreciate' may be too favourable a word—more like tolerate at first. I had to figure out what worked, what didn't, what went over Indians' heads and under their palates.

The food they ate at home or in select Indian restaurants was bold and rich, with strong flavours. The subtleties of Western cuisine would be lost on them. It wasn't that I needed to add fiery chillies, but I did need to play with pumping up the flavour volume. Or maybe it was just that the 'Conti' cuisine people ate at the time was so devoid of even basic fresh herbs and spices that what I cooked with them simply stood out.

Creating a full dinner of several courses, appetizers and desserts forced me to think through how one dish complements the next. Balance is always the key. Even a buffet service has to consist of items that work together.

I was always all about bespoke service. So, while many caterers made their food at their own facility, then brought it to the client's home to empty into stainless steel chafing dishes and put them under heating lamps, I often brought the raw or semi-processed ingredients to their home, took over their kitchen completely much earlier in the day and cooked food fresh whenever I could. It made a big difference, perhaps not to the average diner but to me. Whatever I cooked had to meet my own high bar. And I was and remain my toughest critic.

There are almost too many crazy anecdotes from those years that flew by like an exploding supernova.

I do recall a few juicy ones, though.

I did some extravagant meals for a wealthy Calcutta industrialist family's wedding on the expansive lawns of their family home. These were Marwari vegetarians; they hired me to do the Western food presentation and a local Marwari caterer for the Indian side. With about 500 guests, they suggested I should probably cook for the younger, more adventurous lot of 100 to 150 people who would enjoy my cuisine while the older, more conservative crowd would stick to the more traditional Marwari dishes. My side was what I would loosely call Italian. We set it all out buffet style on long tables and watched from the back tents as guests worked their way through the lines. Very quickly we noticed that most people gravitated to my food, and few were going for the Indian food. We started cranking out more and filling the service dishes as fast as humanly possible. In no time, our platters were empty, we'd totally run out of what we'd prepared, but people were clamouring for more. The mother of the bride came into our back area very concerned and, thank our lucky stars, she had a grand sense of humour as she watched us pull in dishes from the Indian side and rework them. There was a classic jeera aloo, a potato dish, which we took off the buffet, then washed off all the Indian spices, threw in fresh basil and anything else we could put our hands on to turn it into 'Western style potatoes, with an Italian twist'. There was a pulao rice we reconstituted like a risotto, renamed it something or the other and retagged it. This was real 'never tasted before' cooking and the guests gobbled it up. By this point, nothing we sent out had anything to do with our original menu and little to do with anything I'd ever cooked or any self-respecting Western chef would think up in their wildest cross-cultural culinary fantasies. But it worked. People raved. Once again, we'd pulled it off.

On another occasion, I got a call from the wife of another big industrialist in Bombay who asked me to cater a vegetarian meal for their annual (joint) family dinner. We decided the menu together—an elaborate, twenty-odd item spread for eighty people, the price per head and all other requirements for their evening. I prepped, cooked and catered for eighty, with a supporting service staff of waiters, cooks and bartenders to handle the event. Everything went like clockwork that night, except that only twenty of their family showed up for dinner.

I went over the next day with my bill. She handed me a cheque for the equivalent amount for twenty people.

I looked at it in disbelief. 'Was there a problem with the food last night—a shortage, or maybe it didn't meet your expectations? Was any of the food bad?' I asked.

'No, no! In fact there was so much left over, we're still sending it out to all the family who couldn't make it. It was really delicious too,' she said.

'Was there a problem with the service or anything else you contracted me to provide for the evening?'

'No! Everything was perfect and as expected.'

'Then why are you paying me for only twenty people when I provided food and service for eighty people as you contracted me for?'

'Because only twenty people showed up.'

I sat silently for a minute looking at the cheque in my hand. Then I put it down on the coffee table, looked at her, got up and, as I walked out, said, 'Mrs P, I think you need this money more than I do!'

In the time it took me to get home, her driver was already waiting in my building lobby with a cheque for the full amount. I never did another catering job for them. I didn't care. I was a small-time self-made caterer and I had my pride. What's right is right, and she was wrong.

And then there was the time the French consul-general requested me to create 'something different' for the French ambassador from

Delhi, whom he was hosting at a small bespoke dinner at his house. He said he hadn't eaten rabbit in a long time. I checked with my regular meat supplier who said, *'Haan, khargosh milega, bilkul milega'* (Yes, no problem, I can definitely get you rabbit).' The meal went off well and everybody loved it. So, I thought to myself, if I'm able to get rabbit on a regular basis, I should start offering it to people. I asked the supplier where he'd sourced it from. He said, *'Crawford Market ke pet shop se* (from the Crawford Market pet shop)!' That was the last time I served rabbit!

With 20/20 hindsight I can now see that Moveable Feast was a natural and organic marketing strategy to help launch whatever I was going to do next as a chef, even though at that point I had no idea what that would be. All I knew was where my passion lay and all I needed was a venue through which to channel it. Nowadays I would have blasted my catering achievements and clientele on social media platforms, but back then I relied on the oldest form of communication: word of mouth.

KAHLUA (OR RUM) CHOCOLATE MOUSSE

INGREDIENTS FOR 6–8 PORTIONS

½ kg semi-sweet dark chocolate, chopped up (or use chocolate nibs)

50 gm butter (I prefer salted to unsalted, as a little salt always enhances flavour)

2 large egg yolks

5 large egg whites, at room temperature

1 cup heavy whipping cream

2 teaspoons instant coffee powder

⅓ cup Kahlua or dark rum

4 tablespoons castor sugar (you may require less depending on how sweet the chocolate is)

⅓ cup water

DIRECTIONS

Melt the chocolate, coffee powder, butter and water in a double boiler, stirring occasionally. Remove from heat. You can even achieve this by putting the ingredients in a glass bowl and microwaving them for 5 to 10 seconds to warm and soften the chocolate. DO NOT OVERCOOK, or the chocolate will split.

Separately whisk the egg yolks and Kahlua (or dark rum) together, and then add that to the chocolate mixture, whisking as you go. Set aside to cool to room temperature.

Beat the egg whites in a large bowl with an electric mixer (or by hand with a whisk using elbow grease!) till soft peaks form. Add in the sugar a little at a time and continue beating till firm, moist peaks form. Control the amount of sugar added based on how sweet you want the mousse to be. You can even omit the sugar entirely if the chocolate is sweet enough. Spoon the whipped egg whites over the chocolate, but don't mix in.

In the egg white bowl, whip the cream with a mixer or by hand till it thickens and forms soft peaks. Fold the chocolate and egg whites into the cream with a spatula till well combined, making sure there aren't any pockets of unfolded egg white in the mousse.

Pour into one medium-sized bowl or into 6–8 individual ceramic dessert bowls, cover with plastic cling film and refrigerate—4 to 5 hours is good, overnight is better. Serve with chocolate shavings or a dollop of whipped cream, or both ... or anything else your heart desires!

LA GENOVESE (LEG OF LAMB VERSION)

This recipe is only for the meat and onion sauce. Serve it with whatever pasta you want or eat by itself as a stew with crusty bread.

INGREDIENTS (FOR 6–8 PORTIONS)

1 baby lamb or mutton leg with thigh bone ~1.3 kg to 1.5 kg

2½ kg onions, cut in half and sliced thin

6–8 garlic cloves, smashed

1 fennel bulb, quartered and sliced thin (optional)

1 carrot, diced (optional)

2 teaspoons fresh thyme leaves

2 sprigs fresh rosemary

3 bay leaves

2 tablespoons chopped parsley

½ cup deseeded kalamata olives in oil (optional)

2 teaspoons small capers drained (optional)

½ cup olive oil

½ cup white wine

1 cup grated Parmesan cheese

2 litres water or vegetable stock (if you need more, just add water)

Salt and pepper to taste

DIRECTIONS

Heat the olive oil in a large Dutch oven or heavy-bottomed saucepan, big enough to hold the leg of lamb and the onions. When hot, sauté the garlic till it just starts to brown, then sear the outsides of the lamb leg on high heat in the same pot and remove when nicely seared all over. (NOTE: if using the carrot and fennel, add them first after removing the lamb, saute them till they soften, and then add the onions.) Lower the heat and add all the onions to the pot, and cook for about 10–15 minutes till they soften. Keep scraping the bottom of the pot to keep the onions from sticking and to incorporate any caramelized solids that may form. Deglaze the pot with wine, cooking off most of it.

When the onions (and vegetables) have just softened, add the bay leaves, thyme and rosemary, season with salt and plenty of pepper, mix well and then add the seared leg back to the pot, working it into the centre of the onions to cover it. Cover the pot and slow-cook the onions and lamb leg together on low heat for several hours (it'll take 4 to 6) until the onions are totally caramelized and the meat is tender and falls off the bone. The onions should release enough water to keep the pot contents wet and saucy but not too soupy. If the onions or lamb start drying out, add water or vegetable stock ½ cup at a time to keep them nice and moist. Every so often, redistribute the onions in the pot, turn the leg over and scrape all the caramelized solids off the bottom. Towards the end, as the meat tenderizes, tease the thigh bone(s) out and discard, leaving the leg meat boneless. (NOTE: You can add the deseeded Kalamata olives and capers to the pot at this time if using them.)

Cook a little more till the meat is fork-tender—cooked long enough to be so tender as to be pried off the bone and cut using only a fork—the onions caramelized and everything is nicely integrated. Adjust the seasoning. You're done. Either make the pasta right away or set aside the Genovese till you're ready to eat, reheating it when you are.

When ready to eat, make enough pasta for everyone, making sure to plan for second helpings too! When the pasta is boiled al dente and ready, drain and add the Genovese lamb sauce to it, combining well. Mix in half the chopped parsley and grated parmesan and distribute among the pasta plates. Top each plate of pasta alla Genovese with a spoonful of the meat and onions and smother in parmesan and chopped parsley.

7: JUST DESSERTS – NOT JUST ABOUT DESSERTS

mocha fudge torte
granny smith apples
bourbon sauce
cinnamon

NO ONE WOULD HAVE expected the Fort neighbourhood of south Bombay, north of Colaba, to be the backdrop for the next act of my life as a chef: running and co-owning a little place called Just Desserts.

The Fort area (named after Fort George, walls and all), was built in 1769 by the British East India Company in the heart of the city's financial district. The Bombay Stock Exchange, the Reserve Bank of India and the Tata Group headquarters (aka Bombay House) are all located here. The headquarters of Asia's oldest continuously published newspaper, the *Bombay Samachar,* established in 1822, is also there. These imposing institutions from Mumbai's so-called golden period all spoke to our heritage. Today, it's less shiny than its former self when sidewalks were filled with vendors selling books, music cassettes, clothes, imported items such as audio equipment, digital cameras, musical instruments, calculators and so on. The side streets from DN Road lead to schools, playgrounds, restaurants, cinemas and other important business houses. DN Road itself is famous for its software vendors. The whole area is known for street shopping and the bookstalls sell myriad books at huge discounts.

This buttoned-down staid 'suits' scene was not the likely setting for a hip European-style café, serving only desserts and hot caffeinated drinks (without a liquor licence), with live jazz twice a week. Nor would anyone have thought we would become so successful. Yet breaking set norms, going against conventional wisdom and so-called market demographics was exactly why we did so well. And that's probably where my reputation for being 'disruptive' began.

As classic and uninventive a concept as this would have been in 1991 in most major Western cities, it was—confounding as this may sound to a millennial—the first of its kind in Bombay. There were zero cool nightlife cafés—with jazz on top of that—anywhere in this woefully uncool country back in the day. Just Desserts would blend influences from New York clubs, Persian cafés and bistros on the artsy Left Bank of Paris.

All credit for the idea goes to its originator, A.D. Singh, who later became the founder of a small empire of well-known restaurants (the 'Olives'—Olive, Olive Beach and Olive Bistro; the Fatty Bao, Monkey Bar, SodaBottleOpenerWala, Guppy by Ai and many others) and a man with a keen eye for what is about to become the next 'it', often himself the sparkplug igniting a hot trend. It was to be a partnership of two men on the verge of even bigger things.

Back then we were relative nobodies with only dreams and raw ambition. This would be the second business for both of us, if I count Moveable Feast as my first. But it would be my first business partnership. We both had a lot to learn.

At the time AD knew squat about restaurants, by his own confession. After graduating with a degree in electrical engineering from Lafayette College, Pennsylvania, which just happened to be 20 miles from F&M where I went to college (though we never met there), he, like me, had only a vague notion of what to do next. He had been exploring something in the field of agricultural development when he almost literally stumbled into a business opportunity and a niche he saw wasn't being filled. In fact, with his first business venture, Party Lines, he created the niche in India. The concept was simple: parties at sea. He produced banquets, events and other bashes on board ships, boats and barges that floated not that far into the waters off the Mumbai harbour in front of the Gateway of India and the Taj Mahal Palace Hotel. He was not a chef, nor a restaurateur, but he was a natural entrepreneur. He ran that business successfully for fifteen years.

Funny how fate works. Had it not been for my catering business, it might have taken me longer to meet AD, who became such an important part of my life. We've known each other so long that neither one of us can recall exactly where or when we met, but we both assume that since we have a lot of common friends and colleagues, he must have been a guest at one or more of my catering gigs.

AD had read an article noting that one way that Americans were cracking the real estate market was by utilizing spaces that did not do business after hours. He and his partner Naomi Khattau looked at twenty to thirty places around the city with that in mind, but most owners were worried their space would be trashed if they leased or rented to anyone other than family. And, he says, owners resisted as well because it's very hard to get a tenant out of a space once they are ensconced there.

There was an Irani restaurant in the Fort area that closed in the late afternoon, leaving the space empty for the evening, probably because the owners assumed all those downtown business folks go home after work and the last thing they'd want to do was stay there any longer than necessary. One man's unused pocket of real estate is another man's window of opportunity. The owner was willing to let AD in if he would share a percentage of the profits. He cut a deal. And a sweet deal it was; the landlord charged a ridiculously low rent, mainly because he thought this innovative dessert bistro wouldn't work. O, he of little faith.

AD's idea for a dessert spot was also driven by what he refers to as 'a serious chronic ailment called sweet tooth'. He would serve desserts by the slice, desserts only, which was not happening anywhere else. So he had all the pieces in place, but then he panicked. He could not do it alone. He needed someone like ... me.

Of course, the name Just Desserts is a double entendre. Yes, we sold just desserts. But we felt this was a well-deserved reward for hardworking people after a day at the office as well. Also, we were well aware of the near-sacred place sweets hold in the Hindu tradition. Mithai, which includes all sweets containing sugar, milk and ghee, is considered to be sattvic—pure and, as such, offered to the gods and distributed among temple devotees. Mithai is used to break fasts or eaten during a fast and will always be served at times of celebrations. In that spirit, we invited guests to imbibe with a sincere appreciation of the sweetness of life.

When he approached me with the concept, I saw ways I could add to the idea. My role was to handle the food and the overall operation. I would incorporate touches of what I myself had experienced in New York. It would be casual and fun, affordable, but the desserts would be over-the-top in quality. I could bake well ... well enough. But we would tap women in the community we knew who could bake up a storm. We'd buy their products, sell them a slice at a time, turn a profit and keep them in the money too. Inspired by Iranian cafés—in particular Britannia & Company, also in the Fort area and run since its opening in 1923 by a Zoroastrian family originally from Iran—we had marble tables and bentwood chairs. The vibe was to be cosy, intimate and cool. Fun would be the operating paradigm.

Live jazz was AD's idea, since his father loved it. AD concedes that he hated it at first, but he came to love it, enough so that he later opened Jazz by the Bay (now called Pizza by the Bay), which became a staple showcasing live jazz acts. Jazz—in fact American music of all genres—was my thing. Jazz became a signature at Just Desserts, a venue where you could nibble on sweets, imbibe the music and the whole groovy scene, and drag on ciggies (this was before the ban on smoking in public places), the smoke wafting like a mystical cloud overhead, adding to the Parisienne atmosphere. You could almost imagine the legendary French actor Jean-Paul Belmondo, a Gauloises cigarette hanging off the side of his lip, sauntering into the café and fitting right in!

Jazz was live two nights and we played tapes the rest of the week. We attracted some pretty stellar musicians and soon it was like a club for those in the know: if you didn't know how to get there, you didn't belong anyway. It was *like that only*. A veritable who's who of Bombay's hip and cool and successful—but not just those who were making a boatload of money. In fact, that was low on the list of criteria; it drew people doing cutting-edge things in the arts and entertainment space, and entrepreneurially.

To make the owner feel less nervous, we committed to using all our own equipment. We brought in our own cutlery, fridge and coffee machine. I commissioned Philip—remember him from my parents' home and Moveable Feast? Then I found a bunch of Parsi women—amazing home bakers—to whom I could outsource the job of making some of our desserts. I signed up Gulnar Sarkari and Jeroo Shroff. Through social circles I knew Zarina Screwvala, later wife of media guru Ronnie Screwvala, and I knew Zarina's mother made a cake whose name tells it all: Death By Chocolate, soft gooey brownies that made you go *hmmmm*, mainly because your tongue was stuck to your palate. It killed. I filled in with my own recipes—some that I'd brought from my New York years, others I developed.

Running restaurants is not rocket science. But creating a vibe and getting it right depends on the ability to manage a few key factors that, when they come together, set the tone for any diner's experience. You learn a lot about how to make a restaurant successful through your own experiences eating in them. Hopefully you've been fortunate enough to travel, and your experiences have been from across the globe and at all levels of dining, from simple cafés and bistros to Michelin-starred restaurants at the haute-cuisine end of the spectrum. But even if you haven't, it just requires you to think about what makes you happy when you visit a restaurant and try and replicate or improve upon that experience.

Niccolo Lorimer, my freshman roommate at F&M, came from the small village of Scandicci in the hills overlooking Florence, Italy. When we first met while moving into the dorms, we couldn't have been more different. We were chalk and cheese, with me the stuttering, squash-playing, pre-med science nerd to his free-spirited, incense-burning, psychedelic-clothed hippie persona, majoring in religious studies. Yet, we hit it off and bonded right away. Maybe it was because we were both so different from everyone else, the only two with an international upbringing and a world view that stretched further east than the Jersey shore, that we relied and depended on one another to help relate to the others. Whatever the reason, we became really fast friends and roomed together for three of our four years at F&M, on campus and off. Niccolo opened my eyes to living life and doing so on my terms. I learned to laugh at the world with a sense of irreverence and not be so damn serious all the time. He taught me to embrace my individuality, that it was okay to not conform and to be, in the words of the Robert Fripp and David Byrne song 'Under Heavy Manners', 'resplendent in divergence'. I really owe my present freewheeling, risk-taking nature to the time spent with him.

Twinning with Niccolo ... hair today, gone tomorrow. From not too long ago

Niccolo's always been a wheeler-dealer, trader, deal-making kinda guy and not surprisingly, went on to a highly respectable entrepreneurial career in many fields, mostly relating to the import of food and wine from Italy to the US. Today, he's the founder and CEO of Noble Harvest LLC in the US and of USA Export, SRL in Italy. With a rich background in real estate, art dealing and business, he developed a unique approach to the American market, honing his skills with a strong focus on marketing and sales. Noble Harvest is the reference point for many institutions (such as the Italian Trade Commission, Fancy Food Shows, Italian Consortiums, Chambers of Commerce and more) for logistics and compliance. Niccolo is on the board of the Italy–America Chamber of Commerce of Houston, Texas, and an advisor for the prestigious Wine Hunter, part of the Merano Wine Festival in Merano, Italy, where he got me to guest chef in November 2011.

But back in the winter of 1980, during our senior year at college, when I first visited his family, we spent two weeks over Christmas and New Year's in Italy. Following that, he went with me to India for a month, travelling around the south. As a broke college student, I'd managed to save up about $700, which was the budget I set for the two weeks in Italy, but I still found myself flush with funds at the tail end of our sojourn.

'Niccolo,' I proposed, 'I have close to $600 left over and I want to blow it all on a meal at the best restaurant in Florence before we leave for Bombay.'

'I know just the place,' he offered without hesitation. 'It's a fancy starred restaurant in an old villa called La Loggia in Villa San Michele, Fiesole, overlooking Florence. We'll never get a table if I call, but if you call and speak in an American accent, we should be okay.'

I called the restaurant and, in my best Indian-Texan drawl, I managed to get a table for three the next night. Niccolo, his sister Francesca and I were going to dine in style. I couldn't wait.

It rained that Saturday night as we drove from his home in Scandicci up to the villa's front entrance in his brother's beat-up, tiny, grey Fiat Cinquecento. The car, no bigger than an inverted bathtub, had a totally torn and open convertible roof which we covered with an old shower curtain we held tight to keep it from flying off. We got out of the car—dressed in jeans, muddy hiking boots and heavy Florentine sweaters—and with as much swag as we could muster, casually tossed the keys in the valet's direction.

Everyone in the restaurant was dressed to the hilt in dark jackets and ties, the staff even more so in black tie with white waistcoats and jackets. Formal and stuffy were la moda. A piano player crooned old, clichéd Italian songs like 'O Sole Mio', in the centre of the dining room. Even dining couples had serious faces and spoke in whispers with each other. Everything felt strained and uncomfortable, when it should have been joyous and celebratory. Taking one look at us post-bohemian hippies, the maître d' quickly sat us at a cramped table near the kitchen entrance, as far away from the gaze of the dining room as he possibly could. The staff all but ignored us; service was terrible. That is until we ordered our first bottle of champagne ... then everything changed.

First, I sent a glass of champagne to the piano player with a song request, after which we ordered our second bottle; then the third, fourth and fifth. With each bottle, we sent glasses of bubbly to almost everyone in the dining room and some for the staff too. Now the staff was fawning over us. Even the chef sent us several dishes on the house. By late in the evening, jackets and ties had come off, now draped casually over the backs of chairs.

The piano player was pounding out The Beatles' 'I Saw Her Standing There ...': 'Well, she was just seventeen, You know what I mean, And the way she looked was way beyond compare ... '

Couples were actually dancing near the piano. Some had gotten up and were chatting with others at their tables. The whole vibe transformed in the restaurant that night. It suddenly became friendly, warm and convivial—casual even—without taking away from the seriousness of the dining experience. People let their guard down and were enjoying themselves. I blew my entire $600 wad and Niccolo must have easily dropped another $600 between the two of them. But man oh man, did we have fun that night! It was never about the money, it was all about the experience. And we'd engineered that.

This taught me never to be stuffy and formal, no matter how serious I want the overall experience to be for the diner. We may take our food seriously, we may take our service and hospitality seriously, but we never take ourselves too seriously. In other words, the takeaway for anyone is: take what you do seriously, but learn to have fun. Lose the formality, but not the attention to detail. It is possible to do both and it always creates a sexy, stylish vibe. I began realizing that at Just Desserts.

Almost from day one, we had people waiting to get in. Our word of mouth, through customers from my catering business and from AD's extensive list of people who'd been to a Party Line event, worked wonders. Word of mouth was all we had; we could not afford advertising, and social media was light years away. It's amazing what you learn when you have limited resources.

Watch the Books

While I was laser-focused on the food and the wait staff, when I did look at our cash flows, I noticed some holes. It turned out that AD and I had opposite approaches to 'comps'—that generous act of giving freebies to some guests, which also serves as payback for their past (and hopefully) future loyalty, loyalty that would not require comping their next visit. AD concedes that he picked up the tab for far too many of his family, friends and customers from his previous business. He's just that kind of friendly guy. I, on the other hand, played it strictly by the book, nice guy though I also am. My family and friends had to pay, just like everyone else. Even when there was a line outside, I did not give preference to those I knew. When two friends came to me and asked me to let them in ahead of the line, I declined.

'See that elderly couple back in line?' I pointed to a pair. 'They're my parents, and if they can wait in line to get in, so can you.'

I was too self-righteous and AD was not disciplined enough. We both took responsibility for our early flubs. There was no right or wrong; there should just be balance and compromise. We should have discussed this and other policies before we opened and set some internal policies.

You can't abuse your own business. It's larger than you. There's a lot of glam to owning a restaurant from the outside. But the innards, its dirty work, long hours and—if you don't watch the cash flow—not great financial rewards.

Treat Staff like Priceless Guests

As we learned, there's another valuable commodity one has to watch carefully and protect at all costs: one's staff. With the right motivation and inspiration, people will work hard for you, we found. They will go above and beyond your expectations. However, if you don't compensate them fairly and on time, they will not be there for you, figuratively speaking but also possibly literally. Staff will revolt by calling in sick or orchestrating a work slowdown, or simply staging a walkout, as I did back in New York. So don't muck with their salaries. If they see lines out the ying-yang coming to the restaurant, if they see the kitchen slammed most nights and then you tell them you have a 'cash flow problem' and their weekly pay cheques will be delayed ... well, what would you do?

While AD continued with Just Desserts for about two years, I lasted only about three months. We were just not bringing in enough money to compensate me appropriately and I knew I had other culinary mountains to climb. In truth, I was already in conversations with a number of people about my next venture, which was to become Under the Over. But in that short time, I had already learned a few valuable lessons that informed my philosophy about how to run a restaurant business.

RAHUL'S APPLE TART

INGREDIENTS FOR ONE 10-INCH TART PAN OR PIE DISH; 8 PORTIONS

Pastry

1¼ cups all-purpose flour, chilled in the refrigerator

¼ teaspoon salt

150 gm unsalted butter, cold and cut into 1-inch cubes

3–5 tablespoons ice water

Apple Filling

7–8 Granny Smith apples

1 teaspoon freshly grated nutmeg

1 teaspoon cinnamon powder

1 cup golden raisins, soaking in rum

½ cup broken walnuts

½ cup icing sugar

1 cup apricot jam

Juice of 1 lemon

2 tablespoons soft butter

DIRECTIONS

To Make the Pastry:

You can do this by hand or by food processor.

By food processor, add the flour and salt to the bowl. Pulse the processor to combine. Add the butter and pulse 6–9 times in short bursts or until the pieces in the bowl are the size of peas. Add 3 tablespoons of iced water and pulse only until the dough is completely moistened. Do not process till the dough comes together and forms a ball. The dough should hold together when pinched between your fingers but still be crumbly. If it's too crumbly, add a little more water, a tablespoon at a time, and pulse in short bursts till it's moist. Transfer the dough to a plastic bag or overturn the bowl on to plastic cling film, shape the dough into a ball and flatten into a disc. Seal the bag, or cover the dough in plastic and refrigerate.

By hand, stir the flour and salt together with a fork in a medium-sized bowl. Mix in the pieces of butter, combining them with the flour gently with your fingertips to form a crumbly dough with pea-sized pieces. Add 3 tablespoons of iced water and continue gently combining with a fork or your fingertips till the dough is moistened and just starts to form a ball. Gather the dough together with your hands and gently shape into a ball. Wrap in plastic cling wrap or put into a plastic bag, flatten into a disc and refrigerate.

To Prepare the Apples:

Peel and core the apples and cut in half (north-south) through the core. Put the halves into a large stainless-steel bowl with iced water and the lemon juice to keep them from discolouring. When you're ready to make the pie, remove the apples one half at a time, pat dry with paper towels and start the slicing. Slice the apple halves into very thin slices perpendicular to the core, but don't cut them all the way through to separate them. Try to leave them attached at one end.

Tart Base:

Dust your work surface with some flour and place the refrigerated dough disc on it. Dust some flour on the dough and roll out to about a ¼-inch thick disc or 1 inch larger than your pie dish. Lightly butter the inside of your pie dish with your fingers. Carefully roll the dough on to your rolling pin to lift and transfer it to the buttered pie dish and then unroll it across the mould. Gently press the dough into place, making sure you have no air bubbles between the dough and the dish. Trim the edges. Score the entire dough base in the pie dish with a fork, to keep bubbles forming while baking. Refrigerate the dough-filled pie dish to firm up the dough base before filling.

To Construct the Tart:

Heat up the apricot jam with a teaspoon of water to liquify. You can do this either in a microwave or on a stove. Remove the pie dish from the refrigerator and brush some of the apricot glaze across the entire dough face.

Take an apple half, put a few raisins and crumbled walnuts in the core channel and place the apple, flat-side down, with the slices perpendicular to the rim (in a radial orientation) pointing towards the centre of the dish. Complete the outer rim of apple halves, making sure to pack the sliced apple halves tightly together. Then complete another row until you fill as much of the pie dish with sliced apples as possible. Fill the crannies where the apple halves come together with a few rum-soaked raisins and crumbled walnuts. Lightly brush the tops of the cut apples with some apricot glaze. Dust the tart with cinnamon and nutmeg using a tea strainer. Dot each apple half with a small dab of butter and bake the tart in the middle of an oven at 190°C for 30 to

40 minutes or until the apples have softened completely and the crust turns a golden brown. You may need to bake a little longer to dry out any excess liquid released by the apples and raisins, to keep the base from getting soggy, but don't overcook and burn the tart.

Remove from the oven and let cool. As it's cooling, brush the top of the apple tart with the remaining apricot glaze. Refrigerate once cool and serve warm or cold, dusted with icing sugar and with a dollop of vanilla ice cream or whipped cream.

MOCHA FUDGE TORTE WITH BOURBON SAUCE

INGREDIENTS FOR ONE 10-INCH CAKE PAN

Mocha Fudge Torte

500 gm semi-sweet dark chocolate, chopped up (or use chocolate nibs)

400 gm butter (I prefer salted to unsalted, as a little salt always enhances flavour)

7 large eggs

2 tablespoons instant coffee powder

½ cup brown sugar

¼ cup dark rum

1 tsp vanilla essence

Bourbon Sauce (~ 2 Cups)

3 large egg yolks

1½ tablespoon cornflour

¼ cup water

½ cup brown sugar

1 cup whole milk

½ cup bourbon or whisky

1 teaspoon vanilla essence

½ teaspoon grated nutmeg

½ teaspoon cinnamon powder

DIRECTIONS

Mocha Fudge Torte:

Heat the oven to 180°C. Combine chocolate, coffee, butter, rum and vanilla in a non-reactive bowl on low heat, stirring constantly till well combined and melted. Remove from heat. Separately, beat the eggs till thick and foamy with a hand mixer or manually using a whisk and elbow grease, and then fold into the molten chocolate and butter mixture. Continue beating or whisking till well combined.

Pour the chocolate-egg mixture into a 9-inch buttered spring form cake pan and bake in the centre of the oven for 30–40 minutes or until a crust forms around the top edges of the cake and the centre is still quite soft and wobbly. It will look underdone. You want that. Don't overcook. Remove from the oven and let it cool to room temperature. It will sink as it cools. Cover and refrigerate overnight until firm. You're done.

Make a frosting, add berries with a coulis, add ice cream ... whatever you want. Or eat it plain as it is, dusted with powdered sugar and smothered in bourbon sauce.

Bourbon Sauce:

Lightly whisk the egg yolks in a stainless-steel bowl. Dissolve the cornflour in the water and add to the egg yolks. Continue whisking. Whisk in the sugar and milk, cinnamon and nutmeg, and cook over moderate heat till the sauce just comes to a boil and thickens. Make sure you keep whisking. Remove from the heat and whisk in the bourbon and vanilla. Cover with some plastic wrap directly in contact with the surface of the sauce to keep a skin from forming on the surface as it cools. Let it cool to room temperature. Either serve chilled immediately or refrigerate, covered. It will keep for a week if refrigerated and covered.

8: HOW I MET MY PARTNER IN CULINARY CRIME

I INTERRUPT MY MONOPOLY of this book to introduce Malini Vachani-Akerkar, my wife, the mother of our two daughters, a visual visionary who was largely responsible for Indigo's cool look, the concept creator behind our collection of Indigo Delis, a brilliant artist in her own right and a master at keeping me in line.

It was the fall of 1990 and Just Desserts was already *the* hip locale for the cognoscenti of Bombay. In walked this woman and when I saw her, I felt like I already knew her. I had heard through the proverbial grapevine that she was a cousin of fashion designer Tarun Tahiliani, whom I vaguely knew while we were at Doon School. But our connection goes further back as she and I were born at the same hospital, Breach Candy, albeit several years apart.

Malini had come with Tarun's sister Tina. As was almost always the case at that time, there was a long line outside Just Desserts. Tina, who has no shortage of guts, found me and said, 'I'm Tina, Tarun's sister. Do you think you could let us get to the front of the line?'

Malini says I left quite an impression on her, as a man with integrity and family values, when I pointed out my parents standing in line as well. Needless to say, Tina and company got in the back of the line and waited their turn.

After that I met Malini a few times at the café, but we didn't really chat.

She had returned to Bombay when the Gulf War broke out, after working in Abu Dhabi as a numbers' cruncher for PricewaterhouseCoopers. She'd handled a lot of hotel clients in the UAE, doing internal audits, a skill that would come in handy a few years later. Somewhere along the way, after finishing a bachelor's in microbiology from Imperial College in London, a field she later came to hate, she wound up working as a chartered accountant's apprentice at PricewaterhouseCoopers. In Bombay, she joined Tarun and Tina, working as a floor manager at Ensemble, India's first multi-designer boutique.

Our big moment came on New Year's Eve in 1990. Some Doon School classmates had a big party in Bombay. She ended up there and happened to sit next to me. That was when we first really got to know each other. Then, after being up all night, a gang of us went for breakfast to the Shamiana coffee shop at the Taj Mahal Palace, which was 'the thing' to do. Malini was dating a man at the time, which ended pretty soon after I met her. In fact, her guy kept suggesting that we spend time together. Malini didn't know why, but later all the pieces fell together after he realized he was gay.

I continued to stay in touch with her and would do little devious things like get mutual friends to invite her independently to dinners or small parties at home. So, there we'd 'accidentally bump' into each other. Meanwhile, I'd make cassette mixes (remember those?) of my favourite music, demonstrating my great and eclectic taste.

Malini, Cyprus Pier, 1994

You know that line 'the fastest way to a man's heart is through his stomach'? With her and me, it was the opposite. I won *her* heart with my food. On our kinda-sorta first official date, I invited her to my parents' house to cook her dinner. The parents were conveniently out that night. I pulled out the stops, with an incredible mushroom almond pâté accompanied by a bottle of wine, and pasta and a simple but elegant salad. It was divine, IMHO, and hers! Proof: by April 1991 we were living together at my parents' flat.

In the summer of 1992 I took her to Europe on a sailing trip through the Sporades islands in northern Greece. The two of us first flew to Daniela's home in Scilla for a couple of weeks and then, along with six Italians, flew to Athens where we chartered a 15-metre Beneteau sailboat for two weeks. While it was all quite lovely, we hit a bit of a rocky patch. I—subconsciously—was mean to her and in some childish, perverse way almost needed Daniela, Antonio and the other Italians to 'approve' of her. It was enough for her to fly back from Rome after our sailing trip, somewhat pissed off. I, in turn, headed back to Scilla with the Italians. Once in Bombay, Malini came to the rather accurate conclusion that I had little intention of coming back to the city, where we'd already borrowed money for Under the Over, had people waiting for me, partners wondering what I was doing in Italy and when I'd come back after being away several months already. Sure, I was having too good a time while honing my Italian culinary skills. Deep down I feared the enormous responsibility of starting a new restaurant business and also perhaps the deep feelings I had for Malini.

My future wife saw through all my walls and fears.

Thankfully, she felt it was her responsibility to light a fire under my ass. So, she called me. I had already practised some excuses—like I couldn't get a flight, I was still working in an Italian restaurant in Reggio—all of which was total BS. She knew it and went ahead and booked my return flight. I was back in Bombay very shortly thereafter, taking life and her a lot more seriously.

As I went about preparing to open Under the Over, Malini was not officially on the restaurant staff. She was still just 'the girlfriend known to have lit a fire under my butt'. Slowly but surely, she began to influence the look of my first real restaurant in a very significant way.

In the spring of 1992, the pressure to open Under the Over was mounting. Malini saw first-hand how intense the weeks before a restaurant opening get. I, being the perfectionist, take these times extremely seriously. One of our partners could see how stressed out I was and suggested Malini take me to lunch to chill out and distract me. We went to The Chinese Room, a restaurant diagonally across the way at Kemps Corner. That eatery is no longer there but it eternally remains in our minds. We rarely drive by the area without remembering why.

I honestly don't remember most of our lunchtime conversation—nor does she—but my freak-out was palpable to her. In the middle of lunch, over sweet corn soup—hers with asparagus and mine with chicken—I proposed to her.

'Enough of this madness,' I blurted out. 'Let's get married!'

We both started crying into the poor soup, she probably in relief and disbelief that I'd finally asked, I surprised I finally had.

Then I added this caveat that dampened the whole proposal: 'But don't tell anybody.'

Where did that come from? I can't completely answer. Nor could she. Was this the height of my ambivalence? Was I suddenly uncharacteristically shy? Was I building my own out clause? Was I not fully ready? Was this a totally spontaneous ask, with no follow-up plan? Had I realized what exactly I had done ... to my own great horror?

She got no answers that afternoon. I went back to work prepping for a pre-opening dinner party. She went home, completely flummoxed that she couldn't tell anyone.

But all was made crystal clear when I came back home that night. At three in the morning I got down on one knee and formally proposed. I did not proffer a ring and she was okay with that, knowing better than most people that I could not afford one. She then asked if she could tell her parents at last. Of course she could, I said, all smiles.

The next morning I shouted the announcement to my mother, who happened to be in the bathroom.

'Mom, I proposed to Malini last night.'

'Well done,' she shouted back in her no-nonsense style. 'You finally decided to make an honest woman out of her.'

She then, in her equally generous style, gave me one of her mother's diamond rings to give to Malini. It was a family heirloom that they, like so many other Jewish refugees, smuggled out of Germany when they fled the war in Europe. In December of that year we got married. It was the happiest day of my life.

On our wedding day, 20 December 1992

Malini and I have a very intense and complex relationship. We call each other on our shit, but we love and respect each other deeply.

We are both creative artists; we are both trained scientists. She is no shrinking violet; no one ever accused me of that either. We are competitive, but we are complementary as well. Her strengths are my weaknesses and vice versa. We have worked together in the most stressful environments, we let off a lot of steam in those moments but we always come out the other end unscathed and still in love.

How do we accomplish that miracle in an industry that takes a major toll on husband-and-wife chef–manager teams, many ending in divorce?

One by-now-familiar word: Balance. As in so much of my cooking, as in so much that I preach throughout this book, the key is not to go overboard in any direction. And to be open to an opposing opinion, at the same time without completely letting go of one's own. If that sounds too Zen, so be it. I bow to any higher authority—as long as he or she sees it my way. LOL. But seriously, all of nature always tries to achieve and maintain that balance. The body has mechanisms to safeguard a state of balance. In biology, this is called homeostasis. From the *Encyclopedia Britannica*: 'Homeostasis is any self-regulating process by which biological systems tend to maintain stability while adjusting to conditions that are optimal for survival. If homeostasis is successful, life continues; if unsuccessful, disaster or death ensures.'[1]

Or look at ancient Chinese philosophy. Yin and yang is a concept of dualism, describing how seemingly opposite or contrary forces may actually be complementary, interconnected and interdependent in the natural world, and how they may give rise to each other as they interrelate.

Yin is usually associated with female energy, yang with male. While from the outside, one would think I'm the yang to Malini's yin, she actually has a lot of male energy; and I, though I look like a WWE wrestler, exhibit many female qualities. And in fact, we both flip-flop between the two energies.

Another reason we work so well together: she gets me going when I tend to vacillate, as you saw when she got me off my butt to return to India from Italy. This scenario continues right up to yesterday. Also, when I get caught up in details due to my OCD tendencies, she comes in and in one fell swoop gets me to look at the bigger picture. She micromanages my inclination to micromanage!

Despite all that lovey-dovey new-agey stuff, there are days when we want to strangle each other. Then, at the edge of the outbreak of Akerkar World War Three, one of us will make a physical gesture that does more to make peace than Kissinger could ever have done. I'm like a raging lion, then she comes over and kisses my bald head and I start to purr.

Through learning these lessons of collaboration as a couple and as working partners, we conquered many obstacles. We felt ready to take on our greatest challenge and what turned out to be our biggest achievement.

Elated and exhausted at the Indigo Deli, Palladium, Mumbai on opening night

Being given feedback at a wine dinner at Tote

Malu and me at the opening night of Blue Frog, December 2007

'Your children are not your children.
They are sons and daughters of Life's longing for itself.
They come through you but not from you.
And though they are with you yet they belong not to you.
You may give them your love but not your thoughts,
For they have their own thoughts.
You may house their bodies but not their souls,
For their souls dwell in the house of tomorrow, which you cannot visit, not even in your dreams.'

~ From *The Prophet* by Kahlil Gibran

All of this intensity, along with meaningful time to reflect, brought me back to thinking—not, for once, about menus or my role as a chef, restaurateur and businessman—but about my role as a father. Let's go way back to the beginning ...

Malini was in her last trimester, pregnant with our first, and we'd already decided that boy or girl, we'd name our child Shaan, meaning 'glory, peaceful and pride'. A few months before her birth, I'd taken apart a pair of Sennheiser headphones; each evening I'd come home from work at Under the Over and play different musical genres through the speakers placed on Malu's belly.

I always started these sessions with, 'Hi Shaan, this is Daddy,' as I rested my face on the mother-to-be's belly. I'd tell her about my day, world events, food, the restaurant, the type of music she was listening to ... just about anything, really. Shaan would respond by kicking against Malu's belly with joy. Contact with my first offspring! I was immediately hooked on fatherhood.

Waiting patiently (perhaps even reluctantly) to be born, relaxing in her prenatal private sound studio, she loved classic rock of the 1960s and '70s and jazz—kicking to their rhythms with greater frequency than to other forms of music. This ritual played out daily until she was born almost two months later by caesarean section. I stayed in the operating room, photographing the whole process. When Shaan was returned to Malini after being cleaned up and wrapped, she cried as all newborn babies do. I walked over and whispered, 'Hi Shaan, this is Daddy.' Eyes closed, she turned her head in the direction of my voice. Her face and body relaxed and she immediately fell silent and asleep. Calm and secure in the familiarity of my voice, I presumed. It ripped my heart out of my chest. I felt like Superman. Was this the new happiest day of my life? It sure felt like it.

She was a happy, curious baby and we did a lot together. She was independent but shy, a very gentle child. Like I was in many ways, also an introspective observer. Through the years and our many moves and changes, our ups and downs as a family, and her own changes, Shaan has remained that way.

Alibaug here we come...

Aja and Charlie ... nose to nose

When only daddy's shirt will do

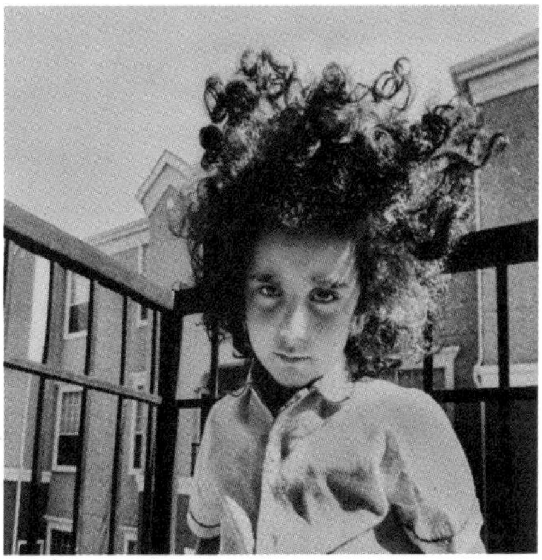

Seriously bad hair day

Birthday in Goa

Shaan in Alibaug

Shaan

Putting daddy to sleep post lunch, Alibaug

Sulking in Ranthambore

Hanging out in Alibaug

In the woods, Kodaikanal

Tummy-tickling a full-grown Burmese tiger, Tiger Monastery, Thailand

Amalia

Shaan and Amalia

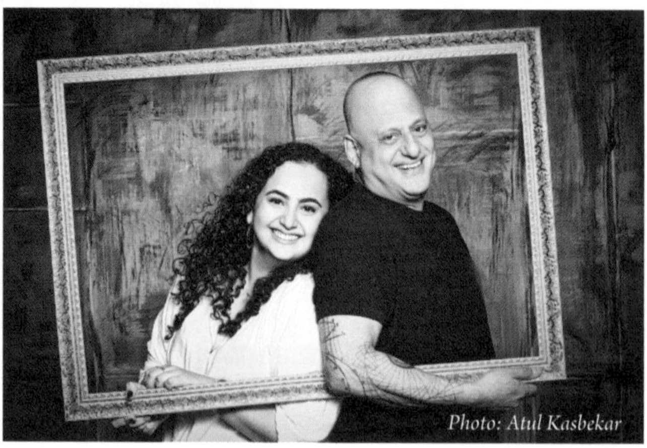

Bob and Shaan

Photo: Atul Kasbekar

AMRAS family portrait

Amalia, our second-born, is five years younger than Shaan. Malini wanted a Hebrew name to celebrate that part of her heritage and Amalia, meaning 'Work of the Lord', fit the bill. By the time of her birth, Malu and I knew—or thought we did—the parenting drill with a tad bit more education and experience. Yet, in my naïveté, I thought that my second-born would be like my first. I was in for a not-so-rude awakening. Where Shaan was a gentle child, introspective and observant of life, Amalia was the cheeky rascal, headstrong, brazen and full of élan. The physical setback she suffered later did not subdue her joie de vivre.

Adjusting to this new person, I could only say vive la différence. Who is to say which personality is better or worse than the other's? The cliché is true: we are all unique snowflakes.

The lesson for me, an admitted control freak who often believes there is either my way or the highway, was and remains to let go of what I want my girls to become, both professionally and as independent personalities. After all, who am I—the man who headed in one direction professionally only to end up in an entirely different one—to suggest to anyone, especially my daughters, what they should do? Would I actually be able to say with any credibility, 'Do what I say, not what I do' or even 'Do what I do, not what I say?'

It's just like how Kahlil Gibran put it:

'You may strive to be like them, but seek not to make them like you.
For life goes not backward nor tarries with yesterday.
You are the bows from which your children as living arrows
are sent forth.'

Long before he becomes a father, a man wonders what kind of parent he'll be—wonders and worries whether he will be up to the challenge and responsibility. In my mind I was following in some mighty big footsteps: my role model, my own dad. Could I be as good a father as I perceived him to be for me and Avantika?

I thought I was a great father through my daughters' prepubescent childhood years. I took them everywhere, let them do whatever they wanted to do, encouraged them to take risks and even to be naughty. I related to them at their level, not as an adult guiding father but as a mischievous prankster child. We had a ton of giggles together. I remember travelling to San Francisco with Shaan when she was three or four years old and egging her on to redecorate the interior cabin of the KLM Jumbo with her bag of crayons as I pretended to be asleep and oblivious to her artistic machinations. On another occasion, when she was about five, she and her sleepover girlfriend Shaira woke up early one Sunday, conned their nanny out of ₹50 and headed out alone on Colaba Causeway to buy diamonds for themselves. Lucky for us, the flower vendor near our home recognized Shaan and promptly brought them back before they disappeared in the maze of side streets and shops. I remember chewing on my tongue, trying to keep a straight face later when we and Shaira's parents gave the two girls a dressing-down for the danger in which they'd put themselves. Somehow, I just found the whole thing hilarious and was strangely proud of these young women's fearless exploration.

Amalia took to food more adventurously than Shaan, wolfing down tuna carpaccio at eight months old. She developed very strong likes and dislikes where food was concerned and grew to become the discerning gourmet between the two sisters. She learned to cook early on, making puran poli, pancakes and chocolate-chip cookies and sushi maki rolls with equal skill. When Amalia was in kindergarten, I'd done a cooking activity with her class—we made pancakes from scratch—and all the kids got a chance at making their own. Amalia, dressed in her Indigo chef's jacket, wielding a wooden spoon, immediately pushed me aside, assumed the mantle of sous chef and took over the demo, instructing and controlling her classmates with the confidence and cockiness of a drill sergeant. All I could do was laugh ... and step aside.

'Wait! Don't touch anything ... not till I say so!'

Pancake time... woohoo!

Another time the four of us and Daniela's family, who were holidaying in India that Christmas, made a trip to Ranthambore, the tiger sanctuary in Rajasthan. One game-drive morning, we all watched in hushed silence as a mother and her two cubs ate a deer kill not 20 feet from our SUV. Amalia decided she needed to get a closer look and jumped out of the open Jeep. Luckily, she didn't get far, instead finding herself entangled in a well-placed thorn bush, suspended by the wool of her sweater like a moth caught in a spider's web. The commotion of us trying to extricate her from the bush caused the tigers to abandon their kill and bolt into the vegetation behind them. That evening, as we drank and dined around a bonfire under the stars, laughing at the thought of Amalia being offered up as cat food earlier in the day, she did it again. This time she decided she was going to bartend for the group. She reached for the bottles and glasses—all 3 feet of her—and wound up pulling on the tablecloth, dragging everything off the makeshift bar table, including a large glass candle full of molten wax, which splashed all over her face, fortunately missing her eyes.

I was very easygoing with them while they were young, but later as they navigated their teens and beyond, I became demanding and exacting, expecting perfection from them, albeit in an imperfect world.

I guess I wanted everything for them and I expected them to want it all too. Quite removed from the open, nurturing, encouraging, self-discovering upbringing I had had at that same age. I'm not sure what changed in me and why I became this controlling father. I realize today that I might have micromanaged them driven by my OCD behaviour. I rarely left them to their own devices, to make mistakes, to find their own way. I regret that deeply today.

I was both thrilled and anxious as I watched them gravitate toward careers in the restaurant world, and even more that they would join Malini and me in our company, Shaan on the marketing, management and events planning side, Amalia in the kitchen. Thrilled because I loved the idea of them following in my footsteps. Anxious because I know how tough this business is. It can eat you up and spit you out. And sure, they had a head start, standing on the shoulders of what we had established. But even so I worried that with my accomplishments, I would be a tough act to follow. People would not judge them on their own merits. They would even be judged more critically just because they are my daughters.

But they are strong-willed women. (I wonder who they got *that* from?) So, I have no doubt they will find their own way. I'm really proud of my girls and support their journey of self-discovery and self-determination, be it in the restaurant business or elsewhere. I know they're capable and bright, and I'm confident they will find their way. We have our girls' trust, and they know there's nothing they can't talk to us about.

9: UNDER THE OVER: AN OVER-THE-TOP SUCCESS

cornbread
jalapeños

BACK TO MY PROFESSIONAL journey. The writing was already on the wall with Just Desserts, when I'd started thinking it was time for me to step up my game and take the dive into a restaurant of my own. Aside from a business deal gone bad, I usually know when it's time to leave: I get bored, as though I have reached a creative plateau, and I start coasting—and it's not how I like to feel. In fact, it's a repugnant feeling, as if I'm wasting my life and whatever talent I have been granted by the Big Executive Chef in the Sky.

But like a well-timed soufflé, life served up a lovely coincidence at just the right time. Here's where two degrees of family separation came into play. My mother managed the law offices of American immigration lawyer Michael Phulwani, one of whose friends was Harish Sehgal, who owned a small but flourishing chain of eateries by the name of Open House Gazebo. It was an early Indian foray into burger joints, pizza parlours and pastry shops, with about four outlets in Bombay. One of them, at Kemps Corner, however, was not doing well. My cousin Radha Patkar's husband, Farhad Nathani, who also happened to be a partner in Open House, asked if I wanted to take over the four years left on its lease.

I went for it, after much talk with Malini and my family. By this time Malini and I were quite involved; she was living with me at my parents' home. This was very modern of my parents. What did hers say? Nothing. They lived in Abu Dhabi at the time and didn't know. We did not have the nerve to tell them. They assumed she was living in a room she'd rented in the Opera House area of Bombay.

So our start-up team, working out of my parents' kitchen, was Malini, Philip and me.

This would be the proverbial big bite for me: my first serious restaurant as owner–chef.

Surprisingly, we made few rookie mistakes with this, our first real business deal. The entire initial renovation expenses cost us a mere song—I recall we fit out the entire restaurant for the astronomical sum of ₹16 lakh—including reworking the tiny kitchen with used equipment and covering horrendous dirty white marble tiles in the dining room with plywood sheets that we painted ourselves. The deal was that I would pay for the renovation and run the restaurant, and Open House and I would split profits 50:50. I didn't have that kind of capital, so I borrowed the money from Saraswat Co-Operative Bank with a term loan. Open House at Kemps Corner had never done well and the landlord didn't think I'd do any better. Negotiating the terms with him on our new four-year lease went pretty well because of this. He got 12 per cent of the net revenue, but that was capped at a not-overly-outrageous threshold monthly figure. Without a liquor licence, we would not be able to benefit from alcohol sales, which account for a considerable percentage of overall restaurant gross revenue. In retrospect, I guess we had not considered the fact that our restaurant might actually become a raging success.

It's often said that 'location, location, location' has a lot to do with a restaurant's success. Kemps Corner was literally at the crossroads of an upscale neighbourhood, flanked by Altamount Road on one side, with Peddar Road and Malabar Hill on the other. The crossing roads are Breach Candy, Warden Road, Peddar Road and Nepean Sea Road. The predominant architecture of the area—other than Charles Correa's iconic Kanchenjunga Apartments, the three-towered twenty-eight-storeyed Grand Paradi Towers, and Reliance Industries, Chairman Mukesh Ambani's ostentatious private residence, Antilla, on Altamount Road (which actually was built some fourteen years later)—was India's first flyover (which Americans call an overpass), which opened in 1965. When we started thinking of what to call the restaurant, we wanted to let the name suggest the neighbourhood. Located as we were, almost literally in the shadow of the flyover, one name jumped out: Left of

Over. Cute as it was, 'left overs' wouldn't work to promote a restaurant. So we came up with Under the Over (UTO).

It was a longish rectangular box of a space. We had room for sixty-four seats in three rows, with two-tops along the walls that we could bring together as needed. Malu, whose magnificent aesthetic eye became increasingly invaluable, took over the 'look' of the place. In a very real sense, Malini became Under the Over's curator of art. Sunil Vijayakar—the same Sunil who had inadvertently launched my catering career a year earlier—was also a hobbyist painter with a unique abstract-modernist, pop-art style that was best imagined or described as Keith Haring meets Miró and Henri Matisse's *Blue Nudes*. We convinced him to let us copy a painting of his to use as a template for our paper table mats and also commissioned two gigantic 7x5 foot abstract canvasses for the dining room walls. So, as soon as you walked in, you were already struck by an avant-garde vibe not seen in Bombay before. The food would have to match that. Later on, we used those walls to showcase the artwork of several new and upcoming local artists. We got their permission to hang and sell their paintings in exchange for a percentage of the sale price.

What I had in mind was something similar to what we had been cooking at the Saloon in New York—a variety of cuisines from around the world, a sort of 'cooking global, eating local' theme—minus Indian food per se. Of course, there would be India-informed spices and tastes, but not stereotypical Indian food. This in itself would be a departure from what Mumbaikars could find in the city back then.

At the time, Indians were almost starved of real Western food that was 'true to taste' and served in a European-style casual café setting—beyond our familiar 'Conti'. They had Shamiana at the Taj Mahal Palace in Colaba. They had Gaylord's, and the Trattoria at the President Hotel. There was also 'fine dining' at the Society restaurant off the lobby of the Ambassador Hotel in Churchgate, much more famous for its rooftop rotating restaurant. At these places you could find typical English pub food—the ubiquitous variety of baked dishes with rich white sauces, overcooked vegetables, pompous roast beef or chewy beef wellington.

My initial menu would be simple but, under the circumstances, radical: Texas-style barbequed chicken with cornbread, Louisiana blackened pomfret, Mexican nachos, calzone and real pizza that combined my New York and Italy experiences. I would run it with the same level of correctness that I had learned in New York. The service staff would be friendly and attentive but not overwhelmingly fawning, hanging onto every guest's move and gesture. I would also leave a third of the tables unreserved to accommodate walk-ins, a practice I saw work extremely well in New York.

Like all good Indians, we picked an auspicious day to open, one for which I didn't need to consult with an astrologer: my birthday (6 April, for those who want to send me a gift every year) seemed good enough. It turned out to be the opposite of auspicious. I got to work on the sixth and there were no chefs in the kitchen, none, *koi nahin*. Where the fuck was my entire kitchen team? I'd hired a senior sous chef a month earlier, and over the next few weeks built up our team as we did food trials and planned the menu at home. We'd even gone through a couple of weeks of soft openings before we officially opened. It turned out that the sneaky Chef Gomes, who'd joined me as my second-in-command, actually was part of a team waiting in Bombay for its travel papers to come in for jobs in the Gulf. They'd signed up individually over the two weeks and I hadn't a clue. Back to the shit at hand … in a panic, I called my friend Ricky Lamba, who had an offshore catering business with people rotating on and off the oil rigs quite regularly.

'Ricky—I'm fucked,' I shouted, skipping the small talk. 'Send me chefs, cooks, kitchen help, whoever you can!'

While he scrambled to help me, I called my catering friends Sunil and Nikki and also sent a '*HELP ME!*' flare to Philip, who still worked for my parents and me. With them, we pulled together a small skeletal kitchen staff. Malu worked the front door as hostess. Friends waited on tables. It was only when things settled down that I learned where my—ahem—dedicated staff disappeared to. They'd got the call apparently the day before and just left. I guess 6 April was auspicious for Gomes and his team too. They were gone—onto greener pastures or parched, sandy deserts, as I really hoped. Not even a phone call. But there was nothing we could do except press on.

Luckily for us, we hit pay dirt and Under the Over took off from day one. My followers—basically the loyal and growing group of high-rollers who'd hired me for catering gigs and the people who ate at them—paid off. Word-of-mouth back then actually worked.

In our first year, 1992, Under the Over was named among *TIME* magazine's Best of Asia. We were the only stand-alone (non-hotel) restaurant from India to make the guide.

This was a wake-up call for India's five-star hotel-based restaurants, suggesting that perhaps they were out of step with emerging food trends and diners' tastes. Complacency was not an option for them any more.

In fact, we created a bit of a menu war. Chef Hemant Oberoi, who oversaw all Taj Hotels' restaurant programmes as corporate executive chef, immediately changed the entire menu at the Shamiana, Bombay's then popular coffee-shop café. Other would-be cafés in town followed suit.

Those were the early years of teaching the city's palate to adapt to Western taste profiles. Diners liked our food but weren't sure why and most had no contemporary vocabulary to explain it, even if they knew. Then there were the people who had travelled to Europe and—living up to the saying 'a little bit of knowledge is a dangerous thing'—would claim, for example, that my cream sauce was too lumpy and broken. I would patiently explain that it's not a broken cream sauce, but one made from ricotta.

Later, at Indigo, I again faced this issue of serving well-travelled people my original versions of recipes they thought they knew and getting criticism for it not being just like what they'd had before in what I assume was an overseas restaurant. We are creatures of habit, all of us, especially when it comes to food. Nothing tastes as good as your mother's homemade *anything*. That's why we call it comfort food. But I don't see my job to be replicating those exact tastes. I aim to invent, create, originate based on tradition but tweaked to reflect my personality. Granted, I myself may not be everybody's cuppa chai. I am not cut from a traditional mould and some people may think me to be too much Rahul for their comfort. I can live with that. Can they? It may not be market-savvy of me, though. I think not—and history proves me right. I feel the same about what I cook. Perhaps my motto should be: 'Cook it my way and they will come ... or not.'

I was introduced to what happens when you turn away some VIPs who don't have a reservation shortly after we opened. It was a Friday night and we were slammed. A rather dignified gentleman with a distinguished goatee approached Malu, who worked the front of the house. He told her he had a reservation under his name. Malu did not recognize his name, nor did she see it on the list.

'No,' she politely responded. 'I don't see your name. I'm sorry but we have nothing available now.'

'Just tell him I came by and was turned away,' he said tersely.

Malu came back to find me in the kitchen.

'Who is this guy?' she asked me.

'Damned if I know,' I said.

And that was that. But not quite. Two days later, in a prominent newspaper, we read—in disbelief—a pan of Under the Over by that very chap. He wrote that the food and service was terrible. The minor problem was that we knew he'd never tasted our food. I was livid. Every fibre in me wanted to retaliate, to call him out. I planned to write a rejoinder and have the paper publish it and retract his so-called review. My father, the astute public relations Yoda, told me to forget it—people will not remember it tomorrow. He was so right.

Under the Over went from strength to strength. The lesson for me was to avoid knee-jerk reactions when people criticized me or, more specifically, my food. Despite my outer bravado, it's still hard to handle negative media, but after twenty years of withstanding some criticism, my skin has grown thicker. I now understand it goes with the territory; if you innovate, you will have naysayers. You know what I say? Fuck 'em. But I would phrase it much more diplomatically.

The wide range and variety of people who walk into my eating establishments never ceases to amaze me. How to accommodate their idiosyncrasies is a skill acquired only by experience. Early in the game, I did not know how to handle the situation when in walked the offspring of a prominent Bombay doctor. She entered as though all cameras were on her, wearing white jeans so tight they looked like her skin and a translucent matching white muslin top. She and her entourage also did little to suppress their loud voices and giggles. Their attention-getting ploy seemed to be working—but in a negative way for other guests.

She excused herself from the group to go to the bathroom, which required walking through our kitchen. The cooks could not take their eyes off her; I worried some of them might chop off their fingers.

When she returned to her table, my most reliable and dignified restaurant manager, Shabbir, a portly, soft-spoken guy who took his job quite seriously, approached the group. He began to take orders, starting with her.

'I'll have the grilled penis,' she said and giggled, her voice several decibels above the dim of the crowd.

Shabbir went totally deadpan.

'Sorry, we don't grill it, we only serve it raw.'

Watching this all from a neighbouring table where I was taking an order, I almost fell over backwards. It was so incongruous of him, not to mention that it might have offended her and anyone within ear range.

But the only comeback was silence. That shut her and her groupies up.

Later, Shabbir came into the back where I was sitting in my little office and said, 'I need to talk to you.'

I got up. 'If it's about what happened at that table, I salute you.'

It was now he who went silent, taken aback and almost in disbelief.

'Let me shake your hand,' I went on, robustly grabbing it. 'Well done. I could not have come up with a better comeback.'

The journey of a chef and restaurateur involves working with many people along the way. Mostly for short periods of time, mainly because the job is so physically and mentally demanding that people just burn out and move on. Occasionally, however, you're fortunate to work with someone who makes an impression on you; who's dedicated, driven, trustworthy and with whom you just click. Someone you take under your wing and mentor, letting whatever you know rub off on him or her in the hope they'll blossom and take it all forward. Irfan Pabaney is one such guy.

We first crossed paths in the winter of 1991 when, as a student in his last year at Sophia Polytechnic's Hotel Administration & Food Technology (HAFT) programme, he joined me on one of my private catering jobs in the kitchen. As a one-man-show caterer, I have regularly hired culinary students from the Institute of Hotel Management, Dadar (IHM), and Sophia's HAFT to help me with service and in the kitchen on a per-job basis. We hit it off that night and I gave him my card, telling him that I was planning on opening a restaurant the following year and would gladly offer him a job. I never heard from him until September, six months after we'd opened Under the Over, when he just showed up out of the blue one afternoon and asked to see me.

'I don't know if you remember ...' he started to say nervously.

I cut him off: 'I was wondering when you'd come by. You can start in the kitchen tomorrow.'

And that's how Irfan came to work with me. Like the postman's oath—'Neither snow nor rain nor heat nor gloom of night ...'—nothing ever kept Irfan from coming in to work. Not the weather, nor his health, nor personal issues, nothing. You could always count on him to be there, dependable, responsible, giving it 100 per cent. Always. This is something about him that has never wavered, regardless of how far up the restaurant ladder he's climbed—from cook to chef to manager to business partner. He's always led from the front, with a smile on his face, never asking of his team anything that he himself wouldn't do.

Needless to say, he grew rapidly and eventually became my sous chef at Under the Over, even managing the entire restaurant operation when we first moved to Bangalore in 1995. Later, when UTO closed, he came to Bangalore and ran the Bookery Cafe for us while we ran Kuteeram, a boutique, ten-room hotel and restaurant 40 kilometres out of the city in Hessaraghatta. When we closed shop and moved back to Bombay before setting up Indigo two years later, he'd moved on and joined the Hakkasan Group, helping them set up and run their restaurants. After jumping around for a while he came back to us in 2007 at Indigo in the kitchen, where he stayed for another three years before heading out to partner and helm a new restaurant called Sassy Spoon.

Irfy, as I've always known him (or as the Chef in Shorts, a moniker lovingly bestowed on him by his peers because he's always in shorts and a bandana, even in the kitchen) is a dear friend. In an industry rife with cutthroat competition and backstabbers, he's been my rock and my confidante, keeping me going through my periods of snow and rain and heat and gloom.

Chef Irfy ... always smiling, always happy, always in shorts

Irfan assisting me plating for a private dinner

Under the Over had a four-year run, not bad in my industry and for a first time chef–owner. But in 1995 my comfort zone began to rake against my need to create and reinvent and challenge myself. I got complacent. I wasn't pushing myself. When that itchy gotta-move-on feeling hits me it's hard to contain, restrain or tie me down. I get into my own chalta hai state of mind. And though I remain half Indian in blood and culture, it ain't me, babe, as Bob Dylan groaned. My antsy American side reared its head. And since we were doing well, better than expected, I had no impetus to change. I'd gotten what I'd hoped for from Under the Over; it had validated me as an owner–chef and given me the confidence to do something bigger and better.

Any relationship between a restaurant owner and a landlord is rife with problems. Our landlord was, in my opinion, a terrible guy who made our every move difficult. Why? Because he could. So the timing was perfect when my landlord reminded me in late 1994 that my lease was coming to an end in a few months. As he saw how well we were doing, he got greedy and wanted to make a new lease so that he had a larger stake in the revenues. We'd originally agreed to the 12 per cent revenue share, with a cap on that. But now he'd spent the last few years burning mad with the smell of money he wasn't making on our success. His new offer was to come in as a partner, as well as jack up the rent.

My response was simple.

'I might as well get a job,' I said. 'I'd have nothing left. I'm not working for you. That's not happening.'

He tried to play hardball. I said I'd rather close the place than become his indentured slave. He thought I was joking. Several weeks went by without any engagement from me on the lease renewal topic and in early 1995 he started getting antsy.

'What about me and the space?' he now implored, the threat becoming real to him.

'You can have it back—all four walls,' I replied. Later, in a moment during which he developed those famous Italian 'coglioni quadrati' or 'cubic balls', he exclaimed with hollow confidence, 'Okay, I'll buy the business from you.' Bingo! 'Better than walking away empty-handed,' I thought. So I sold him the restaurant name and the business. I think he ran it into the ground, as I had suspected he would.

Recently, on a bit of a sentimental journey to see how far I'd come, I drove by Kemps Corner. Today at that location there's a retail store for Reliance Jewels tucked in next to a FabricSpa dry-cleaner, among other businesses, in a little strip. I walked in. It was like visiting the house you grew up in—I could not believe how truly small it was.

But standing on the street, where cars are parked in front of an odd silver fence, I was reminded of one of the little advantages of owning a popular restaurant in Mumbai, where *bakshish* can buy almost anything, including a precious parking space. That curb had had a 'No Parking' sign when we had been here in the 1990s. We had made a little deal with the local police precinct. Whenever a tow truck came by, the driver would look to our front-door security guard, who would give a nod or a headshake to each car parked in front. A nod meant that car did not belong to any current guest in Under the Over, so they could tow it. A headshake meant it belonged to one of our guests, so not to tow it. For myself, the police gave me a piece of paper stamped with something that had no obvious meaning, but that implied 'FRIEND OF THE PRECINCT'. This meant I could park anywhere in the precinct without fear of being towed ... or so I thought.

One day I was parked in front of my restaurant and the guard, a bit frantic, found me in my office.

'Sir, they are towing your car,' he said, all in a tizzy.

'Not to worry,' I tried to calm him down and gave him my FOP paper. But it was too late. My car was gone.

I called someone at the precinct headquarters. I'll sum up my side of the conversation in three letters: 'WTF?!'

I added, 'Why am I paying you guys?'

The gentleman on the other end of the phone apologized profusely, explaining that there was a new inspector and it might take him a week or so to get educated as to how things worked. He asked me to have my car keys sent over. Shortly thereafter my car reappeared and my parking ticket magically disappeared. They'd paid for my parking ticket and towing charges from their neighbourhood slush fund.

To those who might argue that this compromised my ethical values, I would respond that there remains honour among thieves.

Another incident at UTO served as my first introduction to the darker underbelly of the restaurant business in Bombay—no different, in the end, from anywhere else in the world. It's just that earlier I was merely an employee and never really had to deal with these things head-on, as a restaurant owner does. It had to do with our monthly water bill.

One afternoon I was sitting in our tiny back office post lunch when we were visited by a gentleman from the municipal corporation's water department. After chai was served and we'd gotten over pleasantries, he got down to business.

'I can reduce your monthly water bill from ₹18,000 to ₹12,000,' he said matter-of-factly.

'That's great,' I replied, curious where this was going. 'And what do I have to do to achieve this?'

'You pay me ₹3,000 a month in cash, and I'll make your bill less.'

I thought about it and replied that I wasn't interested. I explained, 'My real savings is only ₹3,000 a month, plus I cannot expense the ₹3,000 I'd pay you as it's an off-the-books cash transaction. It doesn't make any real sense to me. So, thanks but no thanks, I'll pay my monthly bill as is.'

Thereafter we started getting water bills of upwards of ₹60,000 a month. The guy was so upset that we'd cut him out of his monthly take that to spite us, he was screwing us. Unfortunately the way it works here is if and when you dispute a utility bill, you need to first pay it and then dispute it, or the utility service is cut off. So we wound up going to court for the better part of a year to fight this. The municipal water supply only came for an hour or two each day, during which we filled up the five water tanks we had in the restaurant loft. We functioned off this water storage for twenty-four hours till the water supply resumed the next day. To generate a bill of ₹60,000 a month, we showed that we would have had almost two feet of water flooding the entire restaurant perpetually. We were able to win eventually, but it was a total waste of time and energy. Is it worth holding on to an ideal? Or do experiences like this start blurring or forcing a shift in the sand of your ethics and values? When do you finally yield, justifying such actions and pass off such demands as part of the cost of doing business? I don't have an answer to this question. I can only say it's hard to be Gandhi and at the same time run a business in India. Corruption and bribes and pay-offs are so embedded in our system that sometimes it feels like the cards are stacked against an honest person trying to make an honest living. We just have to try harder.

One tries to find that balance between generosity, acceptance and forgiveness, *and* protecting one's family, one's work and one's personal space. I had to find my understanding of give-and-take when a problem made life at UTO difficult.

There was an aggressive group of street people and beggars who had taken up residence on the sidewalks and curb right in front of my restaurant. They were cooking and even defecating out there on the sidewalk. It got to the point where they were terrorizing anyone who walked around Kemps Corner. They even threatened us. After our security guard tried to shoo them away, they refused, got really aggressive and went so far as to warn us that if we messed with them, they would throw human faeces at our frontage and more.

So one day I gathered the courage to go talk to them. Introducing myself as the owner, I found the woman who appeared to be the head of their matriarchal clan.

'This is not a nice or considerate thing you are doing,' I suggested. 'Let's work this out.'

Her first response was basically, 'Who cares what you think? We have been marginalized and, worse, ignored forever. So tough shit and we will do what we need to do to stay alive and feed ourselves.'

I am obviously paraphrasing this for you, but that was the essence. I took her last comment as a cue.

'What if I fed all of you three times a day?' I suggested. 'If I did, would you keep your area spotless? Would you stop harassing people? Would you make sure others don't replace you? And even better, would you move everyone to a different location?'

She agreed. We delivered. It was like my version of mafia-style protection.

I admit there was some quid pro quo to my generosity in that tale. But we have done a lot in the altruism arena. For example, with filmmaker Mira Nair's Salaam Baalak Trust, the NGO she founded in 1988 to support children of the streets and other marginalized youth in the inner cities of New Delhi and Bombay. We know Mira through some other friends in the film industry. We took in a few young people and put them through our training programme many years later when we created the Indigo Delis. Along with how to work in a restaurant, they learned the basics of personal hygiene. All were illiterate so we helped them to read and write Hindi and even to speak [kitchen] English.

They worked mainly at our Indigo Deli at the Palladium Mall in Bombay, and in other Deli locations too.

There was one instance that showed me how a simple thing they'd learned could inspire them to who knows what kind of heights. A young girl came up to me, her eyes full of enthusiasm and wonder. 'Uncle, uncle,' she called to me. Of course I was not her uncle, but that was how she addressed me with affectionate respect. 'Today I learned how to make fusilli pasta with tomato sauce!'

But the payback for us was to see how far some of them did rise. One wound up a senior chef on a cruise ship in the Mediterranean. This kid who did not know what lay beyond the slums of Dharavi in the heart of Greater Mumbai has now probably seen more of the world than I have.

As it turns out, these young men and women were some of our best employees—every employer's dream. They were hardworking, responsible, dependable and loyal. For them, every day at work was a window into a new world and a new life. Our restaurants were microcosms of how things work. They sucked it up as though it was a lifeline itself.

Because of our philosophy—that you are as good or as bad as the work you do, not the caste or economic class you come from—this might have been the first time they were treated as equals. Or even recognized at all as human beings.

In India, we deal with the poor with blinkers on. We look away. We disavow. We deny. Until they come to the window of our cars or knock on our doors. Then we shoo them away. That is wrong. I do not have a solution, but I know that giving to others feeds oneself. I felt more pride training and giving those kids aspirations than in almost anything else I've ever done.

I had just opened Under the Over but it was getting such great reviews and the public loved it so much that I was thrust into the limelight, up there with well-known Indian chefs from the major five-star hotels. As a result, I was invited to attend the first ever All-India Chefs Congress. In one session, the discussion was about what they called 'The bastardization of Indian food overseas'. They were quite upset that restaurants in London, for example, run by Bangladeshis, were cooking dishes like rogan josh, a traditional lamb recipe, the signature of Kashmiri cuisine. What was being served had 'neither rogan nor josh (neither flavour nor fire)', one of the chefs declared condescendingly.

Another chef suggested the need to create standardized recipes, like from the French cooking encyclopedia *Larousse Gastronomique*, 'or we will lose our culinary heritage'.

I listened to this drivel for a while, then could not help myself.

'Sirs,' I started with respect. '*Larousse Gastronomique* standardized cooking techniques, not actual recipes. Look at our own ubiquitous chapati. The ingredients are exactly the same everywhere in India: flour, water, maybe some oil and salt. Yet, rarely have you ever eaten a chapati that tastes the same from one region—from one kitchen—to another. But they all are good. Which is the right one? Every grandmother makes a bhindi masala (spiced okra), yet they all taste different and all are delicious. Which is the right one?

'The beauty of food is in its diversity,' I continued, now on a roll ... or on a chapati. 'We are not here sweating our butts off in the kitchen shooting for homogeneity. I say hats off to the Bangladeshis in the UK for bastardizing our food. It's more than any of you are doing. None of you here are innovating, nor experimenting, nor creating new taste memories for diners. Our cuisine must grow and evolve.'

I thought I had surely burned some bridges and stepped on some toes. But many came up to me afterwards and told me I was right. Not surprisingly, though, nothing changed on most of their menus.

BLACKENED POMFRET, TOBACCO ONIONS and CORNBREAD (From Under The Over)

INGREDIENTS FOR 4 PORTIONS

Blackened Fish

4 boneless pomfret fillets, skin on, ~125gm each (or use red snapper, or any other firm, white fish)

3 tablespoons onion purée

1 teaspoon garlic purée

½ teaspoon chilli powder

½ teaspoon coriander seed powder

½ teaspoon cumin seed powder

¼ teaspoon thyme leaves

¼ teaspoon dried oregano leaves

¼ teaspoon freshly ground black pepper powder

¼ teaspoon white pepper powder (optional)

2 tablespoons salt

Juice of 1 lemon

1 tablespoon apple cider or white wine vinegar

Olive oil for searing fish

Tobacco Onions

2 large onions cut in half and sliced thin

4 tablespoons plain flour

2 teaspoons cayenne pepper

½ teaspoon salt

Vegetable oil, for frying

Cornbread

1 cup finely ground cornmeal

1 cup all-purpose flour

½ cup yoghurt

2 eggs

⅔ cup brown sugar

½ teaspoon baking powder

½ teaspoon baking soda

½ teaspoon salt

1–2 tablespoon chopped fresh coriander

1 tablespoon boiled corn kernels (off the cob)

1 roasted green bell pepper-capsicum (skinned, de-seeded and chopped)

1 tablespoon olive oil (approx.) to coat the capsicum

1 small green chili, de-seeded and chopped fine or 1 teaspoon chopped jalapeño

Butter to grease the tray

DIRECTIONS

Cornbread:

Preheat the oven to 180°C. Grease a baking tray with butter and line it with greaseproof paper.

Rub the green bell peppers with olive oil, salt and pepper. Roast them over an open flame till charred. Once all the peppers are charred, immediately put them in a bowl and cover with plastic cling wrap so they collect some steam. Let them cool. Once the peppers are cooled enough to handle, peel the charred skin, de-seed and finely chop. Also, de-seed and finely chop the green chillies (or jalapeños) and add to the roasted capsicum.

In a large bowl, whisk the yoghurt and brown sugar together till smooth and well combined. Add both the cornmeal and all-purpose flour and whisk well. Add the baking soda and baking powder. Add chillies, chopped roasted peppers, boiled corn kernels and chopped fresh coriander. Mix really well and pour into a greased, 2-inch walled baking tray.

Bake at 180°C for 30–40 minutes or till a toothpick inserted comes out clean. After it is baked, remove the tray from the oven, cool for 15 minutes, then turn it out on to a wire rack or serving plate. Cut into cubes and serve immediately—it's unbelievably good when it's grilled, hot and slathered with butter!

Tobacco Onions:

Heat oil in a pan or electric deep-fat fryer. Mix the flour, cayenne pepper and salt in a bowl. Thinly slice whole onions into rings or cut them in half and slice thin (half-moon shapes). Toss and dredge the sliced onion in the seasoned flour, shake off the excess and deep-fry until they're golden-brown and look like tobacco ... get it? Drain well on paper towels and serve with your blackened fish.

Blackened Fish:

For the onion purée, peel and slice onions and process in a blender to a purée or thick paste consistency. Use the same procedure to make the garlic purée as well. You may need to add a teaspoon or two of water to the onions and garlic when blending to get the desired consistency, but don't add too much. If your onion-and-garlic paste is too watery, drain out the excess liquid by letting it sit for a short while in a fine mesh strainer.

To make the blackened spice paste, in a bowl, mix the onion-and-garlic paste along with chilli powder, coriander powder, cumin powder, thyme and oregano.

Season the fish fillets with lemon juice, salt and pepper. After seasoning the fillets, generously apply a thick layer of the blackening paste on to the non-skin side only for all the fillets.

Put a non-stick or cast-iron skillet on high heat and let it get nice and hot. Pour some olive oil in it. It'll start smoking pretty quickly. Carefully place your fillets in the pan, paste-side down, and let them cook for 3 to 5 minutes till the paste chars. It will get quite smoky, so you might want to open a window and turn up the exhaust! Turn the heat down to medium and deglaze the pan with a healthy splash of white wine vinegar or apple cider vinegar. Carefully flip your fish over on to the skin side, making sure that the blackened paste stays stuck to the fish, and continue cooking for another 4 to 5 minutes to crisp the skin. Don't overcook the fish.

Serve with hot, buttered cornbread and crispy tobacco onions.

lemongrass

10: A DETOUR TO BANGALORE

SHE HAD A DREAM and she figured out a way to make it work.

That was the life lesson Malini and I learned in 1995–96 from what at first glance might seem like a diversion from our journey to Indigo in Mumbai.

The 'she' above was Protima Bedi, the renowned model, Indian classical dancer and teacher who showcased Odissi, the traditional dance from the state of Odisha. We knew her through my parents; they were good friends. She had established a dance school called Nrityagram 40 kilometres outside Bangalore, our country's first modern gurukul (residential school) for Indian classical dance, and an intentional community set up as a village. She owned 10 acres across the dirt road and set out developing a jewel of a boutique hotel there. It was called Kuteeram (meaning 'hut' in Telugu and Tamil), a ten-room retreat. What both amazed and impressed me was her conviction and passion; she sold everything she had, begged, borrowed and just short of stole to realize this dream.

Protima had seen what we did at Under the Over and loved it. She offered us a contract to join her as resident hoteliers and chef–managers of the restaurant connected to it. At the outset, we knew jack shit about most of this. This would be a steep educational climb, my equivalent of an advanced degree in hotel management, albeit hands-on. When we started meeting with Protima, we asked a lot of questions, most of which she could not answer. We quickly realized she was in over her head. As much as we also felt the water rising to our chins, when she begged us to 'sort it all out', we signed on.

Sometimes the Great Culinary Gods work in strange and timely ways. The timing was perfect for us, as we'd hit another roadblock in our lives. We had just left Under the Over. A year earlier we'd had our first daughter, Shaan, a bundle of joy. We were still living with my parents but the situation was becoming untenable, if only due to the lack of private space for our little family of three. Besides, Mom had also made it clear early on that thrilled as she was to be a grandmother, she wanted to be able to either visit her grandchild or have her grandchild visit her. She was certain that parents need to rear their kids on their own terms without constant interference or influence. We didn't have enough money to rent our own place and buying was so far out of our vision that it was like a hurtful joke. So this opportunity attracted us on several levels. Not only would we make and save money, but it would also add to our growing experience in the world of hospitality.

It was during this period that we officially set up deGustibus Hospitality Pvt. Ltd. At the same time, we ran a café at a bookstore called The Bookery in Bangalore. The café did all-day dining with a simple snacky menu. I'd prep the food at Kuteeram and have it shipped into the city. Protima took a percentage of that for providing the workspace and I did the work on her clock, which she approved.

Along with learning to go for my Big Dreams rather than stay with the conservative logical thought process I was trained to follow as a scientist, I learned about P&L statements, balance sheets and such. I do not come from an entrepreneurial or business family, so watching the books was not a high priority. But this experience of running the ship and, frankly, Protima's ambitiousness opened my mind to the possibility that minding a budget is a good, even an essential thing. One saw zeroes in a whole new way. A lot of them after commas could mean big profits or big losses. These lessons were indispensable when we came to realizing some of our Big Dreams.

Malu went ahead of me with baby Shaan. Dear friends of ours gave us their company guest house to stay in in Bangalore; every other day we drove 40 kilometres to the village of Hessaraghatta and then to Protima's Nrityagram. Once I arrived and while we waited for our house to be built on the property, we moved into the kathak gurukul, the house that was usually reserved for the teacher in a residential school setting. Right away my wife, aka Ms Organization, made our abode gorgeous. When Protima saw what she'd done, she asked Malu to do the interiors of the whole ten-room hotel and dining room. It was the vote of confidence my wife needed to realize her capabilities as an interior designer. Amazing how motivational someone else's compliments to your vision can be—especially from such a talented woman as Protima.

'She gave me the courage to embrace that yet-unexpressed part of myself,' Malu said later. This part of her blossomed again years later when a serious illness in our family caused a great deal of stress for us all. Malu dealt with it by expressing her anxiety on canvas. 'One day, I don't know what got into me—I bought some paint and started to paint ... and it took off. It was my therapy.' She's been painting ever since and went on to have her art exhibited, even launched a line of art deco-inspired jewellery.

But it all began with Protima's initial belief in Malu. Protima took her to Delhi, gave her several lakhs in cash and names of furniture sources in Shekhawati in northern Rajasthan, and sent her off to buy what would be needed to furnish and decorate Kuteeram.

Malu's destination was the old and conservative small town Churu, in the Thar Desert of Rajasthan, about 250 kilometres west of New Delhi. Protima knew of a furniture maker who made wrought-iron, wood and camel-leather furniture, which they also sold to Pottery Barn. It would have been a shopper's dream, except that my young wife was a woman travelling alone with so many rupees that she needed a second bag. As a precaution, Malini asked a young employee of her father's family to accompany her and act as her bodyguard for the trip. They travelled by train from Delhi to Jaipur and upon arrival in Churu, she went shopping right away. That night, in true Rajasthani hospitality, she stayed as a guest in the haveli of the family that owned the factory. Hospitable as her hosts were, the one thing she noticed was the absence of any women in their midst. They were all in purdah,

(*Above*) The entrance foyer of Indigo, looking at the yellow dining room
Photo: Sheena Sippy

(*Below*) Indigo's yellow dining room
Photo: Sheena Sippy

(*Above*) The Indigo entrance and bar with Jitish Kallat's painting
Photo: Sheena Sippy

(*Below*) The Indigo bar with stairs leading to the terrace and black lounge
Photo: Sheena Sippy

(*Above*) Indigo's main dining room looking towards the bar
Photo: Sheena Sippy

(*Below*) Getting set for service
Photo: Sheena Sippy

(*Above*) Filling the Shiva blue pond with fresh marigolds—a daily ritual
Photo: Sheena Sippy

(*Below*) Terrace dining at Indigo
Photo: Sheena Sippy

(*Above*) Entrance signage of the first Indigo Deli in Colaba, Mumbai
Photo: Sheena Sippy

(*Below*) The retail wall, Indigo Deli, Colaba, Mumbai
Photo: Sheena Sippy

(*Above*) Indigo Deli at the Palladium Mall, Mumbai

(*Below*) Indigo Deli at the R-City Mall, Ghatkopar, Mumbai

Looking down at the Tote Bar from the mezzanine lounge
Photo: Sheena Sippy

(*Above*) Dining al fresco under 100-year-old rain trees at Neel
Photo: Sheena Sippy

(*Below*) Neel veranda lounge at night
Photo: Sheena Sippy

(*Above*) Entrance foyer at Indigo, New Delhi
Photo: Sheena Sippy

(*Below*) Bar with patio at Indigo, New Delhi
Photo: Sheena Sippy

(*Above*) Dining room at Indigo, New Delhi
Photo: Sheena Sippy

(*Below*) All lit up against the night sky…Indigo, New Delhi
Photo: Sheena Sippy

(*Above*) Shaking it up at the Qualia bar
Photo: Jordi Huisman

(*Below*) Qualia bar detail
Photo: Jordi Huisman

(*Above*) Qualia's open kitchen with its wood burning hearth and oven, lined with hundreds of pickle jars
Photo: Jordi Huisman

(*Below*) 'Qualia Qurbside'...one of the few outdoor, sidewalk café dining set-ups in Mumbai city during the COVID pandemic

Qualia dining room with open kitchen
Photo: Jordi Huisman

Ode bar
Photo: Niveditaa Gupta

(*Above and below*) Ode bar lounge, dining room and open kitchen
Photo: Niveditaa Gupta

Shadow play with the wire mesh cloud installation at Ode
Photo: Niveditaa Gupta

behind closed doors and absent from the revelry. As the evening went on and the booze flowed, she became increasingly uncomfortable and when her young bodyguard came back to her room drunk and insistent on spending the night, her nervous feeling grew worse. She packed and left alone that night by train for Delhi, leaving him behind.

Designed by award-winning Goa-based architect Gerard da Cunha, the Kuteeram buildings had a touch of Spain in design elements like spiral pillars, the details of which came from Da Cunha's visit to the Goth Quarter of Barcelona. It looked like nothing anyone had seen on Earth or any other planet—a cross between The Flintstones and Star Wars on LSD. The materials used were traditional: thatch woven by local craftsmen set against exposed granite and brick, red oxide and mud mortar. Domes over each room and arched walkways dominated the landscape. Flagstone floors, wrought-iron lighting fixtures, planter's chairs—the details were breathtaking. All the buildings, except for the water tower, were low to the ground, following the contour of the land, and wrapped around an open space of an inner courtyard. Terracotta figures by the Malayali sculptor Alex Chandy faced an ornamental pool. There was a terrace above the restaurant, where performing artists danced.

Striking as it was, it needed help to bring it to completion. We took over the rest of the construction. I redesigned the kitchen, while Malu oversaw interior decorating.

Guest rooms had mother-of-pearl shutters and tinted glass panes in the style of traditional Goan Portuguese homes. Some rooms had Balinese bamboo chairs that came from Protima's own collection. There was a mural by Anand Sayam, from the Karnataka Chitrakala Parishath, or even things Malu had found, like a carved box she discovered on one of our many furnishing forays in Rajasthan and elsewhere.

Amid the mishmash of mixed design influences, there was one motif that tried to hold them all together: broken tile mosaics that moved from bathroom floors and counters to everywhere else. I recall one mosaic featuring a frog leaping toward a fish. They started out as one way to use leftover broken tiles, but under the creative and whimsical eye of Gerard's resident architect Mona Madan, they quickly became something of a signature detail.

To prep the kitchen, first I cancelled orders for kitchen equipment because the Delhi manufacturers were cheating Protima on pricing and even components. She'd been conned into giving them 100 per cent of the cost upfront, so naturally they took their sweet-ass time in delivering. When I went up to Delhi to inspect the equipment readiness in their factory I noticed that the fridges lacked compressors. When asked about that they replied, 'That's additional!' Eventually they fell in line once we had their company blacklisted by the Karnataka State Finance Corporation, the company that was controlling the purse strings of the Kuteeram project. Malu and I became plumber, electrician, contractor, gardener, chef, hostess, server and clean-up crew. I remember once even donning a snorkel and mask and diving down into the water tank, underwater torch in hand, to seal a crack from the inside. The hotel was full of guests and draining the water tank to undertake repairs was out of the question. It was that nuts.

The restaurant, my main domain, had an indoor–outdoor feel. Dining tables made of rough-hewn sheesham wood were surrounded by interesting chairs upholstered in camel hide. A bench for two was inset with ceramic tiles in the backrest. We did a constantly changing five- to seven- course set meal for dinner. We figured, if you're driving out over an hour from the city to come dine with us, you're there for the duration. It was priced really well too, Bangalore being such a price-sensitive market, at ₹500 or so per head. The thing was, we didn't realize just how price-sensitive most Bangaloreans were. The Bombaywallah or Delhiite who happened to dine with us was flummoxed at how cheap our food was. The Bangalorean would say, 'Give us less, but charge us less.' Less than ₹500 for a five- to seven-course meal … really?!

As far as cooking went, it was a time of experimentation. I'd grown complacent once again and knew I needed to learn some new tricks. We'd built a beautiful open-air grill and tandoor 'food bar' that allowed me to experiment with smoke and wood cooking (something that we finessed much later with Qualia). Fundamentally, I kept trying to marry Indian and Western. The results, to my mind, were interesting but not amazing. I was looking for amazing. That said, I did a couple of chicken dishes that would stand the test of time ...

For Malini there was another lesson that later served us well with Indigo. She got actively involved in marketing and public relations, about which she and I knew little to nothing back then. But she worked on intuition and her natural instinct for networking. With a very small budget, we knew word-of-mouth recommendations would be our strongest play. And we played it to the hilt. We hosted influential people like the folks from Cox & Kings; we also invited the wealthy investment broker Jonathan Soros, son of the even wealthier investor and philanthropist George Soros.

We saw that we could use events as pretexts to bring people in and garner publicity and bookings, so of course we hosted many dance performances at the amphitheatre on the property. We had an amazing launch for the press, bringing in a dance troupe from Malaysia. This crash course in marketing and PR set the stage for Indigo.

However, in a relatively short time, perhaps two years, we grew tired of being there. I didn't want to be a gentleman farmer or a glorified B&B host. And the idea to develop this as a Michelin-starred Relais & Châteaux kind of place, the type that Malu and I would either like to run or retreat to ourselves, was never going to happen. Protima just didn't have the capital to do that; she was already undercapitalized. More than that, I knew it was time to get serious about my own restaurant. Taking Protima's cue, I had a dream and was going to figure out a way to make it work, despite whatever odds.

I was thirty-eight years old at the time. The rest of my life was calling.

TANDOOR ROASTED CHICKEN, ROSEMARY POTATOES, CHILLI-HONEY CARROTS, DATE AND TAMARIND REDUCTION (From Indigo via Kuteeram)

INGREDIENTS FOR 4 PORTIONS

Tandoori Chicken

2 chickens ~800 gm each, skin on

1 tablespoon fresh ginger paste

1 tablespoon garlic paste

Fresh rosemary leaves from 8 sprigs

2 tablespoons honey

1 teaspoon red chilli flakes

1 cup yoghurt

¼ cup cooking oil

Salt and pepper

Rosemary Potatoes

300 gm potatoes

Fresh rosemary leaves from 3–4 sprigs

2 teaspoons finely chopped garlic

1 teaspoon smoked paprika

1 tablespoon chopped parsley

2 tablespoons soft butter

Salt and pepper

Chilli-Honey Carrots

250 gm carrots

2 tablespoons honey

2 teaspoons fresh thyme leaves

2 teaspoons chopped parsley

2 tablespoons butter

¼ cup white wine

½ teaspoon red chilli flakes

1 teaspoon chopped garlic

Salt and pepper

Date and Tamarind Reduction

500 ml brown chicken stock

100 gm seedless dates

50 gm tamarind pulp

1½ cups dark rum

1½ cups port

150 gm sliced onions

1 teaspoon garam masala

1 tablespoon butter

Salt and pepper

DIRECTIONS

Tandoori Chicken:

Clean and cut the chickens in half through the back and breast bone, length-wise, leaving the right breast, leg and thigh joined together and the left breast, leg and thigh joined together. With a sharp paring knife, score and slit the skin and cut deeper into the flesh beneath, to allow the marinade to penetrate down to the bone. Combine the marinade ingredients together in a non-reactive mixing bowl and rub it on to and into the half-chickens, making sure it penetrates everywhere. Marinate for at least 4 hours, refrigerated, prior to cooking. Just before cooking, skewer each half-chicken with two parallelly placed tandoor skewers to keep the halves splayed open and flat and rotating around a single skewer. Cook in a hot tandoor till done and nicely charred—for about 8–10 minutes. Alternatively, cook the halves over either a charcoal or gas grill, or in the oven at 180°C till well-cooked and charred. Remember to frequently baste the chicken with a mixture of chicken stock and leftover marinade to keep the meat from drying out. Either serve a whole half chicken or tear in half to serve the legs and breasts separately. Serve hot and well done.

Rosemary Potatoes:

Wash and scrub the potatoes to clean them of all dirt. Pat them dry with a paper towel and cut them into wedges, length-wise, leaving the skin on. Combine the rest of the ingredients in a bowl and rub the potato wedges with the dressing generously. Spread them out on a baking tray covered with aluminium foil and roast in a medium oven ~180°C, uncovered, for about 20–30 minutes or until golden-brown and cooked.

Keep agitating the tray in the oven while they cook to keep them from sticking. Remove from the oven and keep warm till service.

Chilli-Honey Carrots:

Peel the carrots and cut into juliennes using a mandolin slicer or by hand, showing off your knife skills. In a pan, sauté the garlic and chilli flakes in the butter on medium heat. As the garlic browns, add in the carrots and combine well. Add the white wine and cook to evaporate most of it. Then add in the honey and continue cooking the carrots till they're sticky-glazed and done. Take off the stove, add in the thyme and chopped parsley and combine well. Serve warm.

Date and Tamarind Sauce:

Soak the tamarind and dates in a little bit of cold water for about 10 minutes till they soften. Make sure there are no seeds or woody bits present. Purée the soaked fruit and the soaking water in a food processor to form a smooth paste. In a heavy-bottomed saucepan, melt butter and sauté the sliced onions till light brown. Add the port and half the quantity of dark rum to the sautéed onions and cook to reduce and deglaze. Add the puréed tamarind and date mixture to the pan and cook well. Once the mixture starts bubbling add the chicken stock, mix well and further reduce, whisking as you go, till a sauce consistency is reached. Add the remaining quantity of dark rum with garam masala and season well. Reduce further for about 10 minutes, take off the flame and strain with a fine mesh strainer. Hold warm till service.

GINGER LEMONGRASS CHICKEN, TOMATO PULAO, ZUCCHINI SATAY, LEMON-CORIANDER EMULSION (From Indigo via Kuteeram)

INGREDIENTS FOR 4 PORTIONS

The order of the ingredients is:

Grilled Chicken

Tomato Pulao

Zucchini Satay

Lemon-Coriander Emulsion

Grilled Chicken

4 chicken breasts, deboned, wing bone in, skinless

4 chicken legs, boneless, skinless

3 stalks lemongrass, chopped

⅓ cup chopped fresh ginger

¼ cup chopped garlic

½ cup fresh basil

Juice and zest of 2 lemons

Salt and pepper

Zucchini Satay

250 gm zucchini

2 tablespoons chunky peanut butter (or add 1 tablespoon of crushed peanuts if using smooth peanut butter)

1 tablespoon garlic

2½ tablespoons butter

½ cup white wine

2 tablespoons honey

1 tablespoon sesame oil

1 teaspoon red chilli flakes

1 tablespoon chopped fresh coriander (cilantro)

Tomato Pulao

250 gm boiled Basmati rice

2½ tablespoons butter

80 gm diced onion

20 gm diced garlic

1 tablespoon pommery (grainy) mustard

80 gm spring onion bulbs or shallots

6 medium tomatoes, blanched, deseeded, deskinned and cut into ½-inch dice

¼ cup chopped fresh coriander

¼ cup chopped fresh basil

80 ml white wine

80 ml white wine vinegar

1 tablespoon honey

Lemon-Coriander Emulsion

200 ml olive oil

4–6 garlic cloves, crushed

½ cup roasted coriander seeds

1 packed cup fresh coriander (cilantro) leaves

4 green chillies, split and deseeded

200 ml red wine

200 ml port

Zest and juice of 4 lemons

DIRECTIONS

Grilled Chicken:

Blend lemongrass and ginger in a mixer to make a coarse paste. Add a little water if required. Spoon the paste into several layers of muslin cloth, wrap tightly around the paste and keep twisting to squeeze out the ginger and lemongrass juice. Blend the lemongrass-ginger juice with the basil, salt, pepper, garlic and lemon juice to make a paste. Marinate the chicken breasts and leg pieces in this paste for at least 3 hours, refrigerated. When ready to serve, cook the chicken over a hot grill for approximately 4–5 minutes on either side till nicely done.

Tomato Pulao:

Boil Basmati rice in water till cooked. Strain and reserve. Separately, melt butter in a saucepan (large enough to hold the rice), add onion and garlic and sauté till translucent. Add the mustard, shallots and chopped, blanched tomatoes. Cook for 3 to 4 minutes, then add the white wine, vinegar and honey and reduce till the pan contents become thickish and paste-like. Add the cooked Basmati rice to the pan, mix well, then add fresh coriander and basil leaves and combine well. Check seasoning and hold warm.

Zucchini Satay:

Using a mandolin slicer, cut the zucchini into long thin julienne ribbons. Separately, melt butter in a pan, add chopped garlic and sauté till it just starts to brown. Add the peanut butter and chilli flakes and mix well. Add white wine and some water to the pan, mixing well to make a thick sauce. Finish with honey and sesame oil and check the sweet-sour balance and seasoning. Add in the zucchini ribbons, combine well to coat the zucchini and cook for a short while more till they wilt and soften but still maintain a slight crunch. Reserve till ready to plate.

Lemon-Coriander Emulsion:

Mix the red wine and port together in a non-reactive saucepan on high heat, and cook the wines until they reduce to a third or quarter their volume and become syrupy. Separately, dry-roast the coriander seeds in a pan, crush them in a mortar and pestle, and set aside. Separately, heat the oil in a pan, add crushed garlic, green chillies and fresh coriander, and cook for a bit. Remove from the flame when the coriander leaves start turning dark green. When off the flame but still hot, add in the toasted coriander seeds, port and red wine reduction and lemon zest. Blend everything and finish with lemon juice, checking for balance. Reserve the lemon-coriander dressing.

11: INDIGO RAISES THE BAR

grouper
charred red pepper
kashmiri chillies
kokum

NOW, WRITING THIS MORE than twenty years after Indigo opened and considering how much the dining-out experience in India has matured and expanded in the interim, it's almost impossible to imagine how groundbreaking Indigo was and remained until the time we finally sold the restaurant. I had had no idea it would become so disruptive to the Indian restaurant world, perhaps because I knew what was happening in the US, Europe and other parts of Asia. I did know there was no other stand-alone restaurant in India doing Western-style cuisine at our level. I knew I was a good chef, but would not have had the chutzpah to say I was a great chef and certainly would never have believed Indigo would go on to win awards and a vast international following—not to mention show two-digit per cent growth every year for some ten years.

Yet, that is exactly what happened. Here's how.

Once our two-year management contract expired towards the end of 1996, we gave up running Protima's Kuteeram Retreat and fled the boonies to move into a beautiful apartment in the cantonment neighbourhood of (where else?) Cooke Town in Bangalore for a couple of months. I was done being a gentleman farmer, and it was time to reinvent myself and build that food-focused, serious restaurant I knew I had to. The plan was to settle in Bangalore, at the time the fastest-growing city in Asia, and we managed to convince our family and friends to invest in our newly formed company, deGustibus Hospitality Pvt. Ltd.

When we left Bombay for Bangalore, Mom said she wanted to help us put a roof over our heads and offered to gift Malini and me about ₹70-odd lakh to do this. I convinced her not to buy us a flat but to invest instead in our restaurant company, so that the business could one day put a roof over our heads. She did, and that's how my parents became the first investors in deGustibus Hospitality after Malini and I founded the company in 1996. Malini's parents and a few friends of theirs did so too. The money was in, we'd raised between ₹2–3 crore of seed capital and were raring to go.

We spent our days and nights eating, drinking, hanging out and people-watching at almost all the bars and restaurants in buzzing Bangalore, attempting to understand customers and consumption patterns as we honed our business plan. One thing soon became alarmingly clear—there wasn't much consumption. We couldn't believe it. Yes, it was true that bars, pubs and eateries were heaving with young, partying techies, but when you looked closely, they weren't really buying anything. They'd nurse a pitcher of beer and a plate of kebabs all night long as they conversed and hung out. Definitely not good customer behaviour if you were planning to open a new restaurant. I grew increasingly unsure of sinking our money into this deceptively booming market, and constantly debated this with our friends in Bangalore. One such evening we were chatting with dear friends Anna and Milind Thakker and had an epiphany of sorts, leading to a decision that would change our lives forever. Our twenty-minute back-of-a-paper-napkin calculation went something like this:

There wasn't a major difference in the set-up costs of a restaurant in Bangalore versus Bombay at the time. Interiors cost roughly the same, equipment cost the same, labour was about the same ... the only real difference lay in the rental of prime real estate. Bombay was about ₹150 per square foot compared to ₹50 per square foot in Bangalore. For a 3,000-square-foot place, the difference in rent worked out to ₹3,00,000 per month. Dividing that over thirty days a month, that worked out to ₹10,000 per day; if you split 50:50 between lunch and dinner, that meant about ₹5,000 per shift. For a 100-seater eatery, this translated to ₹50 per person ... which was approximately the price of a Coca-Cola in a restaurant. So the question became, 'Can you get people in Bombay to drink more Cokes than the people in Bangalore?' The answer was an unequivocal 'YES'. We packed up and moved back to Bombay in two weeks.

So there we were, back to living with my parents but with one difference this time—we were actively looking for restaurant space, with money in the bank to back us. Malini and I were very clear that we wanted a space with character, old-world charm with high ceilings, good frontage and such, and not just a boring four-walled box. We were working with several brokers and had a bunch of questions that our lawyers had drafted for prospective landlords to substantiate clear and marketable title of their spaces. Before we even got down to discussing or negotiating, we needed those questions answered, and it was amazing how many stunning places we were forced to walk away from due to financing. Either the landlord wanted a huge component of 'black money' (ours was only 'white'), or their places were tied up in some legal proceedings. Whatever the reason, we must have seen more than thirty attractive spaces with no joy on the title front. By the summer of 1997 we were all but broke, having gone through our meagre savings like a hot knife through butter. I was beginning to think that opening a restaurant in Bombay was a non-starter. Ironic, considering we had money in the bank to do so. It was depressing to say the least, and if Malini's brother Rajeev hadn't decided to get married at the end of that summer, in Texas, I'm not sure how we'd have maintained our sanity. The trip to the US provided us the break we so desperately needed to refresh our minds and reflect on what we were doing with our lives.

After the wedding we went to San Francisco to hang with Malini's sister Radhika and her husband Jay. It was my first time on the American West Coast and I loved every minute of it. Can you imagine? I'd spent almost ten years through the late 1970s and 1980s between Pennsylvania and New York City, but never once did I venture out west. Go figure! While there, I cooked several successful meals for restaurateurs and friends of theirs and it got me thinking: if nothing was happening on the Bombay front, what would it be like to open a restaurant in San Francisco? We started watching how people ate, as we'd done in Bangalore a year earlier, going out to many different restaurants and bars over the better part of a month. I noticed that San Francisco at the time seemed to have a huge shortage of hotel rooms, so we started exploring the idea of doing a small boutique hotel with a restaurant. We somehow met the owner of an old twenty-room colonial mansion on the corner of Van Ness and Broadway, if my fading memory serves me correctly. It needed a ton of work, but our collective minds started buzzing. We envisioned a British Raj-style B&B, with all the antique furniture from Malini's Rajasthani sources in India and moustached turban-clad doormen in bright red flowing achkans and jodhpurs. It had a beautiful restaurant space on the ground floor. I saw the possibility of an eclectic, Indian-inspired restaurant and bar there. The owner loved the idea and agreed to even carry paper on the project. He wanted in, to partner with us, and was willing to help underwrite a chunk of the investment too. Malini's dad and I created a detailed business plan and we met Jay and Radhika's business bankers to raise capital in addition to the funds we already had. All good. They bought into the project and suddenly we were good to go. It had taken all of four weeks to create a plan, find a space, raise the capital and start the build-out. It was that easy. But something was wrong. We'd been at this for well over eight months in Bombay, dealing with disappointment after frustrating disappointment, and had achieved bollocks, and here we were in San Francisco, ready to get going.

What could be wrong, then?

It was my mind. I panicked, I froze, I started asking myself what was I doing. I'd been gone from the US for almost ten years and was totally out of touch with the way things worked there, the way Americans ate, the way restaurants ran, the American work ethic, you name it. It was clearly simple to open a restaurant or small hotel business in the US compared to Bombay, but what after opening it? The 'running it' would have killed us. In contrast, I later realized, as much as a pain in the ass it was to start a restaurant business in India, it was that much easier to sustain and grow it in the absence of any real competition.

Would this be my Rubicon? Was I about to bite off more than I could chew? Was America too big a stage for me to test my ability as a chef and restaurateur? Was I chickening out, or was my gut telling me something?

So Malini and I sat down and had a powwow with our investors. We decided that if we were really going to make a go of it in the US, I needed to get back into working in American restaurants again. I needed the work and a refresher course in Western cuisine, technique, service, management and—oh, yes—cooking. So in the early fall of 1997, I left Malini and Shaan in San Francisco and headed to New York, where I called Chef Michael Romano and got a job working at the Union Square Café as a line cook. Actually, I bounced around all the departments of the restaurant—front and back—but spent most of that five-month period in the kitchen with him. It was a great learning, one that shaped my approach to work for years to come.

I recall with great fondness the chats we'd have in the late afternoons post lunch service in his tiny office, discussing what it meant to be a chef and restaurateur. He shared insights with me that defined his work ethic: how he approached his food and built a menu; how he interpreted classical cooking, modernizing and expressing it for the current times; how he elevated dishes to make them restaurant-worthy without losing their underlying essence; his attention to detail; and his treatment of his team, among many other pearls of culinary wisdom. He was a taskmaster, but there was a Zen-like correctness and a single-mindedness in everything he did, from sharpening his soft-carbon steel Japanese Misono knives to planning and teaching the daily specials to his team, to being head chef and culinary director of Union Square Café.

I spoke with him many years later, after we opened Indigo. I was having a hard time wearing the hats of creative chef and restaurateur–businessman; the internal conflict led to a rash of ambivalence. I explained that when I was with other chefs, I'd let the creative artist in me come to the fore. Yet when I was with restaurateurs or businessmen, the restaurateur avatar surfaced in an almost schizophrenic dominance over my creative foodie personality. I felt I was a Jack of all trades, but master of none. Michael's response was golden for me: 'Maybe being the generalist—the Jack of all trades, the chef and restaurateur—is your speciality. It's hard enough doing one of them well enough, let alone doing both together and competently at that. You have special skills to be able to look at the big picture, and need to embrace them. Much like a good general practice physician looks at the human body as a complete organism and treats illness holistically rather than in isolation as a specialist might.'

It was one of many lessons I learned from him at a critical turning point in my life. In that regard, I consider him my mentor, making so many of his best practices mine in later years. Mentors are hard to come by in my field, maybe because we are all so competitive, fearing our recipes will be stolen. Or maybe we just don't have the time to raise a next gen of chefs. Other than Michael, I have had none. So my gratitude to him is even more profound.

After that crash course in cooking excellence, let's get back to what we'd decided to do ...

The plan was for Malini to go back to Bombay with Shaan, who was starting school, and continue to look for a restaurant space in Bombay while I cooked in New York. We gave ourselves a cut-off date, the end of that financial year, to find a restaurant space, after which if she hadn't found anything, Malini was to pack up our worldly possessions and move to New York with Shaan. We were going to emigrate lock, stock and barrel to New York if she didn't find anything by the last day of March 1998.

It was a pivotal time for me in New York. Ideas were percolating in my thick brain but not yet congealing. I knew I had to get serious about cooking and stop with gimmicking and duplicating what I'd seen along the way. I needed to create my own signature culinary identity, and that period working with Michael Romano helped the process no end.

I had been lucky enough to be in New York just when food was becoming a thing—with a focus on truly fine dining, well-cooked meals at home, a healthier consciousness about what we actually ingest. Remember, this was after the word 'foodie' had entered our lexicon, thanks in no small part to New York food critics Paul Levy and Ann Barr's 1985 *The Official Foodie Handbook*,[1] which defined this new breed of eaters thus: 'Foodies are children of the consumer boom who consider food to be an art, on a level with painting or drama.' Today I consider 'foodie' one of the most misunderstood and abused words in the culinary dictionary.

Whether foodies were bourgeois capitalist pigs or not, I could identify with the idea that food should be inspired art—should be art itself. I already knew that did not mean nose-bleeding vertical presentations or foamy gimmicks or calligraphic strokes of aioli paint-brushed along the borders of plates. It meant creating dishes that actually tasted like inspired art.

Meanwhile, my business and life partner was combing the back alleys and boulevards of Bombay, keeping her ear to the ground on real estate possibilities. She'd gotten wind of a charming but ill-kept colonial bungalow in Colaba, one of the last such buildings from the nineteenth century still standing in the neighbourhood behind the Taj Mahal Palace Hotel. The day after it went on the market, Malini rushed over, chequebook in purse, just in case. The owner of the building, Essa Sham, admitted to having some financial woes we didn't want to know too much about, but it meant he needed to rent out the property fast. We just happened to be first in line. Malu signed a memorandum of understanding, then called me in New York.

'Come home; we have a place,' were her first words.

My first thought was, 'Oh shit, now it's time to put my money where my mouth is.' Or, in a chef's case, was that vice versa? My second thought was: 'Yessssss ... Bring it on!'

We signed the lease on my mother's birthday—23 February 1998.

I wrapped things up in New York as fast as I could. Two weeks later I was on a plane from JFK to BOM. I think I went right from the airport to Number 4, Mandlik Road, where I had the same reaction as Malini: love at first sight. I truly fell in love with the place, the space and, like her, I could instantly envision a cosy, cool, gorgeous centre for great food, libation and company. We'd been looking for a space with gravitas and she had found it. It felt like the right location to create a food-focused restaurant, where some serious cooking could be done but in a casual chilled-out environment. We felt this funky place could play a symbiotic role, that is, the space itself and how we design it could inspire the food, rather than vice versa. The potential was there; we just had to make it just right.

But it was a mess when we first saw it. Rats running around. Filth everywhere. The upstairs, which would become one of the city's coolest al fresco rooftop venues, was in a shambles. The downstairs looked nothing like what it would become known for. We reconfigured the rooms and the entryway. Walls came down; new walls went up. The bar area required special attention, because we knew we wanted to showcase original drinks that would knock Mumbaikars' socks (maybe even their clothes) off. So we decided that the bar would be the first thing in the diner's line of sight as soon as they entered the main foyer.

The Indigo logo designed by Itu Chaudhuri representing grain, vegetable and protein

The Indigo bungalow circa 1920s. Not much changed since then ...

While Malu started working on interior design concepts with Bijoy Jain, our dear friend and architect, I began actively exploring the tastes of India, buying spices and other Indian delicacies in the local markets. Not that I did not know them, but now my nose and palate experienced them anew, filtered through my recent Western influences. I noticed flavour profiles for the first time. It's like how Indians are accustomed to the homeless on the streets, but when you leave the country for a while and return, suddenly the sight and plight of the destitute rips your heart out. You see the desperate hope in their eyes. You see the beauty in their souls. The produce and spices I saw in the marketplaces spoke to me *like that only*.

As you know, I loved my Aji's food, but at that young age I did not analyse how she made it, what ingredients she used and how much of each went into her recipes. Now I could apply my well-honed academic mind to intellectualize the process. I don't think creativity comes like a bolt of lightning; it's built on an intellectual exercise that informs the creative juices. My mind was spinning with how to combine tastes from the East and the West.

The Team: The Essential Ingredient of Restaurant Success

Every great chef needs a great chef de cuisine or sous chef. Basically, the core of a good working kitchen consists of two cooks who complement each other, who get along well side by side in a kitchen and, most importantly, see eye to eye—or rather taste bud to taste bud—on what makes for a great dish. The word 'sous' means 'under' in French, but without a solid under there would be no over.

I did not go to the Auguste Escoffier School of Culinary Arts but I heartily agree with Escoffier's definition: 'While the executive chef is technically in charge of the kitchen, it's often the sous chef who performs much of the hands-on management. Ideally, a sous chef will be able to train and supervise the kitchen staff and then help them carry out the executive chef's intentions for cooking and plating the meal.'[2]

Second-in-command doesn't garner the coveted marquee chef spotlight, isn't mentioned in reviews, doesn't get to compete in Iron Chef challenges or write the award-winning cookbooks, but is critical to the success of a restaurant. And any executive chef who does not bow in the direction of his chef de cuisine or sous should either turn in his toque blanche ... or fire the dude.

Nitin Kulkarni came to me in a roundabout manner. I was desperately in search of my second-in-command. I'd even placed an ad in several Mumbai daily newspapers. From it, I got a fax from a woman who wrote that her husband was currently the executive sous chef on a Carnival Cruise ship out at sea. 'Ah,' I thought, 'he's had Western exposure.' She wrote that he really wanted to come home to Bombay. I could tell in her writing that she might have wanted him home even more than he did. I know this because she wrote to me without him knowing. She asked if she could submit his résumé to me. He was going to be on a shore leave in a few weeks and she urged me to meet with him then.

His résumé showed extensive experience in traditional restaurant settings; he'd worked for the Oberoi Hotel on Marine Drive in south Bombay for five years before shipping out to sea. For Carnival, he told me later when we met, he would cook seven different international cuisines, one for each night of the week. Before that he'd trained at the Institute of Hotel Management, Catering Technology and Applied Nutrition, Mumbai, generally known as IHM. This was both impressive and concerning. The IHM, established in 1954, was the first institute of higher education in India that taught anything close to hospitality management and culinary training. Hotel management and training of chefs and food service professionals was still a young discipline in those days, even in the West. The now famous Cornell School of Hotel Administration, right up there with Lausanne, was founded in 1954, and officially separated from the Department of Home Economics. IHM has a strange history in itself: the All India Women's Central Food Council had launched a chain of restaurants called Annapoorna, a precursor to health-conscious nutritionally beneficial snacks. Today they'd be called energy bars. A great idea to educate the people, right? The problem was there weren't enough folks knowledgeable enough about nutrition or how to run and manage these franchises on a self-financing basis. Hence the birth of IHM, Mumbai. Considered the godfather and godmother of India's hospitality training programmes, it went from a first graduating class of six to now having produced thousands of grads working at the Taj, Oberoi, ITC, Hyatt, Marriott and even hotels in Dubai. It spawned other such institutes around India. Today there are more than twenty IHMs affiliated to the National Council for Hotel Management & Catering Technology, New Delhi.

Why was this of any concern to me? Did it not sound like a classic foundation for Nitin? It did, but that also was the problem, to my mind. It was possible that mediocrity could well have been trained into him, for all the reasons I believe cooking and service at many of the India-based chain hotels and restaurants are not extraordinary. And while its website still claims that 'the course curriculum has undergone revision over the years keeping pace with the ever-changing industry ... with modern equipment, up-to-date curriculum and dedicated faculty', one wondered how au currant the curriculum could be.

The proof would lie in how he cooked the proverbial pudding. Nitin and I first met in the living room of my parents' flat, where Malu and I were still living. We chatted casually about food and cooking. You can tell a lot about a cook's familiarity and skill with basic cooking techniques not by what he says, but by watching his hands. They will move unconsciously in a way that demonstrates that technique as they speak about prepping or sautéing. The hands hold the muscle memory from doing this chore so many times that it becomes part of the chef's body, like second nature, instinctual; and if executed properly, the movements will be elegantly expressive, like the hands of the great mime Marcel Marceau. I watched Nitin's hands and knew he could handle the job. After chatting a while, I recall asking him to make a lobster bisque. You get a lot of applications from people aspiring to cook, even some with impressive résumés, but when you get them in a kitchen there is a huge disconnect between résumé and reality. With Nitin, I knew from the first sip of the bisque that this was my man.

He remembers our salary negotiations better than I do.

'You asked me what I was expecting,' he recalled as we sat a few years ago in the empty dining room of The Clearing House, the restaurant that was about to open at that time in south Mumbai's Ballard Estate area. My nephew Rishad, the son of Farhad Nathani (remember him from Under the Over?) who had been a director on the board of deGustibus and our business manager at Indigo, had convinced Nitin to head the kitchen there when he left Indigo.

'I have no idea,' he'd said during his interview. 'Whatever you offer will be fine.'

'Are you sure?' I asked. In negotiating such matters, Indians know that 'sure' could mean anything from 'we've got a deal' to 'not on your life'.

'Yes I'm sure,' Nitin said at the time. Now, though, he confided, 'I had a figure in my mind. Mind you, I was making a lot by comparison working for Carnival. But money was not my main objective; my priority was to come back to Mumbai. I was done with being at sea. As glamorous as that may sound, it took me from my wife and my family.

'But you surpassed that number in my head,' Nitin said, smiling at me like a cat who had swallowed the canary.

It was my turn to smile like a cat—I probably would have offered more. He was more than worth it.

His cooking was sound; he worked efficiently. More important to me was his dedication, dependability and reliability. He was never late for work and if he missed a day, I knew something extremely serious was happening at home. Over the seventeen years he worked with me, our relationship grew to the point where it felt like I didn't even have to say what taste I was looking for; he'd just intuit, as though we shared one palate. I could create a dish in my head, convey it in words to him and he would translate that into a delicious rendition, sometimes even better than what my palate had imagined.

The truth is, I could never have created Indigo, nor perhaps even grown the company initially, without Nitin by my side. He gave me the room to wander creatively and think of the big picture because he handled the nitty-gritty of daily operations resolutely and completely, without fail. I will forever remain deeply indebted to him.

We were the perfect entrepreneurial team—two individuals who proved that the team is greater than the sum of its parts. This was a good example of the visionary and the implementer, the dreamer and the numbers' cruncher. Like Steve Jobs and Steve Wozniak of Apple legend.

A happy Nitin meant a smooth-sailing Indigo kitchen, and vice versa

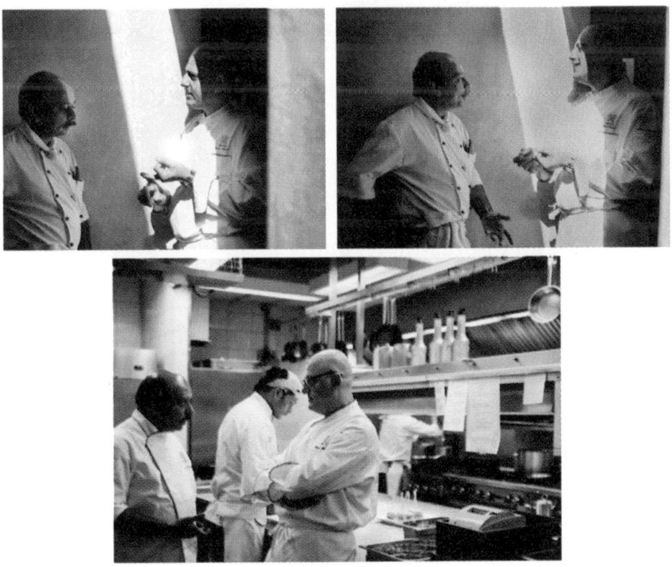

The daily huddle with Nitin

Photos: Sheena Sippy

We worked together by a sort of osmosis, hard to explain. I would say I want to do something with duck or quail; he would throw in ideas and I would throw in ideas. Then the sourcing would begin, a Sherlock Holmesian mystery of where to find the best product in the Mumbai of the late 1990s and early 2000s, a growing metropolis of 180 million but still a naïve food town for professional restaurateurs and chefs.

The week Indigo opened in April 1999

Working on the principle that less is more, our menu initially would be very small, especially compared to typical Mumbai menus that run to book length, though interestingly, many dishes are only slight variations of others. When you see seventy items on a menu, you tell me: don't you start to wonder whether any one executive chef can claim mastery, or even competency, of all of them?

We wanted to go in a different direction altogether.

The first thing to consider was the mix of vegetarian and non-vegetarian. Even that nomenclature suggests a difference between the West and the East. We start with vegetarian, our default diet. In the West it's presumed that you eat meat, fish, poultry, eggs, dairy—

these people are called meat eaters or carnivores—but eating meat is so much the norm you have to assert you are a vegetarian if that is the case.

Malu is vegetarian; I will eat anything that has eyes and is not moving. I eat raw fish in sushi and raw meat in steak tartare. So I was not necessarily the typical eater we were aiming at. Our target diners would be somewhere between myself and my wife.

We decided we needed close to 50 per cent representation of vegetarian offerings. In India, that means no meat, no fish, no poultry, no eggs, no chicken or beef stock. However, times have changed since we opened Indigo. Now, according to three large-scale government surveys, 23 to 37 per cent of Indians are vegetarian. But a 2018 study by US-based anthropologist Balmurli Natrajan and India-based economist Suraj Jacob points to a heap of evidence that even these are inflated estimations because of 'cultural and political pressures'.[3] People under-report eating meat, particularly beef, and over-report eating vegetarian food. Taking this into account, these researchers estimate that only about 20 per cent of Indians are actually vegetarian.

Back in 1999, we chose to break down the menu to one beef, one lamb, two to three seafood entrées, two chicken, one duck and the occasional quail or partridge. We excluded pork simply because it did not sell well, though that too has changed.

We also distinguished ourselves by seeing the menu as part of a whole meal, with tastes and textures complementing each other even if not eaten together. I wanted you to hold the menu in your hand, scan the appetizers and entrées, sides and desserts and understand—if not directly, then intuitively—what our overall concept was ... without the aid of a restaurant review or some pithy, cutesy jargon-filled explanation at the bottom of the menu.

Talking about restaurant reviews, we garnered our fair share of them. Every paper and magazine was talking about the new dining phenomenon, Indigo, that was turning Mumbai's food scene on its head. From straightforward vanilla food reviews to several-page editorials describing the restaurant, its interiors, culinary ethos—every aspect of our operation was written about. And all of it was unsolicited. Yes, you read that correctly. We never asked to be written about. In fact, I didn't make a lot of friends with the food critics and restaurant reviewers because whenever I was asked when someone should come to review the restaurant, I always said I didn't want to know. The conversation typically went like this: 'You don't understand,' the reviewer would say. 'I want to come and review your restaurant.'

'But I do understand,' was always my reply. 'You want me to invite you to come in for a meal, and then expect me to wine and dine you so you give us a stellar review. Well, that's not how it works. You need to call and make a reservation like anyone else, come in like anyone else, order from the menu like anyone else, be served like anyone else, eat your meal like anyone else, pay your bill like anyone else and then write whatever you want about your experience.' *Boom!* Few ever understood this. Why wouldn't we want to control the narrative? Simple. It wouldn't be an honest critique that we could learn from, and that just wasn't my way. Haughty? Arrogant? Maybe so, but I genuinely believe that reviewing needs to be a neutral process for it to mean anything at all.

I knew we had truly arrived when Hemant Morparia, the sociopolitical cartoonist from the *Mumbai Mirror* newspaper, lampooned Indigo and me.

Morparia cartoon in the Mumbai Mirror

Hardly any chefs consciously think about the mix of flavours among all the dishes on their menu. There is usually no consideration of complementary tastes, no thread that ties them all together. To me that means there is no overarching identity to the restaurant. Chefs just tick off what they think is needed. Prawns? Check. Beef or mutton? Got it. Chicken in three styles? Check, check and done.

In the end, though, one cannot detect the soul of those restaurants. Even before you ate, we wanted you to know Indigo's soul. We hoped you would be able to sense our identity. Seeing the totality of the dining experience required us to consciously create recipes that, if they did happen to appear on the same plate, would taste fabulous. We were doing with Indigo what The Beatles did with their ground-breaking 1967 album, *Sgt. Pepper's Lonely Hearts Club Band*, rock's first long-playing concept album, one song melding and blending with the next, so that to anyone who listened to the album non-stop, as I did, it's impossible to think of the title song without immediately following it with 'With a Little Help from My Friends'. Okay, it may be conceited to compare Indigo with *Sgt. Pepper's* ... All we wanted was to have you walk away from the table fully sated, filling not just your belly but also your sense of enjoyment.

And who can deny that part of the fun of dining out together is to exchange tastes from each other's dishes? Though some uptight folks who like to look proper may claim it's déclassé, or maybe they have health safety issues, most couples like to share, and even friends can always find a way: using their own silverware, shifting a bit to a side plate, etc. When did people get so frou-frou and faux polite about this?

I believe this was an important reason for our success at Indigo: we thought about the process. We looked at it from high on, objectively, as the scientist I could have become would approach a situation. This wisdom took us a long way. Every business needs to have that perspective to succeed.

This kind of menu—integrated or holistic, if you will—expanded the dining opportunity, in our opinion. We wanted to encourage the idea that we're all in this eating experience together, and more importantly we're all in *this* together. More tastes equal more fun; more shared tastes lead to more bonding, which, speaking somewhat anthropologically, is the point of dining together. And if there is harmony between your entrée and your dining companion's, it elevates the experience to an almost spiritual level. Almost.

The High(est) Art of Staff Training

As with any industry, staff and employee training is the critical yet unsung hero in making any business successful. B2B (business to business), to my mind, is never so valuable as B2C (business to consumer). It's all the more important in the service industry and no more important than in our area, the prepping and serving of food. There is nothing more intimate, other than sex, than the interaction among cook, server and eater. We're talking primal relationships here. Who feeds you and how, are the bonds that tie mother to children and all of us to each other. As the saying goes, we do not 'bite the hand that feeds us' because that hand is a loving and giving hand. So it is of utmost consequence to honour that exchange.

Karan Suvarna, our restaurant manager who knew everyone by name and could sell them anything

Greg D'Souza, Indigo's bar manager who knew everyone's tipple and made sure they always had one

Indigo's men in white in 2008. L to R: Rashmiraj Rego, Keyur Chandorkar, Suresh Kumar, Nitin Kulkarni, Irfan Pabaney and Bapi

Teaching wait-staff skills is easy—fork goes here, serve from the right, etc.—but if we were going to deliver on our vision of style and atmosphere as well as world-class service, we knew we had to bring in someone singularly skilled at training waiters and waitresses, someone with whom we were in sync creatively, who shared our philosophy and was an original thinker. We knew that the bigger objective was training a different kind of behaviour and attitude in relation to service.

Arunesh Maiyar had been coming to our restaurants as far back as Under the Over. A former food stylist and writer, active in theatre for social change, and president of the Sangama Board, a group working for the rights of the working-class minorities and sex workers, he had spent fifteen years in the area of employee training, largely for the hospitality industry. We lucked out by getting him on board to train our start-up Indigo staff and he continued on a yearly basis for about seven years. Arunesh taught all the typical stuff, like what to do and what to say, but he was much more concerned with helping them overcome the taboo of being a 'server'.

'We are a male-dominated and hierarchical society that outsources caregiving, mostly to women, so most men feel it's a clash with their upbringing to end up waiters,' he'd say. 'The culture does not respect those who serve, because it implies they are less powerful. So we have to change that mindset. To be of service is a noble act. We can give lip service to the old adage that "guest is God" but to mean it is quite another thing. And, it turns out, in that act there is an intangible benefit that goes much deeper than a hefty tip: serving makes us feel good and there's research to prove it.

'Unless you can find meaning in your work, you will live a life without meaning.'

Arunesh was echoing what I had learned intuitively in New York working for Danny Meyer and Michael Romano. His way to achieve that was to first encourage the staff to respect themselves and then earn the respect of customers. This is a lifelong lesson that goes way beyond being a waiter; we could all benefit from a little more self-respect.

He shared ways to break down the barrier between waiter or bartender and guest, to overcome the us-versus-them mentality, the haves-versus-the have-nots or not-enoughs that permeates Indian society. Little 'tricks', like saying a few words to guests as they were walked to their table, so that the guests didn't feel like the person leading them was a robot—even if it was just 'Save some room for our amazing desserts'.

Blowing off some steam post a week-long training session in the black lounge with Arunesh (front and centre with hat)

In early 2000, the nascent Indian wine scene was dominated by the Chougule family, led by the visionary Shamrao Chougule, accompanied by his two sons Vikrant and Ranjit. Some ten years earlier he'd set up the first Indian winery, Château Indage, in his hometown of Narayangaon near Pune. They produced a bubbly called Omar Khayam for export and another one called Marquis de Pompadour exclusively for the Indian market. They also made several still wines—cabernets, merlots, sauvignon blancs, chardonnays, chenin blancs and blends thereof.

Their wine-maker, John Locke, an American from California's Napa Valley, and I became good friends. He'd dine with us at Indigo each time he came down to Mumbai from the boonies, seeking out a bit of urban nightlife. Over a couple of years John grew increasingly frustrated with work, complaining that the Chougules weren't concerned with producing a quality wine. So, he threw in the towel, pulled out the cork—whatever the analogy—packed up and left for the US of A, where he went on to make wines at the amazing Bonny Doon Winery in Santa Cruz, California, before moving on again.

While all this was happening, Vikrant and Ranjit started diversifying, setting up a handful of restaurants and bars in and around Bombay.

Athena was their latest nightclub in Colaba, a stone's throw from Indigo. As it grew in popularity, we started losing bar staff to them on a regular basis. This pissed off me and Eric Lobo, our bar manager at Indigo, no end. We were investing time and money training our people and each Thursday or Friday someone would suddenly bail before the weekend crush. This happened to us with A.D. Singh's Olive Bar & Kitchen too when they first opened, until I called AD and Henry Tham (his partner and my good friend) to say they had to stop stealing our servers. Unfortunately, I didn't know the Chougule boys that well, so I had to take a different approach. I invited Ranjit Chougule to lunch one afternoon at Indigo and as we dined and generally caught up, I got Eric to line up all our bar staff at the bar. As we finished lunch, I took Ranjit into the bar.

'Ranjit, here's my entire bar team,' I began. 'Please take whoever you want right now. I can't handle the slow and random erosion of our staff each week, as it's making it very difficult for us to manage our bar roster. I'd rather you do this in one fell swoop so we can get on with running our restaurant and bar.' I also asked all of our bar staff to take a step forward and leave now, if there were any among them that planned on doing so later. No one moved.

'What are you talking about?' Ranjit stuttered, clearly embarrassed and very awkward.

'You guys keep poaching my people and it's making operational staffing at the bar very difficult to manage. I can't run the restaurant and especially do weekends, wondering who's going to show up for work. It's too unsettling.'

Ranjit sheepishly offered: 'I'll make sure this doesn't happen anymore and will instruct my managers and people to lay off *all* Indigo staff going forward. Really sorry about this. I had no idea it was happening.'

'Glad to hear that and many thanks for understanding,' I heard myself saying, though I was thinking, 'Yeah right, you really had no idea this was happening?! That's BS if ever I heard it.'

Whatever the truth, the poaching finally stopped, and we all lived happily ever after!

Lessons in Hospitality

Hospitality, I had to learn, sometimes the hard way, is nothing more than a simple contract between the service provider (in our case, our restaurants and catering) and the customer, which goes something like this:

We deliver a menu, with the promise that the food we list is available, that it matches what we describe, that it's the best we can cook, that service will be excellent, that the hygiene will meet the highest standards.

Your part as our guest is to pay the bill and generally meet the standards of appropriate dress code and behaviour befitting an appreciative diner—or if you are not appreciative, to let us know so in a kindly manner and allow us to correct any errors on our part.

Simple. When all goes according to that agreement, smiles and high-fives all around. Failing that implicit if not explicit contract, things can escalate rapidly and make for a bad time for both parties, as well as others in the kitchen and at surrounding tables. But if we do fail at our end, it is within reason for the guest not to pay and to even make a ruckus. Here are examples on both ends of the spectrum from our Indigo years.

We had a small satellite dining room upstairs from the main dining floor at Indigo when we first opened the restaurant in 1999. It was removed from all the groovy action downstairs and it was also admittedly a tad dark and gloomy, a concern we later addressed with a redesign when Malini converted it to a lounge bar, which came to be known as the Black Lounge. But on this particular night that had not happened yet.

It was one of those slam-bam nights; we were packed to the gills. A group of six that consisted of some Mumbai high-fliers entertaining their international visitors arrived at 9.45 p.m. for their 10 p.m. reservation. Half a dozen women were having a rocking time at the table we had planned for this next party, and they seemed far from paying and leaving. No matter how much we enticed them to vacate their table in the main dining room, the six women were just partying too hard and refused to leave. It was now 10.30 p.m. and the 10 p.m. reservation grew irritated and tired of 'having drinks at the bar' as their table was supposedly readied. With no other option, and much against their wishes, we sent the waiting party upstairs with drinks on us as we were bordering on violating our 'contract' of seating them at the time of their reservation.

All got sorted out and the new party was seated, being paid special attention as we took orders straight away and served them. Near the end of their meal, Malini, the quintessential hostess, approached the group and told the host we would 'comp' the whole evening—meals, drinks, wine, everything. The bill would easily top ₹45,000. But to our minds, it was the only right thing to do: we had broken our agreement to seat them at a time very close to their reservations, and we would rather eat the bill than have these obviously well-heeled and well-connected people go home and badmouth our service.

'We possibly ruined your evening,' Malini explained to the dumbfounded guests. To us, the ₹45,000 was not worth losing our reputation.

The host, still blown away, said, 'I have travelled and done business all over the world, have dined at some of the finest restaurants, entertained VIPs, and I have never *ever* heard of a restaurant doing such a thing.'

He came back many times after that with various guests, and others came mentioning this gentleman, whose word of mouth had sent them to Indigo.

Our parent hospitality company was called deGustibus, short for the Latin phrase *de gustibus non disputandum est*, which means 'In matters of taste, there can be no dispute'. We meant it and we certainly witnessed and experienced it.

One night at Indigo we served another guest and his wife. Word came back to me in the kitchen that he was not happy with anything we were sending out, complaining vociferously and frequently to the waiter without the least respect or concern for anyone. Every course we served brought new reasons for him to loudly voice his disappointment. I could hear his voice even from the noisy kitchen. I finally left the stove and went to the table.

The guest quickly asked who I was, probably ready to lambast me as well, assuming I was the chef or manager. I explained I was the chef *and* the owner, with my wife. He did not seem taken aback.

I politely began, 'Sir, it's clear that nothing we prepare for you tonight will satisfy you and that you are actually suffering. Why don't you save your suffering and leave?'

'Are you throwing me out?' he asked, indignant.

'That's one way of putting it,' I replied. 'But why are you forcing yourself to stay if you are obviously not enjoying yourself or the food we are serving? You're not enjoying yourself and everyone around you is being forced to suffer your disgruntlement. Do yourself and the rest of us a favour.'

I got the usual response from an insulted Indian of means: 'Do you know who I am?'

'It does not matter,' I did not flinch (thank you, Stewart Rosen). 'Come back another time when perhaps our dishes and your palate will find a better connect, or perhaps when the planets and stars are more aligned and conducive to your enjoying your dining experience.'

I extended my hand to help him get up. He rebuffed my gesture, but got up with obvious resentment and I walked him and his wife to the door. I was wondering to myself if I had actually done the right thing

... until I returned to the dining room. The whole room stood up and applauded me.

So Many Stories, So Little Time

Celebrities came in so often we almost got used to it. Almost. There was the time Brad Pitt and Angelina Jolie were in town for the filming of *A Mighty Heart,* in which she starred and that he produced. They threw a small dinner party on the terrace and Black Lounge at Indigo for some of their crew because Daniel Pearl, the murdered American journalist on whom the 2007 film was based, was an accomplished musician who used to jam regularly with others, on Jazz Thursdays, our open-mic nights. He played the violin. Some scenes for the film were shot at Indigo, but they never made it into the final movie.

Whatever. The two American superstars were dining with *us* at a small private party in our upstairs room. It was all hush-hush—no press knew about it. They had a few South African ex-Special Services bodyguards you did not want to mess with. Yet, I almost did when I went upstairs to greet them, as an owner should do with such film royalty.

A bodyguard stopped me dead in my tracks.

'Where are you going?' he bluntly asked.

'It's my freakin 'restaurant,' I replied equally bluntly. 'I will go where I want to ... to welcome my guests.'

He let me through begrudgingly.

I gave Ms Jolie a quick little peck on the cheek as I humbly welcomed her to our fine establishment. She returned the gesture.

Then Malu, not one to miss out on her chance, did the same with Mr Pitt. He returned the gesture.

Malini floated back downstairs, all 'oooohhhhs' and 'aaahhhhhs', swearing to never wash her cheek ever again.

Maybe we never did get used to such visitations.

There have been celebrities we have turned away when there was no seating available. Indians go into shock when I recount the story of the time legendary stage and film actor–director Naseeruddin Shah and Bollywood powerhouse Shah Rukh Khan walked in together, unannounced, on a crazy busy Saturday night, and asked if they could get a table. I told them, 'I'm really sorry, but as you can see we're chock-a-block, and short of asking someone to leave, I just don't have a table for you.' I still gave no preference just because someone could probably buy my restaurant.

Another dignitary who fell prey to Indigo's policy of treating everyone equally with understated but attentive service, regardless of position, was David Cameron, prime minister of the United Kingdom from 2010 to 2016. He dined with us in February 2013 when he visited Mumbai. We had a couple of his MI6 Special Branch security detail come by in the afternoon saying that the PM and his trade delegation, including their aides, might have dinner with us that evening and they wanted to be treated like any other guests. They selected two tables for six near each other on Indigo's open-air terrace, and another smaller table nearby for the three agents in the PM's security detail. We were excited, but weren't sure they were really coming since we hadn't heard anything further since the afternoon. Also, we wondered if his secret service detail really would choose an open-air seating location in full view of all the surrounding taller buildings. It didn't seem right. But then at around 8 p.m. we were suddenly met by several flustered and exasperated officers from the Mumbai police and municipal corporation who let us know that the PM and his group were on their way—in fact, literally walking over to Indigo from the Taj Mahal Palace Hotel where they were staying. I welcomed them at our entrance and then showed them to their table on the terrace, where I eventually took their order before heading back to the kitchen to cook their food.

It was a normal busy night at Indigo and the added pressure of cooking for the PM and his group wasn't helping. Adding to the chaos in the kitchen, we had some official from the municipal corporation's health department overseeing all the food being cooked that night for some reason. He asked us to cook a little extra of each dish that was being served to the PM, which he dutifully dumped into a plastic takeaway container before tying the box with a piece of hemp twine and then sealing it for posterity with an official-looking wax seal. Really? I asked him why he was doing this.

'To have a sample of the food he ate in case he gets sick later,' I was told with absolute foreboding authority.

'How do you know what I'm giving you is in fact going to his table, let alone being consumed by him?' I inquired, fucking with his head just a little for the fun of it.

Silence.

So I further asked: 'Also, shouldn't you be refrigerating these sample containers to prevent their contents from spoiling, left out in the ambient heat of the kitchen?'

'Yes, good idea,' he said as we took the containers and refrigerated them for him.

About this time, just after we'd served the PM's table their first course we had a visit from one of his agents, a dreadlocked Uzi-packing Rastafarian woman.

'What are ya doin', mon?,' she exclaimed. 'Ya can't be feedin da PM before ya feed us, mon!'

'Huh? Why's that? Isn't he the PM, after all?'

'Ya mon, but when he's done eatin and gets up ta go, we have ta go too ... and we want to eat our dinner ... so don't be feedin us after him, mon!'

Couldn't argue with that logic. So, mid-course we switched the service flow. The secret service agents got served their main course first, the aides next, and by the time we got to the PM's table the kitchen got backed up with a ton of other orders and we were in the shit. The entire service flow had gone for a toss and his table's food got delayed.

He actually had to get our manager's attention and ask how long it was going to be. Our manager responded, in true nonchalant Indigo style, 'I'm terribly sorry sir, the kitchen is a bit backed up right now and your food will be out shortly.'

Hey, the PM did ask to be treated like any other guest after all!

After dinner photo-op with Prime Minister David Cameron ; menu signed by the prime minister

The Time I Told Chelsea Clinton that Indigo's Bread Was Good

Indigo had been open about a year in 2000. Somehow then President Bill Clinton had already heard about us and wanted to dine with us. However, Colaba Causeway was being concretized and Mandlik Road was closed off on one end creating a cul-de-sac, due to which his security team decided it was not a secure environment for him. So instead his daughter, Chelsea, came. Nonetheless, honoured as we were to serve her, we kept the whole thing very low-key.

Accompanying them were the then US Commerce Secretary William Daley, American Ambassador Richard Celeste, some others and a gaggle of Secret Service guys, who stuck out like sore thumbs with dark suits and conspicuous spiral cords dangling from their ears.

Over that time we actually became friendly with Ambassador Celeste and his wife Jacqueline Lundquist, a former Washington, DC, public-relations consultant.

I remember it was a Friday night because we were slammed, especially in the bar area where the hotties and wannabes of both sexes hung out. Chelsea and her entourage settled in my favourite room, to the left as you walked into the restaurant. The journalists and Secret Service people remained in the bar area. The seats are low there, colonial style. That meant that the eyes of seated guests were at about butt- or crotch-level of those standing. As I walked by at one point, I saw them ogling at the cute women gathered around. 'Focus, focus,' I said to a few of them as I moved past.

These people had been with the President and his daughter for about two weeks, seeing folk dances in Rajasthani villages and that sort of thing. They'd not witnessed the new urban India and Indigo was its epicentre at the time.

'We had no idea India was this cool,' one of them said.

With slight nervousness, I approached the Clinton party table to introduce myself and welcome Chelsea. I had been told ahead of her arrival that she is vegetarian, a dietary choice I read she gave up when she was twenty-nine.

'What's good?' she asked.

Do you know how weird a chef feels when a guest asks that? What was I supposed to say? Would I serve anything if I thought it didn't taste great? Do you promote your signature dish? Boring. Do you recommend dishes you know you want to move from your refrigerator before they go bad? Not my style. Do you suggest a new innovative entrée and pray the guests are adventurous eaters?

I chose none of the above.

Instead, perhaps in an uncharacteristic moment of panic, I mustered the lame reply: 'The bread is good.'

The stupid things you say when you are nervous and greeting the daughter of the President of the United States at your humble eating establishment!

I also remember exactly what she had. I was happy to see her order come into the kitchen for our homemade pappardelle with roast cauliflower and cheese.

Walking back to the kitchen, I saw the not-so-Secret Service guys still ogling our local treasures. I stopped and asked no one in particular, 'What part of the circus are you?'

One fellow, eager to engage, turned quickly and with a wry smile, said, 'I'm the guy who follows the elephant out of the ring, cleaning up its dung.' I could tell from his accent that he was from Brooklyn.

That band of men stayed until well after the Clinton party had packed up and returned to their hotel.

You know how a snowball picks up mass and speed as it rolls down a hill? That's what began to happen with Indigo. It just kept gaining momentum. Word began to spread from Mumbai to the rest of India to the world. It was becoming more than the sum of its parts. People came from far and wide. And the amazing stories and coincidences became the rule, not the exception. Like this one:

One night I espied a stodgy white-haired British-looking fellow sitting with a buxom blonde at a table in our main dining room. Even after things had died down in the kitchen and other guests had left, I saw them still there. So I walked over to the table, as I often do as host, to thank them for their patronage and tell them to stay as long as they liked. The man seemed interesting and as we drank a little more, one subject leading to the next, I shared my love of rock music, some of it quite esoteric, always on the hunt for more offbeat bands. I mentioned I was a fan of a 1978 song titled 'Walking in the Rain' by an Australian New Wave band called Flash and the Pan. You've never heard of them or it, right? At the age of twenty, one foot in India, the other in the US, I must have related to some of the lyrics: '*Summing up the people, checking out the race, doing what I'm doing, feeling out of place.*' Well, when I said Flash and the Pan, this gentleman whose name I cannot recall almost dropped his spoon.

'How do you know them?' he asked, incredulous.

'Wait,' I countered. '*You* know them? How do *you* know them?'

His response floored me—and it still does.

'I produced them. That was my record label,' he said. Turns out he was a record industry executive. Coincidence or karma? I thought, 'How does this stuff happen to me?'

This, of course, catapulted us into even deeper conversation and bonding, and we continued drinking and talking till three in the morning.

This was not an uncommon event at Indigo.

There is one memory—and a connection to a guest at our Indigo Deli in Colaba whose identity only surfaced later—we would rather erase from our minds, but cannot. The infamous night of 26 November 2008—which universally came to be known as '26/11'—will never be forgotten by all of us who call India home, nor by all humans who abhor terrorism in all its forms. When Pakistani terrorists attacked several key locations in Mumbai—the closest being the Taj Mahal Palace Hotel, less than one block from Indigo—Malini and I happened to be attending a wedding. We got a phone call from our restaurant manager, telling us there was some shooting going on nearby. They could hear the gunfire. At first, everyone thought it was some sort of gang war. We rushed home to drop off the kids and then planned to run over to Indigo, which was not far from where we were living in Colaba. When we heard explosions, we were compelled to stay at home, but remained in constant touch with our staff.

Two of them had taken a break and gone over to Leopold Café, around the corner from Indigo. They had stepped out of the café for a smoke when all hell broke loose inside; terrorists sprayed gunfire and threw grenades inside the restaurant, killing ten persons and injuring many more. The terrorists, as reports showed, then moved on to the Taj. My guys snuck along back alleys to Indigo and immediately had all the lights turned off. All of our guests got down on the floor and huddled close together. No one knew what was going on but they knew it could not be good. Outside, my team saw a woman running by, then she collapsed in front of Indigo. She had three gunshot wounds in her leg. They took her inside and administered first aid. An attempt to call an ambulance was for naught, as they were all being called to targeted locales throughout south Mumbai—including the Oberoi Trident, Chhatrapati Shivaji Terminus train station, the Mumbai Chabad House, Cama Hospital, the Metro Cinema and the Taj.

Close to seventy of our restaurant guests spent the night in darkness at Indigo as we fed them whatever we had or they needed—including all the booze they wanted. None of our staff left. Meanwhile, in one of the most surreal moments of my life, I sat at home, helpless in my boxer shorts and drinking single malt whisky, glued to CNN, watching the drama unfold so close yet so far away. We could see the iconic dome of the Taj ablaze, dark smoke billowing into the sky. We flinched every time we heard gunshots or explosions.

It was, as I said, a night to forget, but one indelibly etched into my mind and our country's collective conscience.

And then, not much later, we learned that our Indigo Deli had inadvertently played a small role in this mess. Investigators trying to piece together what had happened came to us and asked us for the Deli credit card receipts from a certain week. They were tracking down a man they suspected was involved in the planning of the attacks. Upon turning over the paperwork, we learned that one David Coleman Headley, a Pakistani American affiliated with the deadly Lashkar-e-Taiba Islamist militant group that orchestrated the attacks, spent hours at our Deli drinking coffee and combing over intelligence he had gathered from careful surveillance of the entire neighbourhood. He'd actually even been a guest at the Taj, shooting videos while on in-house tours.

Had we known who he was and his plot, who knows what we would have spiked his coffee with. Sometimes the guest is *not* God, but rather His evil opposite. But let's leave that sordid memory to fade.

On a sweet and sentimental note, I recall an American couple who called from New York and made reservations many months in advance. They came for dinner with their two daughters around Christmas of 2010 or 2011. They told us they had been to Indigo many years earlier as backpackers travelling around India. Their last luxury indulgence before going home was dinner at our restaurant, where the then young man had proposed to his girlfriend. Now they made the long journey back for their tenth wedding anniversary to show their kids where it all began. When they told us this poignant story, I personally cooked their dinner. And their tale touched Malini and me so much that we told them the whole dinner tab was on us. They were shocked but as I told them, 'We are so flattered that you came all this way—how can we NOT show our gratitude for such loyal patronage?'

Hoisting a few with Australian cricket bad boy Shane Warne

With Keith Richards post The Rolling Stones' Mumbai concert

At the Kenneth Cole India launch party at Indigo

With Marisa Tomei

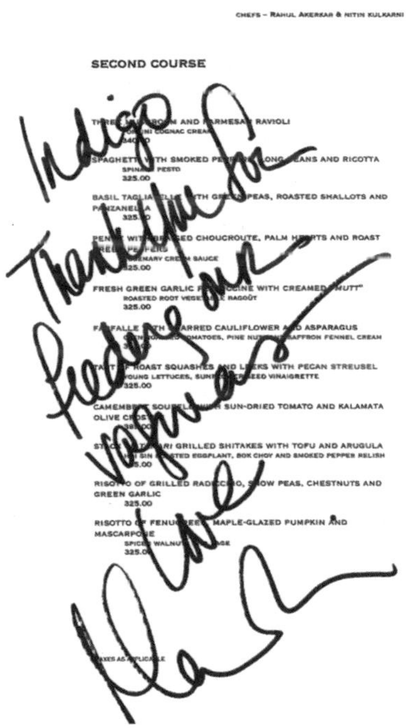

Thank you for Feeding Our Vaginas, signed by Marisa Tomei

Sure, we had Eve Ensler, Jane Fonda and Marisa Tomei at a luncheon celebrating the anniversary of the hundredth performance of the Indian version of *The Vagina Monologues* in which my sister appeared alongside them. Yes, there were the Rolling Stones, minus Mick Jagger, but I got to see Keith Richards close up, with his iguana-like neck. Of course we played host to all kinds of Indian and international sports legends—cricketers, footballers, Olympic champions, Hollywood and Bollywood stars, royalty, artists, industrialists, politicians and such. Yet, it was guests like that American family that really made our hearts sing.

But even with all these visits by celebrities, dignitaries and assorted other attention-getters, the rock stars of Indigo remained the food, the bar scene and the general ambience. It would be easy to take credit for finding the right balance that contributed to our success, but the truth is we lucked out. We put all these ingredients together and then let good old chemistry take over. That's all you can do. Like with two people falling in love, there is no science that assures that magical alchemy. Many restaurants can put the same ingredients together and not achieve what we did. In defence, they can claim they chose a bad location, or that the timing for their innovative cuisine was too early or too late.

Sometimes a person's career and whole reputation can be defined by one endeavour. You never know what that will be. We had a feeling Indigo would be special. How special we did not know. Though we had done great things before Indigo and went on to do very good things after, it will stand as a turning point in the history of dining out in India. If Indigo remains my most widely recognized contribution to India's dining, I will still die a happy and fulfilled man.

PAN-SEARED GROUPER, BASIL POHA, PRAWN AND SQUID BALCHÃO, SOLACHIKADI (KOKUM KADI)

This dish, which I created at Indigo, is influenced by several Konkan coast dishes that Aji made. Her solachikadi, poha and balchão were some I loved; and while not made here in the traditional way, they certainly embrace the textures and flavours of their traditional heritage. A traditional balchão masala (spice mixture) is done with tomatoes and local Goan vinegar and is fiery hot and quite pungent. We toned down the pungency and acidity and rounded off the dish, balancing it with sweet roasted red peppers to allow the prawns and squid to not overpower but complement. Poha, which is traditionally made with Indian spices and grated coconut, was made with a basil pesto likeness and cream, but retained its texture. And solachikadi, a traditional digestive drink made from the dried skin of the kokum fruit (similar to mangosteen) and drunk cold, was adapted as a sauce or dressing for the fish.

INGREDIENTS FOR 4 PORTIONS

Solachikadi

75 gm wet kokum

2 cups coconut milk

3 green chillies, slit down the middle

1 tablespoon sugar

1 teaspoon rock salt

½ cup fresh coriander leaves, chopped

1½–2 tablespoons refined cooking oil

8–10 fresh green curry leaves

1 teaspoon black mustard seeds (rai)

1 pinch asafoetida powder (hing)

Basil Poha

150 gm poha (flattened, beaten rice)

1 large potato, peeled and cut into ¼-inch dice (~1 cup)

¾ cup fresh basil leaves

1½ tablespoons chopped, rehydrated, sundried tomatoes

1 cup olive oil

¼ cup cooking cream

1 teaspoon chopped garlic

1 tablespoon roasted pine nuts

Salt and pepper

Prawn and Squid Balchão

12–15 small prawns, peeled and deveined and cleaned (~400 gm)

½ cup cleaned squid, cut into rings

2 red bell peppers, char-roasted, skinned, deseeded and julienned

8–10 whole, dry, red Kashmiri chillies, stems removed and roasted

1 teaspoon roasted coriander seeds

1 teaspoon roasted cumin seeds

1 teaspoon black peppercorns

½ teaspoon turmeric powder

½ teaspoon cinnamon powder

¼ teaspoon ground cloves

1 tablespoon sugar

1 tablespoon fresh ginger–garlic paste

½ cup apple cider vinegar or white wine vinegar

2 tablespoons olive oil

Rock salt

Grouper Fillets

4 Grouper fillets (120–130 gm each, skin on, or substitute any flaky white fish)

20 ml olive oil

20 gm butter

Juice of 2 lemons

4 sprigs fresh thyme

Salt and pepper

DIRECTIONS

Solachikadi:

Wash and drain the kokum skins under running water to remove any grit or extra salt present in the skins. In a bowl add the washed kokum, green chillies, sugar and rock salt and enough potable water to just cover the kokum skins. Set aside covered for several hours. Regularly press down on the kokum with the back of a spoon to extract as much of the purple kokum juice in the water. After a couple of hours, when the water is nice and pink, add in the coconut milk and refrigerate for another couple of hours till the coconut milk turns a bright purple from the kokum. The length of time you soak the kokum in water and coconut milk determines how strong the colour and flavour of kokum is in your solachikadi.

Remove from the fridge, strain and discard the kokum skins and green chillies. Heat the oil in a small pan and when very hot add the mustard seeds, curry leaves and asafoetida till they splutter and pop, making a tempering. Immediately pour the tempering over the pink coconut milk, add the chopped fresh coriander and refrigerate till ready to use, removing it about an hour before to get it to room temperature. When you're ready to serve, gently warm the solachikadi on very low heat, or put it in a double boiler on low heat. Be careful not to overheat and cause the coconut milk to split ... you just want it tepid for the fish.

Basil Poha:

Rinse the poha in cold water and then drain the excess, using a strainer. Put a pot of water on to boil and blanch the diced potatoes till parboiled. Immediately remove and shock in an ice bath to stop them from cooking further. Rehydrate the sundried tomatoes in a little cold water till soft. Drain and cut into small dice. In a blender-mixer or using a hand immersion blender, purée the fresh basil and half the olive oil to make a smooth paste.

In a heavy-bottomed sauté pan, heat the remaining olive oil and sauté garlic till it's a light golden colour. Add the blanched diced potatoes and sundried tomatoes and sauté well. Lower the heat, add basil purée and fresh cream and simmer for a few minutes, making sure not to overheat or let it boil, as it will discolour. Add the softened poha, toasted pine nuts and mix well. Remove from the fire, check for salt and hold warm till service.

Prawn and Squid Balchão:

In a sieve, under running cold water, rinse the prawns and squid and let drain. In a non-reactive bowl, mix the prawns and squid with turmeric and salt, cover and refrigerate till you finish making the balchão spice mixture.

Roast and char the red peppers on an open flame and then place them in a covered bowl, letting them soften in their steam. When cool enough to handle, remove the stalks, peel and deseed them, reserving any juices that collect in the bowl. Julienne the skinned red peppers and let them sit in their juices.

Roast all the dry spice powders and Kashmiri chillies together. Pour the vinegar, half the olive oil and the ginger-garlic paste into a mixer-blender, followed by the dry roasted chillies and spices, and blend to a smooth paste. Remove and combine with the julienned red peppers and their juices and add a little sugar as needed to adjust the sweet–chilli balance of the balchão spice mixture.

Grouper:

Lightly score the skin of the Grouper fillets, making sure not to cut too deeply into the flesh. Pat-dry the Grouper fillets with a paper towel and season them with a little salt, pepper and lemon juice on the flesh side. Keep the skin side dry. Heat some oil in a non-stick frying pan and sauté the fish fillets, skin side down on low to medium heat. When the edges of the flesh above the browning skin start turning opaque white, the fish is almost cooked. Add in the butter and thyme sprigs to the pan and once melted, use a tablespoon to baste the top flesh side of the fish with the butter-oil mixture to cook and finish it. The skin should be crispy at this stage. Remove from the heat, dab with a paper towel to remove any excess oil, flip the fillet over (skin side up) and let it rest while you start plating the dish.

tandoori
tiger prawn
ATEAU MARGAUX
tadkewali
pomfret
curry
leaf
mustard
seeds

12: MAKING WAVES WITH FOOD & WINE

'Food without wine is a corpse; wine without food is a ghost; united and well matched they are as body and soul, living partners.'

—Andre Simon, twentieth-century French wine merchant

SANJAY MENON, OWNER OF Sonary's and Sansula, a man considered the preeminent Indian authority on imported and domestic wine, recently told me a 'Rahul story' even I did not know he'd witnessed. One night, he was dining at Under the Over when he overheard a gentleman complaining so much about his order of steak with pepper sauce that I came out of the kitchen to see what the trouble was. Those were the days when the chef was just an asshole cook who sweated and smelled bad and knew his place. The gentleman started telling me how he'd travelled all over the world and eaten in fine dining restaurants and this just wasn't the way steak with pepper sauce was supposed to taste. I explained that, well, I too had eaten around the world, even cooked in New York at good restaurants and that was the way I meant the dish to taste.

Sanjay and I had not met at that time, but he told me later, 'This was just not done by a chef in India. That was when I knew I would like this guy.'

Thanks to that moment and thanks to Sanjay, because by the time I was ready to launch Indigo, he too was moving the business he took over from his father more towards wine than spirits. So when he approached us to sell us wines, we were all ears.

In general and for generations, wine-drinking had not been part of Indian culture. The tradition is to drink beer and other spirits such as Scotch whisky, gin, rum and brandy. The reasons have more to do with the lack of availability of good wines at reasonable prices than moral issues regarding abstinence and sobriety. That said, with alcohol sales prohibited in five of India's twenty-nine states (Tamil Nadu has a partial ban), one could make a case for there being some cultural taboo about the consumption of any alcoholic beverage.

Wine was considered too high-brow and sophisticated. There was also the theory that wine did not go well with Indian food—a theory Sanjay and I roundly rejected and proved false in pairings and tasting after tasting.

India's economic liberalization, initiated in 1991, also meant reduced import tariffs, deregulation of markets, lower taxes and greater foreign investment, thus opening the door to import some of the world's greatest wines. All we needed here was an audience.

It's not to say there are no wines from India. Château Indage dominated and monopolized the fledgling wine scene in India for many years before fizzling out, much like their bubbly. Around the same time, Sula Vineyards had opened their winery in Nashik; it now produces 80 per cent of India's wines, about 1 million cases a year. Grover Zampa, which began in 1988 in Bangalore, produced about 2,20,000 cases in 2018. Fratelli, located outside Pune, came along in 2007; by 2016–17, it was producing 1,70,000 cases annually. Others have also entered the market. However, ambitious as these companies were, the quality of the product rarely compared with the historic old-world wines of France, Italy, Germany, Spain, or other up-and-comer wine producers such as Argentina, Chile, New Zealand, the US and Australia. But that's all changed now with a few Indian wine producers genuinely in the business of making good wines, while others are only in the business of business.

Anyway, Sanjay became our outsourced de facto sommelier, designing a wine programme that could be affordable but cutting edge—at least in India. Actually, since no other restaurants were doing wines in India to the extent we wanted to, we ourselves defined the cutting edge.

So when Malu (pregnant with our second daughter Amalia) and I sat down with Sanjay in 1999, the stage was set for us to do something new and exciting and introduce wines to a growing segment of the Indian population eager to widen their experience at the table.

Sanjay pulled out a map of France to show Malu and me where great varietals of grapes grew. Even though she could not drink wine then, Malu showed such interest—even more than food and beverage managers at the hotels he serviced, Sanjay told us—that he knew we would be his best clients.

When we first opened in April 1999, we were unable to serve imported wines, as they were restricted under the law. The Indian government's trade and import policies did not permit independent, stand-alone restaurants to purchase and serve imported wines and spirits. However, by November 1999, in recognition of our success vis-à-vis foreign exchange earned through tourists who dined at Indigo, we received special permission from the Ministry of Tourism to buy and serve imported wine and liquor.

The first programme Sanjay laid out—of wines we should offer—though, was beyond what we could afford, even beyond what we could stock. I also doubted the clientele would be up to speed on his selections enough to appreciate them, much less buy them. Even local food writers at the time had neither the experience nor expertise to write intelligently about wine. Heck, they did not even have a working vocabulary of wine terminology. I recognized that part of any type of wine programme we decided on would have to be accompanied by several educational series of wine tastings, wine-and-food pairings and wine flights. I would even have to explain the concept of wine flights—offers of short pours to compare different vintages (verticals) of the same wines.

The challenge for us in a predominantly spirit-drinking nation devoid of any semblance of a wine culture was several-fold. We needed to educate and inculcate in our diners and staff an appreciation of the joy of pairing wine with food—to demystify wine—and do this without appearing intimidating or overbearing. Wine had to become part of their regular dining vocabulary.

We began cautiously by offering only a few 'safe' wines on our list and spent a lot of effort organizing regular tutored tasting programmes and winemaker dinners, where we paired our food with wines from around the world. Financial and space considerations and a lack of confidence in guests' interest forced us to cut down Sanjay's original list of wines by a third, to about forty, and temper his ambitious suggestions to more conservative labels. We sold out in three or four months, much to our surprise and elation. Encouraged, Sanjay suggested we become more adventurous and ambitious. The success of these programmes and the encouragement we got from our emerging wine-loving diners provided us the impetus to embark on an ambitious expansion of our wine list in the middle of that year.

So we went with several French and Italian wines; from the US we added some cabernet reserves from the Mondavi cellars of California's Napa Valley. Sanjay said the brand name of Mondavi was so well known, even here where brand names seem to mean more than the quality of the product, that it would sell well. We deliberately avoided entry-level wines from our suppliers' somewhat limited portfolios and went straight to the next level in putting together what we believed was a wine list that complemented our eclectic Euro-Indian cuisine. Coupled with that, we also consciously supported the nascent handful of Indian wine producers by giving prominence to new local wines alongside our international offerings and undertook promotional events with Indian winemakers to encourage their sales and exposure.

As part of its commitment to the World Trade Organization, in March 2001 the Government of India liberalized wine and other alcoholic beverage import taxes for—and I use quotes—'free import'. However, in an exaggerated protectionist measure, state governments increased the local import duties and taxes on wines from about 150 per cent to approximately 600 per cent in April 2001. This effectively upped the cost of a bottle that would wholesale in the USA for $1.50 (approximately ₹70) to more than $30 (around ₹1,400) for the consumer in Maharashtra. Regardless, we priced our wines very competitively with tiny profit margins to push their sales. Later, when import duties reduced, allowing us to purchase wines at lower prices, we slashed our menu prices and passed the savings on to our customers to stimulate sales. In spite of this difficult environment, Indigo continued to maintain its commitment to promoting and furthering wine, hosting an average of five to six annual wine-and-food-related events that attracted and educated a large segment of Indian society, as well as garnering media attention. We also had an active and exhaustive wine-by-the-glass programme, printing a recommended wine pairing on our 'Specials of the Day' menu which changed daily. On the service side, we regularly conducted organized staff training programmes and frequently sent our personnel to specialized seminars and courses on wine appreciation. All these efforts eventually took us to a point where our wine sales matched our spirit sales. We were proud of the fact that Indigo was probably the only restaurant in India where that occurred.

Sanjay recalls that we went up to about 150 labels, which was unheard of at the time. To grow, we needed to expand our offering to encompass more than just the familiar brands and to build a new cave (wine cellar), because up until then Indigo used to store its wines in refrigerators at the bar and on the back service stairs. We built an air-conditioned room off our upstairs terrace—a bona fide wine cave, storing upwards of 5,000 bottles. It was time to get serious about wine.

Sanjay subscribed to *The Wine Spectator*, the premier magazine of the industry, which Marvin Shanken had acquired in 1979, when its panel of experts blind-tasted and reviewed more than 12,000 wines. Its

Restaurant Awards, launched in 1981, rated restaurant wine lists around the world. It is the Michelin star rating system of the wine industry. The Luxury Institute ranked the magazine as the number one business and consumer publication among wealthy readers in 2008.

Sanjay suggested we apply for the restaurant awards. What chance did we have? None, but what the hell—we applied. And lo and behold, we earned the nod, winning their Award of Excellence in 2001. We were the first restaurant in India whose wine programme made the list.

We made the list for the next nine consecutive years too. Naturally, the Taj Group of Hotels, the Oberoi Hotels and other international hotel chains with properties in India jumped on our bandwagon and upped their wine game, if only to compete with us for such acclamation from the industry. In our heyday, Indigo's wine list included more than 430 labels representing regions and grape varietals from across the globe; our wine sales grew at a steady 20–30 per cent annually, hitting almost $1 million (yes, you read that right) in sales in 2007, another 'unheard of' for a stand-alone restaurant in India.

Sanjay Menon surrounded by his true love at an Indigo wine dinner

A typical wine dinner in the Black Lounge of Indigo with the winemaker

The Wine Spectator award was not the only first we achieved. Indigo was the first Mumbai restaurant to host events featuring food-and-wine pairings with prominent winemakers, vineyard and château owners from around the world. The many successful winemaker dinners and tutored tastings we conducted over the years and the recognition we garnered as a serious, wine-focused eating establishment, meant that we'd become the 'must-visit' venue for winemakers coming to India. We played host to Château Latour when its owner Florence Rogers-Pinault and President Frédéric Engerer selected Indigo as the venue to hold the first-ever Latour dinner in India, featuring five grand vintages, including its 1982. Over the years we held many dinners with renowned winery owners, such as Angelo Gaja, Alessia Antinori, Edouard Moueix, Alfred Tesseron, Stephan von Neipperg, Daniel Cathiard, Jean-Guillaume Prats, Olivier Bernard, Pablo Álvarez, Mariano García, Maurice Hennessy and many others whenever they visited India. We were privileged to be selected by Moët-Hennessy as the venue for the India launch of its Dom Pérignon Vintage 1995 over an exclusive banquet at Indigo, and then again by its Chef de Cave Richard Geoffroy for the Asia launch of his 1999 vintage of Dom Pérignon.

The International Wine Academy of Roma brought its renowned certificate course to Mumbai for the first time when we held a week-long Italian wine and food festival at Indigo. We also conducted 'Wine Discovery' events at Indigo where, with the support of our leading vendors, we offered all our wines to our patrons at cost, by the bottle or as tasting pours, allowing people to compare several wines simultaneously with their food.

We held the first ever masterclass in glass tasting by Riedel, the 260-year-old Austrian glassware company, demonstrating the impact that glass shape has on the expression and appreciation of grape varietals and styles of wine. We also launched the luxury glassware collection of Lucaris, Asia's first and only luxury crystal glass brand that creates crystal stemware for wine and spirits glasses, in India. The launch was kickstarted with a blind wine-tasting session followed by the food-and-wine pairing dinner.

And then there was my personal involvement and Indigo's long association with the International Wine & Food Society (IW&FS). Nihal Kaviratne (prominent businessman, oenophile, wine collector and *Commanderie de Bordeaux*), Sanjay and I were the founders of its Bombay branch in June 2006. The IW&FS is a not-for-profit gastronomical organization founded in London in 1933, now with dozens of branches throughout the Americas, Europe and Asia. Calling ourselves The Three Hags after the three witches in Shakespeare's *Macbeth*, we forever wondered, 'When shall we three meet again? In thunder, lightning, or in rain?' As it turned out, the answer was often: we created about half a dozen food-and-wine pairing events a year. All were unique, most were truly memorable for the quality and quantity of wine poured and some simply hit it out of the park, with once-in-a-lifetime impossible-to-have-all-these-wines-at-a-single-dinner extravaganzas.

With Alessia Antinori during one of many dinners at Indigo

With the legend himself... no, no, not me... Angelo Gaja

Barbaresco appreciation with jeroboam and straw a la Federico Ceretto

Sanjay and Frédéric Engerer decanting Château Latour for our dinner

Florence Rogers-Pinault, owner, Château Latour

Malini being schooled by Gildas d'Ollone on Ch. Pichon Longueville Comtesse de Lalande

Aman Dhall, Malini, and Alfred Tesseron (Ch. Pontet-Canet)

The 'Les Cinq' dinner—Sheri Singh, Alfred Tesseron (Ch. Pontet-Canet), me, Malini, Stephan von Neipperg (Ch. Canon-la-Gaffelière), Nicolas de Bailliencourt (Ch. Gazin), Sigweis von Neipperg, Daniel Cathiard (Ch. Smith-Haut-Lafitte)

The Three Hags of the IW&FS, Bombay branch inaugural dinner: Nihal, Sanjay and moi

Our branch's inaugural dinner, in July of 2006, was themed as a Syrah vs Shiraz face-off. The wines of the northern Rhône, made from 100 per cent Syrah, from the appellations of Hermitage and Côte-Rôtie, some of the greatest wines of the world, were paired against the Aussies' elegant, powerful, concentrated Shiraz varietals. The stupendous line-up of the icons of their respective regions were sourced directly from the winemakers' own cellars, a great rarity for some of these wines. The vote was unanimous—the Aussies blew the French out of the water with Henschke's 1990 Hill of Grace declared the hands-down winner, edging out the 1990 Hermitage La Chapelle from Paul Jaboulet Aîné for the top spot ... but please don't tell the French that!

THE INTERNATIONAL WINE & FOOD SOCIETY
Bombay Branch

IW&FS

SYRAH vs. SHIRAZ

IWFS Inaugural Dinner
Tuesday 25th July 2006

WINES

Hermitage Blanc 'Chevalier de Stérimberg' 1991, Paul Jaboulet Aîné
Hermitage Blanc 'Chante Alouette' 1996, Chapoutier
Hermitage Blanc 'Chevalier de Stérimberg' 2003, Paul Jaboulet Aîné
'Aeolia' Beechworth-Victoria Rousanne 2004, Giaconda
'Virgilius' Eden Valley Viognier 2004, Yalumba

❀✿❀

Crozes Hermitage Domaine de Thalabert 1998, Paul Jaboulet Aîné
Crozes Hermitage 2003, E. Guigal
The Struie Barossa Valley Shiraz 2002, Torbreck
Mount Edlestone Eden Valley Shiraz 2002, Henschke

❀✿❀

Cote-Rotie La Mouline 1998, E. Guigal
Cote-Rotie La Blonde 1998, René Rostaing
RunRig Barossa Valley Shiraz-Viognier 1998, Torbreck

❀✿❀

The Grange South Australian Shiraz-Cabernet 1998, Penfolds
Hill Of Grace Eden Valley Shiraz 1990, Henschke
Hermitage La Chapelle 1990, Paul Jaboulet Aîné

❀✿❀

Hermitage La Chapelle 1983, Paul Jaboulet Aîné

❀✿❀

The Bothie' Barossa Valley Muscat de Frontignac, 2004, Torbreck
Muscat de Beaume-de-Venise Les Chante des Griolles 2002,
Paul Jaboulet Aîné

MENU

Tomato *saar* & corn soups

❀✿❀

Tartare of root vegetables with wilted *mutt* & beetroot sauce

Tartare of Yellowfin tuna & Norwegian salmon with pink peppercorn dressing

❀✿❀

Boulangere potatoes, roasted mushrooms and arugula with morel reduction

Braised Ox at 2 ends – tongue & tail, red choucroute, red currant sauce & jus

❀✿❀

Spinach & black bean gnocchi, tabbouleh salsa & red pepper jerky

Shiraz braised shank of New Zealand lamb, tabbouleh salsa & shallot confit

❀✿❀

Cheeses from the Rhône

Vache de Chalais, Rigotte Doree, St. Marcellin

❀✿❀

Stewed peaches, plum jelly, panna cotta, cherry compote & ginger anglaise

The region of Burgundy is vast and far-flung, yet some of the world's best grapes comes from tiny family-owned holdings, which make no more than one or two barrels of wine a year. In contrast to several other regions, the whites are as renowned as the reds, and the grape varietals are far fewer, predominantly Chardonnay and Pinot Noir. Only 1 per cent of the produce comes from vineyards that are classified as Grand Crus, and these were the wines we showcased (with a couple of other notable exceptions) that night. They are notoriously difficult to acquire, but acquire we did.

When does one ever experience a Le Montrachet and a La Romanée-Conti in the same evening? Or a collection of five wines from Domaine de la Romanée-Conti? The dinner was truly historic and magical. To have held it in India, at Indigo, with my menu, made it that much more special.

By 2014, we really knew what we were doing. We did a historical event at Neel starring the iconic Château Margaux, one of the five to achieve Premier Grand Cru status in the Bordeaux Classification of 1855. It took about eighteen months of negotiations and planning to set up what became the official launch of the Margaux in India, but it was so worth it. It was a thirteen-course Awadhi feast, pairing the wine with such classics as Hyderabadi haleem and biryani made with raw jackfruit.

As I said, conventional wisdom was that the nuanced flavours and tannins of wines don't hold up against the heat of chilli and other overpowering spices. And this big Bordeaux is particularly known for its great delicacy and perfumed complexity. But with enough testing and tasting, Sanjay Menon, Chef Mukhtar Qureshi and I managed to find some truly magical pairings that surprised (the late) Paul Pontallier, managing director of Château Margaux; Corinne Mentzelopoulos, the winery owner; and Alexandra Petit-Mentzelopoulos, her daughter, who headed their India projects. Over several months, we sampled many of Chef Qureshi's dishes alongside five wines from Château Margaux, adjusting the spice and heat levels to complement, not compete with, the wines. Along the way we established that in the early sixteenth century, when Awadhi cuisine came into its own in Lucknow, it didn't use much chilli, which was introduced to the subcontinent only when the Portuguese, led by Vasco da Gama, arrived later in the century. This led to a purer experience of some of Chef Qureshi's creations and allowed us to discover fabulous pairings with some of the delicate meaty dishes that are at the heart of Awadhi cuisine. Cabernet Sauvignon, with its rich tannins and firm acidity, considered impossible to pair with Indian cuisine, suddenly started to sing in the glass with the chosen courses.

For the whites, Margaux's fruity Pavillon Blanc 2009 matched with Chef Mukhtar's creamy pine nut soup and light vegetal seared bamboo shoot and water chestnut patties, then with tandoori prawns and broiled pomfret in hung curd (an Indianized version of my Oma's original recipe).

We paired the Margaux 1985, noted for its floral notes and fruity core, with tandoor-roasted baby eggplant, achaar-marinated portobello mushrooms, slow-cooked vegetable and okra stew, and baby goat chops. We put the 2001 Margaux, similar to the '85 though with the added oomph of dark berries, together with sweet couscous-stuffed morel mushrooms, rich black lentil stew and tandoor-roasted spring chicken.

The Margaux launch dinner menu at Neel, 2014

The India launch dinner of Château Margaux. L to R: Thiboult Pontallier, me, Alexandra Mentzelopoulus-Petit, Paul Pontallier

They say imitation is the sincerest form of flattery. It is gratifying to realize that you are responsible for change in the dining habits of people and in furthering the awareness and appreciation of wine. In the years that followed the great successes of the wine events and the amount of wine we sold at Indigo, Tote and Neel, five-star hotels and many stand-alone restaurants stepped up their wine programmes, as I said earlier. But we always remained one step ahead. I believe that was because we stayed true to the idea that wine and food themselves were our business—not the wine and food business. Our hearts and our palates were our North Star; if we followed that as our guide, eventually the financial rewards would come along. And they did.

'There is no love sincerer than the love of food.'
—George Bernard Shaw, from *Man and Superman*

Indigo was becoming as famous for its special dinners and events as it was for its daily menus, bar cocktails and the nightlife crowds queuing up to the bar to imbibe its creative fresh fruit cocktails. And with good reason. We'd pull out all the stops to make any occasion—whether it was a birthday, an anniversary, a graduation, wedding or divorce, whatever—memorable beyond imagination. A little thing like personalizing menus with the diners' names (we printed them in-house) always drew proud smiles from the host and guests in their party. We touched hearts. We made people feel special.

We did a ton of events over the years, but it was always about and underscored by our food on some level. During one Kala Ghoda Arts Festival, we collaborated with renowned contemporary artist Jitish Kallat (whose large stunning painting adorned the bar wall at Indigo) to create 'Art on a Plate', an edible expression of his recent works, which adorned the restaurant walls for the duration of the festival. Other times we held supper theatre productions organized by Avantika, my thespian sister, like Oscar Wilde's *Salomé* (among others), involving the diners as participants in the play's banquet. Malini commissioned several contemporary artists to produce works relating to food and wine, which we auctioned off to raise funds for the farmers affected by severe drought in Latur, a region of Marathwada in Maharashtra.

And then there were the annual Indigo anniversary party bashes—easily *the* party of the city each year. They were always held on the first Sunday in April, close to April Fool's Day, and saw upwards of 400 to 500 of Bombay's who's who partying hard from around noon to well into the wee hours of the night before we finally had to throw out the remaining stragglers at around 2 or 3 in the morning. We had pass-around food on trays, open buffets and live grills set up throughout the property. You ate and drank as much as you could hold, while boogieing to live bands. Around 11 p.m., tradition saw me whip up a batch of six to eight dozen eggs for soft runny scrambled eggs with truffles, for those still present and able to find room in their stomachs. These feasts became stuff of legend.

Even Christmas, Thanksgiving and Valentine's Days were celebrated with equal culinary extravagance and indulgence. Our Valentine's Day menus were as tongue-in-cheek as they were outrageously (though understatedly) sexy extravaganzas.

By understatedly sexy, I mean that our wait staff did not appear tableside wearing their birthday suits. That certainly would have taken diners' attention away from the food and wine, especially if I came out of the kitchen undressed like I'd done back in the day with Ed at Jethro's in Lancaster (they would have lost their appetites if I did that)! What I do mean is our menus contained innuendos that still make my mouth water, as well as stimulate other hormones. Here was one of our early offerings on 14 February 2001:

INDIGO

valentine's day

14th february, 2001

"Her breath is like honey spiced with cloves
Her mouth delicious as a ripened mango.
To press kisses on her skin is to taste the lotus
The deep cave of her navel hides a share of spices
What pleasure lies beyond, the tongue knows
But cannot speak of it."
~ Srngarakarika Kumara Datta (Twelfth century)

On this day, Indigo pays tribute to aphrodisiacs, the food for lovers, with a special menu that is redolent of amorous ingredients. Touted as the perfect 'date destination', the cozy ambiance makes for a truly romantic and memorable experience.

"Properly speaking, there are no aphrodisiacs capable of endowing those blind to life with sight,'" said Napoleon's chef Kurmonsky. But for those with poor eyesight in the matter, there are substances which can act as magnifying lenses.

Folklore is full of magic foods said to awaken that slumbering Greek goddess of love and beauty, Aphrodite. Once an exquisite dinner has been eaten, once the secret warmth of the wine and tickle of the spices are coursing through the bloodstream to a rosy glow, it is time to prolong the encounter with the age-old tradition of imbibing aphrodisiacs. But is there any truth in these old wives' (or husbands') tales? We let you decide. Use the list below to help order your food tonight...**Happy Valentine's Day!**

OYSTERS & SEAFOOD: This goddess of all aphrodisiacs provided the perfect foil for Casanova. Why should you be left behind? Let these jewels glide down your throat tempting you with events yet to come.

ASPARAGUS: Ah to indulge the creative mind! Yet for those of you who need a little prodding, its perfect shape should make for a most scintillating swallow.

MORELS: Not only do they exude a musky odor but more importantly, provide the eater with a taste of pure hedonism.

ARTICHOKE: The perfect feminine counterpoint to the asparagus. Do we really need to spell it out?

INDIGO

BEANS: To the Teutons and Romans beans were nothing but stimulants and their flowers symbolized sexual pleasure. Add the colour white to your bean (and we all know what the colour white symbolizes) and you have a potent mixture.

ONIONS: A bulbous tuber that we associate with bringing tears to our eyes; tears of joy perhaps as we read in Sheik Nefzawi's "The Perfumed Garden," a sixteenth century text, that Abu el Heiloukh ate onions and was thus able to excite many a voluptuous maiden for 30 uninterrupted days!!!

GARLIC: If garlic was good enough as an aphrodisiac for the Egyptians, Greeks, Romans, Chinese and Japanese it is good enough for us too. David Berman, professor of the USC Medical School, tells us why: a potent mixture of crushed garlic mixed with lard applied to a certain unwilling male member resulted in miracles Garlic anyone....

GINGER: What do Pliny, Avicena (two well know Romans), Indian and Turkish texts have in common – their stated belief of the aphrodisiacal powers of Zingiberaceae, or ginger. Making a paste from ginger, gingerly applied will "from the moment [of application] she will have such an affection for you that she can scarcely be a moment without you." And if this remedy does not work, don't look to us.

CLOVES: This rod and bulb spice certainly knew how to excite many a Chinese, even in the Third Century BC, where texts explicate the aphrodisiacal properties of the clove. Many years later, a Danish medieval herbalist, H. Harpenstreng, still discovers the magic of cloves at work again, when he stated, "if a man loses his ability, he should stay sober and drink milk spiced with five grammes of clove. This will fortify him and make him desire his wife."

SAFFRON: One of the most expensive spices, these stigmas of the Crocus Satirus flower are reputedly known to make erogenous zones even more sensitive. Now where's that G-spot?

INDIGO

impotence.

SAGE: We know what happens when sage is rubbed. And so did the Greek soldiers; they were often welcomed home by their wives with a sage tea to stimulate fertility. But don't just take our word for it....

PEPPER: The reputation of pepper being an aphrodisiac goes back to antiquity when it was used by the Egyptians, Greeks and Romans. But the Arabs knew its uses best for it is written, "masticate a little pepper; apply a certain quantity of it and then go to work. This will produce for you, as well as for the woman, a matchless enjoyment." Ladies are you listening?

VANILLA: Is a derivative from the Spanish word 'vainila,' a diminutive of 'vaina' meaning vagina or pod. The Aztecs certainly justified the power of vanilla and its amorous properties, for they knowingly used vanilla in their food to excite their people. Now trust us as we bet on the tried and true Aztecan methods of enticing one's mate.

PEACHES: The peach, like its seductive cousin the plum, has often led many a poet to passionately exclaim its erotic character. Slice it open and you are faced with two juicy cheeks. Sigh....

STRAWBERRY: Considered the ideal complement to champagne in courtship rituals, the strawberry subtly seduces you so that you are never satisfied by eating just one; don't let us stop you...

CHOCOLATE: Cold or hot, the intensely aromatic and sensuous characteristics of chocolate are unparalleled. It was the sacred drink of the Aztecs, related to the Goddess of Fertility, and consumed only by nobility. The Mexican emperor Montezuma introduced it into Spain where its fame as an aphrodisiac was so great that women drank it in secret. Although it may be legal to imbibe chocolate today, we take no responsibilities for the consequences.

CHAMPAGNE: Often considered a "feminine" wine and thought to have more of an effect on women than men, we present you both with a challenge. No matter whom the winner, let it not be said that the senses weren't tickled, the pulse not sent racing and the effervescence highly intoxicating.

INDIGO

valentine's day Menu

14th february, 2001

foreplay

white bean & asparagus soup
saffron, pinenuts & crispy sage...155

cream cheese stuffed morels, balsamic marinated papaya
bitter greens...225

fresh steamed kerala mussels
broth of fennel, leeks, saffron & pernod...245

sliced green tea-scented cold duck breast
grilled shitakes, cranberry sorbet, port reduction...285

inter courses

artichokes, roast fennel, polenta, shitake mushroom "compote" & grilled vegetables in phyllo
frizzed leeks, roast pepper & vanilla vinaigrettes...325

pasta shells with morels, peas & ricotta
sage cream with cloves...375

hot crab and smoked oyster soufflé with roast corn
buttered vegetables, green garlic and scallion toast...375

spice-rubbed flame grilled pork chops
cumin mashed sweet potatoes, long beans, *panch amrut*-inspired sauce ...325

grilled ginger & lemongrass brushed chicken
basil polenta, bok choy with roasted lemon coriander dressing...325

climax

hot, runny bitter chocolate soufflé with hazelnut sauce
oven roasted strawberries and strawberry coulis...215

white chocolate mousse with lemon basil
ricotta sponge, stewed spiced peaches & strawberries...215

'Food is better than sex' became the rallying cry of food fanatics around the mid-1980s in the US and Europe, when celebrity chefs, bestselling cookbooks and multiple Michelin stars had more cache than ... well, name your favourite sex symbols from the East or West. As a professional in the restaurant world, I am too biased to opine on the subject. Actually, I think food makes sex better and sex makes food better.

India took a while to catch up to that notion. But when it did, who better to promote the idea than me, a believer in all things sensory or sensual? Our sexy Valentine's Day menus merely reinforced what was on everyone's mind. And we hoped the food would induce a culinary orgasm on your palate. I'd wager many did achieve that climactic moment after dinner with us on those V-Day celebrations. But what happened at home afterwards shall remain at home, under the covers!

Interestingly, a few years ago a study corroborated this titillating theory. The global survey from advertising company Havas Worldwide found that 54 per cent of millennials think 'eating can be just as pleasurable as sex'. What's more, when given the choice between sex and 'an excellent dinner at a restaurant', 35 per cent would opt for dinner.[1]

Having seduced as many of your sensory experiences as possible, we were ready for an 'after' cigarette and our next venture, which would be a little more down-homey.

But first we had a little brush with the law to deal with ...

The One Venture that Went Up in Smoke: SmokeWater Grill in Juhu

By 2002, Indigo was killing it. We were packed every day and the reservation waitlist had stretched to over two months. Seriously. We were probably the first restaurant in the country that had more than a two-month wait for a table. It was unheard of. Naturally, then, being an entrepreneur as much as a chef, I started to think of the next restaurant. It was time to expand.

I wanted to do a grill and we found a stunning space on the ground floor of a small three-storey building in Juhu. The space had a huge outdoor area right on the beach that we were going to develop for alfresco dining. Bijoy Jain designed what was to be a modern raw concrete- and wood-finished space. We were going to call it the SmokeWater Grill.

We were six weeks from finishing construction when we received a legal 'cease and desist' notice from our landlord's two brothers, stating we were trespassing and to stop work immediately. WTF? We showed the notice to our landlord who said casually, 'Forget about my brothers, I'll manage them. Don't stop your work. Keep the project going and finish the restaurant.'

'Kishen,' I replied, 'we can't ignore your brothers, nor this notice. We're a company and this is a legal notice. What's going on?'

'We've had some family dispute going for years and they always try to prevent me from doing any business from any of our jointly held properties. They own two-thirds of the building, but I own the open-air and covered area where we're doing the restaurant. We settled in court years ago but never registered the settlement.'

'Shit,' I thought. 'Now I know why the encumbrance never showed up in our title search when we signed the lease agreement.'

We met with his brothers separately to understand what we could do to prevent us from being caught up in their family squabble. It was obvious that Kishen, our landlord, did not have a clear title to the premises. They were most apologetic and expressed how sad they were that we were getting caught in the crossfire, but there was absolutely nothing we could do—monetarily or otherwise—that would get them to change their minds or their stance. The resentment they had for their brother was just too deep. They were out to fuck him over. Period. We were collateral damage.

Now what? We were several crores (tens of millions) down. The construction was virtually complete and the finishing work just beginning. The kitchen and HVAC (heat, ventilation and air-cooling) equipment had been ordered and delivery had started too. We couldn't move forward with the project without a legal battle. We'd get embroiled in the courts for years to come. So, we approached our landlord and said he was in breach of our agreement and would have to compensate us for all the costs associated with the project. No dice. This was going nowhere in a hurry, despite our patience and willingness to end this amicably. Instead, he got aggressive with us. Not good. We needed to do something to get him to compensate us pronto.

We consulted a crackerjack lawyer who specialized in lease- and real-estate-related cases. In our first meeting I'd prepared a short case note on the history with the landlord, and as he skimmed through that, our lease, the title documents and the brothers' legal notice—all in about five minutes—he suddenly stopped and looked up at me.

'Rahul, you're my worst kind of client,' he blurted out rather matter-of-factly.

'Why?' I asked self-consciously.

'Because you may not have the stomach to do what you need to do to win this.'

'Try me,' I said, unsure of what he had in mind.

He did tell me. And we followed his lead.

We had physical possession of Kishen's place and there was no way in hell we'd give that up without a fight. He took us to court, except that now we were in the driver's seat and in possession of the premises that he was desperate to win back. In a country where possession is nine-tenths of the law, it was now his fight to establish possession of a premises that was legally ours, based on our lease agreement. We were willing to sit tight and drag it out in court for as long as it took for him to come to the table, repay us our losses and earn his property back. We'd lost a ton of money on the project because of him and it was now his turn to lose as much money on his soon to be unrentable, no-income generating, beachfront property. Tit for tat.

Over two years we bloodied it out in various courts under various sections of the law. In the high court, where the matter of juridical possession of the premises was being fought, he lost repeatedly. I remember the first day in court when the judge cut his lawyers off, saying, 'Let me guess, you're going to try and make the case saying that your locks were on the premises and then they were removed by the defendant and replaced by theirs. Correct?'

'Yes, Your Honour.'

'I'm not interested in any of that. My question is whose locks are on the premises now, as we speak?'

'Theirs, Your Honour.'

'Where in your lease agreement does it state that the premises are always in your (juridical) possession, regardless of whose locks are on the door?'

'It doesn't, Your Honour.'

'Then it's clear that the defendant is in both juridical and physical possession of the premises as per the terms of their agreement with you, and in fact, by preventing their peaceful possession and occupancy of the premises to conduct their business, under the terms of your agreement, it is you who is in breach, not them.'

Ouch! That had to hurt. Later he tried another approach: his lawyers argued that our restaurant was in violation of the agreement because we were going to use the open-air space reserved for parking as an alfresco dining area. This time, a different presiding judge asked, 'Have they started the restaurant and are people being served and presently dining in the designated building parking lot already?'

'No, Your Honour, they're intending on doing this.'

'Intending? I might *intend* to fly unaided like a bird, but that doesn't mean that I am going to, let alone even be able to. Furthermore, please show me where it states in the restaurant licence conditions that open-air dining is not permitted? In a modern city like ours, I'd welcome all efforts to be able to do this, as it's sorely lacking. How lovely to be able to dine under the stars by the seashore.'

Ouch again! Double hurt. Thrown out again. They tried numerous approaches and arguments; every time they were overruled. And every time he lost in the high court, he'd fire his lawyers and refuse to pay them. In a very small and tightly knit community of high court lawyers, word quickly spread that he was a non-paying client, making it increasingly difficult for him to find reputable counsel to defend him.

On other occasions when our case was presented to the judge, even before we got going with opening arguments they stepped down. 'Is the defendant Rahul Akerkar of the Indigo restaurant? I know him personally and as a regular patron of his restaurant, cannot in all fairness sit in judgment on this case. I'm sorry, but I must recuse myself,' they'd state each time. This happened twice, obviously much to Kishen's chagrin. I couldn't help but chuckle inside. We even went up to the Supreme Court of India in Delhi, where once again his case was thrown out and sent back to the lower courts.

Now desperate, Kishen switched strategies, filing in the criminal court against me personally on some idiotic charge, and also in the city civil court, making an untenable case that the lease itself was bad in law and therefore we were trespassing and had no tenancy standing in the first place. We'd engaged a very senior lawyer for arguing our case—in fact, he'd written the Maharashtra Tenancy Act under which our case was being argued. When he walked into court, the judge got up and bowed his head in respect. I'd never seen anything like it in my life. Kishen lost in both courts.

Two years later, we were opening our first Indigo Deli in Colaba. In the midst of our Vastu and Grihashanti pujas, rituals performed to bless and bestow good luck and success upon new business ventures, we received notice that Kishen had finally agreed to settle out of court. I recall the exact moment so well: milk had just boiled over—a wonderful Hindu tradition where you let milk boil over in an open pot on a new stove, symbolizing prosperity and abundance of food, blessing the new home (or in our case the new restaurant), when the news came.

'There is a God,' I thought, wiping away tears of joy.

What God—make that gods, including my Hindus gods or my Jewish God—had in store for me next would please all of them. Especially those who like a juicy Reuben sandwich.

TADKE WALI POMFRET (From Neel at Tote on the Turf)

The creation of this fish dish came to me as an epiphany when Mukhtar and I were working on his Awadhi menu for the Château Margaux dinner. We were looking to do an aromatic but delicate fish preparation with enough fat to hold up to the Pavillon Blanc. I found myself describing my Oma's sole broiled in sour cream with paprika and butter, and realized how easily we could Indianize it with a tempering of black mustard seeds, Byadgi or Kashmiri red chilli powder and curry leaves. While not particularly Awadhi by a long shot, it did make you think of India, and paired beautifully with Margaux's rich, complex sauvignon blanc.

INGREDIENTS FOR 4 PORTIONS

4 pomfret fillets (120–130 gm each, skin off; or any other delicate white fish like flounder or sole)

1½ cup sour cream (or 400 gm plain yoghurt hung in a muslin cloth for several hours to drain and thicken and then beaten with a tablespoon of heavy cream or milk till smooth and spreadable)

1½ teaspoon Byadgi or Kashmiri red chilli powder (aromatic but not very spicy)

1½ teaspoon black mustard seeds

8–10 fresh curry leaves

1 tablespoon cooking oil

4 teaspoons butter

Juice of 1 lemon

Salt and pepper

DIRECTIONS

Rinse the fish fillets in cold water and pat dry with a paper towel. Season with a little lemon juice, salt and pepper, and place flat on an oven tray lined with aluminium foil. Spread an even, 1-cm thick layer of sour cream (or whipped hung curd) over each fillet and sprinkle a couple of pinches of red chilli powder over the sour cream. With the back of a teaspoon, put several tiny dabs of butter on each sour-cream-covered pomfret fillet. Broil under a hot broiler or salamander for 5–7 minutes till the sour cream almost dries out and colours golden-brown in patches (where the butter was). Remove from the broiler and serve the tempering.

While the fillets are broiling, make a tempering of black mustard seeds and curry leaves by cooking them rapidly in very hot oil till they splutter and pop. Remove from heat and spoon a teaspoon of the tempered mustard seed and curry-leaf oil on each broiled fish fillet. Serve immediately.

sourdough
tomato concasse
aubergine
olive baguette
roast potatoes

13: INDIGO DELIS

MY CULINARY HOMAGE TO NEW YORK AND MOM

BY 2004 INDIGO, WHICH was in its fifth year, had taken on a life of its own and basically could have run itself. I needed a new creative itch to scratch.

Our next dining venture made no sense at all. There was no apparent niche for it, no 'market demand' for it, no one begging me to open anything like it. Then again, one could have said the same thing about Indigo—and many did.

I will lay the blame on my mother and the culinary preferences of her East European Jewish (aka Ashkenazi) family upbringing. This project was all for Jinx and me, perhaps the most selfish motivation one could imagine.

You see, in New York, where I spent half my life, the delicatessen was a fixture. Not just any deli but the ones filled with all kinds of Jewish delicacies—pickled herring, gherkins (not to be confused with the many styles of Jewish and kosher cucumber dill pickles), salami, pastrami, corned beef and all the other 'cold cuts' (also known as cold sliced meats), head cheese, sausages of all shapes and contents, chopped liver, potato salad, lox and other smoked and pickled fish, and German mustard loaded with whole mustard seeds that exploded pungently when you bit into them. And then there were the desserts: cheesecakes, coffee cake, black-and-white cookies, éclairs and more.

Delicatessen is a word derived from Germany, the homeland of my mother and the maternal side of my family. The Latin root of the word, *delicatus,* means 'giving pleasure, delightful'. Immigrants to America eventually shortened it to deli. The term is now used internationally and its foods and variations continue to delight the world. Delis, which sell prepared foods, cheeses and the like from curved glass refrigerated display cases on a daily basis, as well as provide dine-in service to tables and booths, first appeared in the US in New York City. With the German-Jewish population increasing in the mid to late 1800s, they started mushrooming all over the five boroughs of the city.

New York delis were like shrines you entered with great reverence; the smells alone upon entering could convert even the non-believers. Carnegie Deli, Stage Deli, Barney Greengrass, Zabar's, the Second Avenue Deli, Katz's Deli ... these were the synagogues of sumptuousness. And, as the famous Levy's 'real Jewish rye' bread commercial used to say, 'you don't have to be Jewish to love [them]'.

I was a true devotee and both my mother and I longed for these tastes. We'd start salivating at just the mention of pickled herring. The bummer was that these products were unavailable in India. So what did we do? A normal person would ask a relative in New York to ship them to India. But we are not normal; we are restaurateurs. My not-so-logical answer: open a deli in Mumbai. But from a logical point of view, who would buy this stuff? Where was the market survey suggesting this would work? What due diligence did we do? (Very little.)

Yet we also knew there were no mid-market casual places that did truly good food in an honest way—homemade from scratch, rich in flavour but affordable—which you could buy to take home or eat there café-style. You couldn't even get a decent sandwich anywhere in Mumbai. We'd even have our own bakery and had mastered the recipe for making bagels, one of the most esoteric of all baked goods. Best of all, we had just the chef to helm our project and give form to our vision of the Indigo Deli. His name is Jaydeep Mukherjee or Chef JD, as he was better known.

Chef Jaydeep 'JD' Mukherjee in the Indigo Deli, Palladium kitchen

JD had joined the Indigo team a year earlier, abandoning a career as one of the junior chefs at the Taj Mahal Hotel's high-blown fine-dine eatery, Zodiac Grill. I remember when I interviewed him during his food trial at Indigo, we talked about how frustrated he was that a restaurant of that stature would serve instant mashed potatoes rather than whipping them up fresh. He saw no future there and was keen to join our merry band of passionate misfits. At the time we were planning the SmokeWater Grill. JD was slated to be the head chef of the restaurant. Needless to say after the events described earlier, that restaurant never got off the ground and we shifted our efforts and focus to the Indigo Deli.

I got along with JD right from the get-go. He was sharp, insightful, eager and understood exactly what we wanted, food-wise and conceptually, with the deli. He was much more than a good chef; he was a Renaissance man of sorts, interested in photography, music, wildlife conservation, travel, biking, the outdoors, and a thinker to boot. I saw a lot of my younger self in him, and we developed a super working equation, a kinship that carried forward for many years as he grew into the role of executive chef overseeing all our Indigo Delis. He ran a tight ship, demanding the moon from his team, but was always fair and even-handed and never asked of someone what he wasn't prepared to do himself. I always admired that about JD. He was a true chef's chef in every way—a skilled cook, teacher and leader.

Indigo Deli opened in Colaba just a few blocks from our Indigo restaurant in 2005. It was close to the Royal Bombay Yacht Club and the Taj Mahal Palace Hotel at the Gateway of India. It was another raging success as soon as it opened, as much to our surprise as anyone's. But it confirmed our belief that great food and a cosy atmosphere have timeless appeal.

Malini got star architect and furniture designer Samira Rathod to design and build out the space with constant inputs from the two of us. The double-height front dining room had huge sun-filled bay windows that framed cosy dining booths on one wall, and a floor-to-ceiling display of retail items with a library-like suspended moving stainless-steel ladder to access them. There was an upstairs seating area in a mezzanine (with more retail of course) for those desiring quieter, more private dining and an overview of all the beautiful people below.

Retail formed an integral part of all our earlier Delis, that offered high-end cheeses, bakery items and desserts, cold cuts and kitchenware. We sold Le Creuset kitchenware, Riedel wine paraphernalia, New York aprons, wine coolers, retro coffee machines, Italian oils, bottled truffles and many varieties of Indigo Deli's own branded jams, chutneys, mustards and vinaigrettes. Oh, and we retailed wines too, by the bottle or the case.

We had refrigerated glass display cases stocked with the day's fresh offerings of salads and such, just like in New York. We had jars of pickled things, again as I recalled from New York. The serving portions were way oversized, New York-style, and as promised, we were affordable. What we did not have were nearly hostile (though well-meaning and good-hearted) waitresses, as in New York. But unlike New York wait staff who are all too familiar with what's served, we had to educate and train our staff about these delicacies, none of which they would have tasted before.

I was especially proud of how close our corned beef and pastrami—all meats made on the premises—came to the real deal in New York, in spite of the meat being buffalo. Our Reuben sandwich was my particular favourite: slabs of meat and Swiss cheese topped with Russian dressing made with mayo and ketchup, spiced up a bit and stuffed with sauerkraut between two pieces of rye or sourdough bread. It was hard to get your mouth around it. We were the only place in India where you could sink your teeth into an authentic Reuben with Russian dressing.

The menu was as exhaustive as it was whimsical; we had something for everyone and of all ages. We did a very popular all-day breakfast, showcasing several avatars of eggs Benedict, waffles, French toast and pancakes. The burgers and sandwiches were creative, delicious and oversized, and our wafer-thin pizzas took on a celebrity status of their own. We had a very popular 'Everyone Loves Potatoes' section on the menu as well. It was all about comfort food.

Everyone loved our in-house bakeries. We did a wonderful bitter lemon meringue tart that I fought about with all the Deli chefs constantly. They wanted it sweeter; I desired more bitter. I won. Our New York-style cheesecake with seasonal berries was to die for, as was the crème Catalan that we served with a shot of flaming Ouzo. Leftover croissants at day's end found themselves starring again in our croissant bread pudding, served piping hot with a bourbon sauce. And did I mention chocolate? You couldn't get a better fudge brownie or mud cake in town. Even our ice creams—with a frequently changing menu of tens of flavours—sold out often.

Another common thread the Indigo Delis shared with the Indigo restaurant: you couldn't get 'Indian food' at the delis. But we did our own interpretations of some classics and in that vein Chef JD and I invented some new recipes as well. I could do a sophisticated version of popular comfort foods like mac 'n' cheese, then try a take on a Westernized version of upma for our breakfast menu, or Buffalo chicken wings, Bombay-style, a successful JD creation.

The irony was that while sales were good, not too many people developed a taste for pickled herring or the sülze (head cheese) that we stocked in the early days and what drove us to develop the delis in the first place, so my mother and I ate our hearts out on those items.

After the unexpected success, we made the decision to roll out Indigo Delis as a small chain, though it had not been our intention at the start. There are inherent problems and dangers in expanding what was still a small operation. Would I be able to continue hands-on quality control in my obsessive way? It was one thing to walk three blocks from my base at Indigo over to our Colaba deli to check on things in the kitchen and our in-house bakeshop, but it would not be easy to bounce around the city to visit our other potential deli sites. Plus, can you train staff fast and well enough? If the delis can't be cookie-cutter versions of one another, do you stand to create 'marketplace brand confusion', as the shirts on Madison Avenue would have put it? That's a dangerous thing.

Nonetheless, again swimming against the tide, we forged ahead, looking for space and opportunity.

We did what you could call a test run of the concept with our next time out. We called it Indigo Café, which opened in Lokhandwala, Andheri, in 2008. It was the same as Indigo Deli, minus the retail arm. With its launch and subsequent success, we ventured further.

The real-estate guru's mantra 'location, location, location' resonated from my third eye directly to my wallet. So when an opportunity opened up at the Palladium Mall, my first reaction was 'no way'. Malls to me represented nearly the opposite of the vibe we'd created at Indigo. Indigo was warm and fuzzy; I wanted the delis to be the same, casually chic and convivial settings for food and drink and talk. Malls were noisy and busy. The idea of intimate space at a mall was antithetical to the whole idea of them. Plus, you had the mechanization of shopping with escalators and elevators; décor was modern flash, mirrors and metals everywhere. The storefronts were gaudy showcases, as far as I was concerned.

The Palladium Mall, part of High Street Phoenix, Mumbai's first luxury retail and entertainment destination opened in 1996, seemed no different. India was late to embrace malls as compared to the West; Spencer Plaza in Chennai is credited with being India's first, opening in 1985 as one of the biggest shopping malls in south Asia when it was built. By comparison, big shopping malls started springing up in the US in the 1950s. India may have been slow on the uptake because we are so used to shopping in outdoor markets and bazaars. Also, the idea of having enough disposable income to just 'shop' as part of one's entertainment needed a rising middle class of consumers. That took a while.

But when the rise in consumer demand hit India, it was like an explosion. By one account, by August 2010, stores in the Phoenix complex had realized ₹100 crore in sales, the best for commercial complexes in the country. That said, there were a lot of visitors who simply wanted to walk around the mall, ogling at designer labels like Gucci, Emporio Armani, Brooks Brothers, Ermenegildo Zegna, which they could not afford. But that only built aspiration.

How would a casual deli fit into that mix? While I was hesitant, the owners, Gayatri and Atul Ruia, were keen on us coming. However, the only space in the mall that we liked was already taken by another restaurant, an American chain focusing on casual dining. We liked the space because it was sort of half in the mall and half outside, and well situated beside an escalator that led to the mall's PVR multiplex cinema theatre. This would be great for pre- or post-moviegoers, so we knew there would be a steady footfall. So desirous were the owners for us to set up at the Palladium that when Malini said we'd only bring the Deli there if they gave us that other restaurant's space, they moved them to a different location even after they'd signed a lease.

Now committed, we brought in well-known award-winning architect Sameep Padora. Malini had a knack for finding and using up-and-coming architects and interior designers for all our early projects. She believed in the importance of developing projects with equal weightage between the design and F&B. We'd done that with Bijoy Jain at Indigo and Samira Rathod for the first Deli. Now Sameep turned the space from mundane retail into something extraordinary—truly otherworldly—from both a design perspective and as an exceptional example of innovative engineering. To separate our deli from the straight lines, rigid geometries and starkness of the rest of the mall, Sameep designed a ceiling of undulating waves formed with interlocking rough textured plywood much like an inverted geographical contour map. Threaded steel rods, affixed into a double thickness vertical plywood panel, held the whole structure together.

You could have been in a protected forest grove, or underwater. Or in a womb. He'd interpreted our design brief—that it should be warm and embracing, like a wine cave—with a modern twist. It was perfect. Simply shaped copper lighting fixtures hung from the ceiling, looking like a small flock of birds. It was double the size of the Colaba deli, with seating for 106 and a larger retail area. We retained the same stone floor as at the Colaba deli, but other than that it was so different from our 'prototype' that you had to wonder if our Colaba regulars would dig the new look and feel. They did. In droves. *CNN Travel Magazine* ranked it among the ten best new restaurants of 2010. One reviewer noted how busy it was, 'making it close to impossible to get a table here without calling ahead. And often even that can't guarantee you a seat'.

We brought on Sameep again in 2012 to design our fourth site in Bandra, which had become the hip Mumbai burb to hang out and dine. Yet, pound for pound in terms of revenue per square foot, Colaba was the most lucrative and remained the highest revenue generator of all our delis.

We went on to build this unexpectedly hot brand under our deGustibus umbrella, adding Indigo Delis in the Mumbai neighbourhoods of Bandra, Ghatkopar, Malad, Lokhandwala and eventually in New Delhi, along with our original in Colaba and at the Palladium. Just as the children of a family are unique individuals but with a shared DNA and soul, our delis followed suit. While they all retained a common menu backbone of many popular sandwiches, salads and dishes that we became known for—signatures like our Reuben, our unique paper-thin pizzas, Bombay chicken wings, and the Indigo Deli chocolate-chip cookies we baked fresh to order—each location had its own design, its own personality and its own chef-driven specials of the day.

Our claim to fame, as much as the food we served, was the fact that we were willing to take chances, to break the mould, to disrupt the marketplace by proving that Indian diners were willing to change their status-quo opinions and attitudes, were open to trying new flavours and ultimately would embrace them given the right ambience, context and food preparation.

I saw that we could leverage the good name of Indigo, the quality service and cuisine that it had come to represent, to expand the possibilities for deGustibus. I could envision Indigo becoming more than a one-hit wonder, with many variations of the theme. It opened doors to more creativity in the kitchen. It got people thinking, 'What will Chef Rahul concoct next?'

Meanwhile, Mom and I gorged on pickled herring, sülze and gherkins.

Here are two of Indigo Deli's sandwich winners ...

ROAST MUSHROOM SANDWICH WITH POTATO, CARAMELIZED ONION AND BRIE IN OLIVE BAGUETTE

INGREDIENTS FOR 4 SANDWICHES

Roast Mushrooms

400 gm mixed mushrooms (button, shitake, oyster, portobello, etc.) cut into thick slices

1 tablespoon extra-virgin olive oil

4–5 whole garlic cloves, roughly smashed

4–5 sprigs of fresh thyme

½ teaspoon grated nutmeg

Salt and freshly ground pepper

Roast Potatoes

2 medium potatoes, peeled and cut into ½-inch thick slices

2 teaspoons extra-virgin olive oil

2 teaspoons butter

½ teaspoon grated nutmeg

1 teaspoon finely chopped parsley

Salt and freshly ground pepper

Caramelized Onions

2 big onions, cut into ½-inch thick roundels

1 tablespoon extra-virgin olive oil

4–5 sprigs of fresh thyme

Salt and freshly ground pepper

Sandwich

4 olive baguettes (6–7-inches long)

1 tablespoon soft butter

100 gm soft, ripe Brie cheese, cut in wedges

1 cup baby arugula leaves

2 tablespoons aïoli (garlic mayonnaise)

DIRECTIONS

Roast Mushrooms:

Mix all the ingredients together in a bowl to coat the mushrooms well. Spread the marinated mushrooms in a single layer on a baking tray and bake for 20 minutes in a preheated medium oven at 180°C till nicely roasted and golden brown. Set aside. Alternatively, sauté them in a heavy-bottomed skillet or pan over high heat till golden brown and set aside on a paper towel to drain off excess oil.

Roast Potatoes:

Wash and pat-dry the potato slices with a paper towel. Sprinkle them with nutmeg, salt and pepper. Heat the olive oil in a frying pan or skillet on low to medium heat, add the butter and when melted, add the potatoes in a single layer and fry, turning them over, till both sides are golden brown and crispy. Check that the insides are cooked by biting into one. Transfer to a bowl and sprinkle with chopped parsley.

Caramelized Onions:

In a bowl mix the onions with a little olive oil, salt and pepper and the thyme to coat well. Heat the remaining olive oil in a frying pan or skillet on low to medium heat, add the onions and sauté till they're brown and caramelized.

Assembly:

Cut the baguette in half lengthwise. Generously apply butter on the cut inside of the baguette, spread open and warm or toast lightly on a pan or in a broiler. Remove and spread the garlic mayonnaise on it.

Layer the roasted mushrooms, potatoes and caramelized onions on the toasted baguette like in an open sandwich and top with the wedges of soft ripe Brie. Transfer the open sandwich to a hot oven or broiler to grill and melt the cheese. Remove from the oven or broiler, top with baby arugula and complete the sandwich with the other toasted baguette half.

TUNA NIÇOISE SALAD SANDWICH

INGREDIENTS FOR 4 SANDWICHES

4 six-inch sourdough baguettes or 8 slices of sourdough farmer's loaf

300–325 gm fresh tuna loin (sushi-grade)

1 cup tomato concassé (deseeded and peeled diced tomatoes)

1 large aubergine, cut into 1-cm thick discs

1 large potato, peeled, sliced and boiled

1 large red onion, thinly sliced

½ cup pitted Kalamata olives

1 cup baby arugula leaves

1 teaspoon finely chopped parsley

½ cup fresh basil leaves

4 hard boiled eggs, cut in slices

⅓ cup French vinaigrette

2 teaspoons butter

1 cup olive oil

Salt and pepper

DIRECTIONS

Slice the aubergine into 1-cm thick slices, sprinkle both sides with salt and spread out in a single layer in a colander for a couple of hours to allow all the bitter juices to drain out. Quickly rinse in water to remove all salt and pat-dry with paper towels. Heat half the olive oil in a shallow frying pan and fry the aubergine till golden brown on both sides. Drain on paper towels or napkins to remove excess oil and set aside.

Rub the tuna loin with salt, pepper and olive oil. Heat a pan and sear over high heat. Remove from the pan and drizzle with a little of the vinaigrette. When cool, slice the loin into thin slices and refrigerate if not using immediately.

Melt the butter in a pan on low heat, add the potato slices and parsley, and immediately remove from the heat. The parsley potato slices should just be warm. Season with salt and pepper.

Cut the baguette in half lengthwise. Sprinkle olive oil on the insides, spread open and grill to char lightly. Smear the tomato concasse on the cut side of the bread, distribute a few Kalamata olives over the concasse and top with the slices of fried aubergine, tuna loin, parsley potatoes and boiled egg slices.

Tear the basil leaves by hand and toss with the baby arugula and the remaining French vinaigrette in a bowl. Add the dressed leaves, drizzle the remaining vinaigrette on to the tuna sandwich and cover with the other half of the bread.

kashmiri
green olive
chutney

14: TOTE & NEEL:

FLIPPING THE SCRIPT ON FAILURE

'... there's no success like failure and failure's no success at all.'

—From 'Love Minus Zero/No Limit' by Bob Dylan

I LEARNED BOB DYLAN'S typically cryptic but bang-on brilliant observation the hard way, as most successful people who fail at something will probably confess if they have the backbone to. Ask Bollywood superstar Amitabh Bachchan, whose production house Amitabh Bachchan Corporation Limited tanked and sent him into bankruptcy until he turned it all around with the TV game show *Kaun Banega Crorepati*. Or Dutch painter Vincent Van Gogh who sold one painting in his life, never getting to experience the joy of success. Also ask J.K. Rowling, whose manuscript for *Harry Potter and the Philosopher's Stone* was rejected by twelve publishers before it was acquired. And just for good measure, there was an American fellow called Thomas Alva Edison, whose teachers said he was 'too stupid to learn anything', who was fired from his first two jobs and made 1,000 unsuccessful attempts at inventing the light bulb. We know how that one ended ... and began.

We seemed to be going from success to success. With Indigo's Deli chain, we added another dimension to my repertoire. But then that damned itch came back, that biting-off-more-than-I can-chew syndrome.

Timing and real estate converged. Malu and I had heard that an incredible 90,000 square feet space with a huge open area, several structures with verandas and a two-floor building was up for redevelopment at the Royal Western India Turf Club's Tote building at the Mahalaxmi Race Course in Mumbai. The tender had been out for months but we only found out five days before the closing when Ajoy Kapoor, a dear friend, called and asked whether we were tendering for it. Who reads tenders for development projects in the papers? I know I don't, but Ajoy said we should take a look regardless, and we did just that.

We visited the space on the Monday before the Friday tender deadline. It was a wet dream project, a jaw-dropping, once-in-a-lifetime kinda space. We drooled at the possibilities of developing multiple F&B, banqueting and event space concepts, and an architectural design that would do justice to it. We came home, called up my parents, asked them to take the kids for a couple of days and locked ourselves up, working on our bid. Four days and sixty-four pages of a business plan, several rounds of discussions and presentations later, we eventually won the deal, beating out twenty-six other bids, including several five-star hotel chains.

Great! Now what? We had no idea how we were going to fund this massive development. Luckily for us, the Turf Club got embroiled in a public-interest litigation, a class action suit against their plans to construct a massive development project that involved converting part of the club into hotels, malls, a golf course, racing track and park. The public was outraged and put a stop to all of it. Somehow, our twenty-year lease managed to slip through the cracks. We lay low for a couple of years, putting the project into hibernation as we developed the concept, got our permissions and raised the funds to build it.

We brought on the fast-rising brilliant team of Chris Lee and Kapil Gupta, partners at Serie Architects, to develop the project. We knew it had to be something entirely different from Indigo and the Delis.

What they did was nothing short of miraculous—miraculous enough to win the international 'Best Bar Design' recognition at the Wallpaper Magazine's Restaurant and Bar Design Awards in London.

Kapil immediately saw this as an urban architectural project in which he and his team could reinvent a late nineteenth-century building and make it relevant in post-colonial India. The team couldn't change the exterior beyond a point, as the building fell under the Heritage Regulations for Greater Bombay, which had been enacted in 1995. They also wanted to respond to what Kapil later called 'the poetics of the place', extending the peaceful vibe of the raintree grove, visible through big glass walls, from the outside to the inside.

Inspired by the trees, they incorporated branching steel columns with an I-shaped section. Entering the dining room, the stark bleached white walls and pillars that looked like trees in modern abstraction were meant to serve as a benign backdrop to the views of the trees outside through high glass windows.

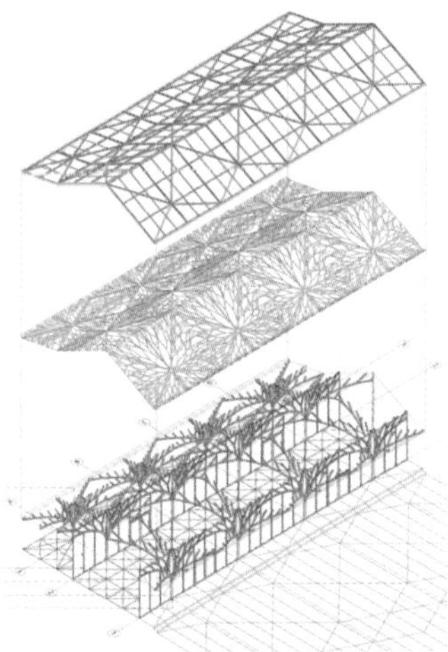

Tote Banquets. Axiomatic plan with the tree-form, branched structural columns by Serie Architects

Tote Banquets mirroring 100-year-old rain trees

As extraordinary as the dining area was, the team went even further with the upper-level lounge, which itself had two floors: the long bar area and a narrow loft with small tables overlooking the wild scene below. It was an intricate arrangement of three-dimensional, faceted wooden panelling, acoustically treated with sound-proofing material. The pattern of the panelling was a series of trees with intersecting branches. The 40-foot-long bar was made of dark chocolate wood, complemented by the wooden wall panels that made you feel as though you were looking out through the top of a geodesic dome.

It was this bar area that won the well-deserved design award. I will go out on a limb and say that Mumbai had seen nothing like it. If the bar at Indigo was a magnet for the hip and cool, the bar at Tote was even more so. On weekends it drew such large crowds of The Beautiful People from near and far, who packed in like sardines, closely rubbed elbows (and more)as they partied into the night.

Helping bartend at the opening night party at Tote on the Turf bar, Mumbai, 2009

It wasn't just the drinks and ambience they came for. We took bar food to new levels. As one reviewer for *CNN Travel Magazine* wrote, 'It's what you might call the city's first true bar menu, with a character of its own, standing out from the mezze platter monotony everywhere else.' I'd designed half the bar as an open satellite kitchen, serving up freshly cooked tapas and nibbles for our guests. That was very new and an instant success.

The restaurant itself, meanwhile, started out well. I had decided to focus on the grill. Everybody likes smoke, fire and charcoal, so you can't go wrong with that. And Bombay didn't have a hardcore grill. So we went with items such as Grilled Baby Rawas, Grilled Mustard Chicken with Jus, and Baby Red Snapper with Saffron and Tomato Jus. We also served emu and rabbit, grilled portobello mushrooms and pork chops; we imported ribs from Germany, lamb from Australia, scallops from the North Atlantic, fish from Chile and a ton of local fresh ingredients. You could order a steak and choose from about ten sides, such as caramelized mushroom and buttermilk mashed potatoes. For all-day dining, we went simple, with the standbys of pizzas, burgers and light sandwiches.

We did a killer Sunday brunch that rivalled the one at Indigo, where we'd been given credit for introducing a New York-style Sunday brunch culture to Mumbai. We featured several live stations where chefs cut meats, barbecued or grilled them as you waited, and made eggs to order. We had Cajun-rubbed chicken, citrus king prawns and beef tenderloin medallions and a surprisingly popular Burmese khow suey. The Indian barbecue menu included the nihari: lamb shanks cooked in a lightly spiced Lucknowi gravy, another traditional breakfast favourite from up north. There was a counter solely for roasted bhutta (corn on the cob), a nod to a traditional Mumbai monsoon street snack. The restaurant's signature gourmet pastas and risottos were also made to order, topped with a variety of sauces and meats. Dessert selections featured white chocolate bread pudding and an original torte of hot chocolate and jalapeño fudge.

To feed the ear, Malini wanted to create a specific sound, a concept similar to Paris' Hotel Costes or Café del Mar in Ibiza. Deejays Nikhil Chinappa and Pearl developed a mix for us that blended Afro-Latino percussive beats, Balearic dance beats, electronica via Paris and Berlin and jazz-tinged house sounds like what you'd hear in London and Paris bars.

Despite all we did, people were not flocking to our restaurant at Tote on the Turf. We wrung our hands trying to figure out what was going wrong. One thing was clear: though we went to extremes to make it look and feel completely different from Indigo, the menu was not different enough. We were, in effect, competing against ourselves.

I guess people thought, 'Why go to the knock-off when we can get the same food at the original where we have so many sweet memories?'

Who knows, really? But the bottom line speaks volumes. As we saw ours going down and some negative reactions in guest comments and restaurant reviewers, I did one of the most audacious, unexpected things in my already audacious career: I admitted I made a mistake. And I apologized. We shifted gears, changed direction entirely, renamed, rebranded and redid the menu. Not only did I apologize to my investors, but I did so publicly. I wrote a letter that we placed on tables, that went out to our mailing list and even in newspapers.

I was entirely surprised and encouraged by the widespread enthusiastic and anticipatory reaction the announcement generated. Tote on the Turf reopened with a focus on the grill, but I soon realized we needed to pivot away from anything remotely Western and create an Indian tandoor and grill restaurant. We closed soon thereafter to redesign the big kitchen area and with that, Tote on the Turf was reincarnated as Neel—the Hindi and Sanskrit word for indigo. (See what we did there?) At long last we finally decided to focus on Indian cuisine. Not just any Indian food but nawabi Awadhi cuisine, historically served to Muslim royalty, which we knew was popular with clients of Moveable Feast, our catering arm which continued to do business. This cuisine comes from the cities in the region of Awadh, and bears similarity to that of Hyderabad and Kashmir. We would go traditional rather than put my trademark East-meets-West fusion spin on it. With one exception: we'd reduce the oil content and control the pasty marination of most Indian kebabs, so that diners could actually taste the base ingredients.

deGustibus Hospitality Pvt. Ltd.
2nd Floor, Badamia Manor, S. K. Rathod Marg, Mahalaxmi, Mumbai - 400034, India.
T + 91 22 4349 0000 / 2354 9888 | F +91 22 2353 9887 | E info@degustibus.com | W www.degustibus.com

deGustibus

October 25th, 2010

Dear Guest,

When you conceive of a new restaurant, you either first design the interior look and feel of a space, and then create a cuisine that compliments the design, or you first know what you want to serve food-wise, and then find and design a space to enable you to deliver that at its best. I have always believed that to have a winning restaurant, the food must come first, with the space and interiors providing the embellishment to augment the dining experience.

Since Tote opened last year, we've gone through a few avatars of its menu in trying to establish the correct culinary identity for the award winning designed restaurant. I now realize that we'd gotten so immersed in the design of what is clearly a world class, unique space, that we somehow let the food play second fiddle to the interiors. We did precisely what I maintained one should never do, and the restaurant suffered a culinary disconnect and identity crisis, and never really took off as it ought to have done.

We've been working on correcting that over the past few months and I believe that we have a delicious new menu that will clearly define what our restaurant Tote is all about. Like the space, it is designed and built from the ground up; it's expansive, but focused; it's contemporary, stylishly refined yet restrained, uncluttered and quite elegant. The cuisine is modern European, infused with a few Indian influences wherever we felt they'd enhance the dish, and our ingredients are as always, fresh as can be expected of my restaurants. Our kitchen has wonderful wood burning grills, ovens and tandoors, and we've tried to grill and roast our food wherever we could to satisfy my love of food cooked this way.

But, talk is cheap, and the real proof of the pudding, as they say, is in the eating...

So, bon appétit, and let us know what you think.

Rahul Akerkar

Page 1 of 1

The Tote's public apology letter

This was when we got to shine a light on our chef, Mukhtar Qureshi, who belongs to the Awadhi region and understands the cuisine well. Originally from Lucknow, since 2008 he had been the Indian cuisine chef for Moveable Feast.

While we did not touch the design of the dining areas or bar, we redesigned the kitchen itself, as it would require rearrangements consistent with the flow of food preparations in an Indian restaurant, as opposed to what I was used to in Western tradition. Unusually, we didn't use a consultant for this. Mukhtar, our Executive Chef Nitin (from Indigo) and I decided to design our kitchen ourselves. We went to various Indian restaurant kitchens to understand the flow, since the cooking techniques were all different.

Working menu ideas with Mukhtar for Neel

Once rebranded and reopened as Neel, we were off, cooking and grilling ... and earning accolades from fans and food reviewers. In an early review in *DNA*, food critic Shakti Salgaokar wrote: 'Neel is a great example of demonstrating its philosophy with its food. With lesser oil, traditional recipes that keep flavours intact ... it could be safe to say that this is a [sic] kind of Indian restaurant Mumbai has been waiting for.[1]'

The feedback was a strong reminder to follow my own food-first commitment. Lesson learned! Vindication! Validation! Furthermore, Vir Sanghvi, the highly influential veteran restaurant critic, declared Neel as the best stand-alone North Indian restaurant in 2016 in his personal annual awards announcement, singling out Chef Qureshi: 'For years, the people of the city ate Punjabi restaurant food and thought it was genuine North Indian. But ever since Neel opened, Chef Mukhtar Qureshi has shown Mumbai what great Awadhi food really tastes like.[2]'

We served a remarkable fifty types of kebabs, twenty of which were vegetarian. Ms Salgaokar's favourite was the kakori kebab 'with its aromatic, melt-in-your-mouth texture'. Her second favourite dish was the gosht ki dum biryani.

We made it a point to serve individual chutneys and condiments with each dish, so guests could personalize the taste to their liking. We did Hyderabadi fish, Jhinga Dum Anari (prawns in almond and pomegranate curry), Adrak ke Panje (lamb chops in a spicy ginger marinade) and Raan-e-Mukhtar (tandoor-roasted leg of baby lamb), slow-cooked haleem, nalli nihari and taar korma, along with chicken tikka and biryani.

Among vegetarian dishes, we made Chilgoze ka Shorba (a thick soup made of pine nuts), Kashmiri Seb ki Sabzi (a curry made of Kashmiri apples), Gucchi ki Biryani (a Basmati rice biryani with stuffed morel mushrooms), Sofiyani Paneer Tikka (cottage cheese prepared with saunf or fennel) and Jaituni Kumbh Tikka (olive-marinated tandoori mushrooms served with a green olive chutney having the consistency of tapenade). 'Olives in this food? No way!' I challenged Mukhtar when he first made the tandoori mushrooms for me. Turns out there are in fact several (uncommon) dishes in the Muslim cuisine of Kashmir that use olives. Olives were ostensibly brought over to India by Alexander the Great when he and his invading hoards paid the country a visit way back in the day. Was it possible? No real way to tell, but it made sense, and the olive-marinated mushrooms were unusually delicious.

We let diners go home with sweetened palates, proffering an assortment of desserts, mostly based on the regional tradition, such as Parde Me Khubani—a dried apricot baked halwa with a crusty phyllo pastry on top. We also indulged in the rabdi ice cream which was, apart from the Dal Q-Man, the only English-sounding dish on the menu. The moderately sweet, smooth, creamy ice cream with a hint of pistachio was a lovely partner to the very coy, yet rich khubani in its phyllo parda or veil.

The move from Tote to Neel worked: it increased bookings, brought in new clientele and earned respect from reviewers and foodies, especially those who had long appreciated—or gained new appreciation of—traditional Awadhi cuisine.

All in all, we were very happy with how Neel turned out. But the biggest takeaway for me was that sometimes, Bob Dylan aside, failure can lead to success. It's about recognizing a mistake, having the courage to 'fess up and then, most importantly, turning it around.

I was embarrassed and humbled by the so-called failure of Tote. It was a big blow to my ego, perhaps a timely comeuppance to keep said ego in check after a string of successes going back even to the early days of Moveable Feast.

The only way to overcome your fear of failure is to face it and stare it down. For Malu and me, that would mean finding another culinary summit to conquer.

JAITUNI KUMBH AND JAITUNI MURG TIKKA

INGREDIENTS FOR 4 PORTIONS

Jaituni Kumbh

1 kg button mushrooms, cleaned and cut through the stalk just under the cap

10 green chillies

25 gm garlic

25 gm fresh ginger

250 gm pitted green olives in oil

50 gm fresh coriander

1 teaspoon crushed black pepper

1 teaspoon green cardamom powder

10 gm mace powder

5 gm ground clove powder

5 gm Lazzat-e-Taam, also known as 'Potli ka Masala'—one of the secret spices from the kitchens of the erstwhile Nawab of Lucknow. It is one of the most important ingredients for making nihari and kebabs and is also used in other curries for added flavour.

15 gm fennel powder

150 gm olive oil

Salt to taste

Jaituni Murg Tikka

1 kg boneless chicken thigh and leg, cut into 30–40 gm per piece

10 green chillies

25 gm garlic

25 gm fresh ginger

250 gm pitted green olives in oil

50 gm fresh coriander

1 teaspoon crushed black pepper

1 teaspoon cardamom green powder

10 gm teaspoon mace powder

5 gm ground clove powder

15 gm fennel powder

15 gm garam masala (see recipe below)*

150 gm olive oil

1 teaspoon lemon juice (juice of 1 lemon) along with zest

Salt to taste

Garam Masala

15 gm coriander seed

10 gm whole cumin seed (shahi jeera)

5 gm black cardamom

5 gm green cardamom

5 gm dry rose petal

1 star anise (3–5 gm)

3 gm cinnamon

5 bay leaves

---

* NOTE: Lazzat-e-Taam masala is omitted in the chicken marinade. Garam masala is used in its place.

Dry-roast all ingredients in a hot pan, agitating constantly. Remove, cool and powder. Yield ~50 gm

DIRECTIONS

Jaituni Kumbh:

Clean and trim the stalks of the mushrooms, cutting through them just below the cap. Make the olive marinade for the mushrooms by combining olive oil, pitted olives, ginger, garlic, coriander and green chillies in a blender and pulsing repeatedly into a coarse paste. Set some aside to serve with the mushrooms later. Alternatively, use a stone grinder or mortar and pestle and pulverize into a coarse paste. Add all the dry spice powders to the olive paste and mix well.

Combine the olive paste with the mushroom caps, making sure to work in the marinade well, and refrigerate well covered in a glass or non-reactive bowl for half an hour. When you're ready to serve, remove the mushrooms, skewer through their caps and either cook in a hot tandoor or over coal in a barbeque, or grill till the mushrooms and olive paste just start to brown and partially dry out. Serve with green olive chutney.

Jaituni Murg Tikka:

Marinate the chicken pieces in a paste made by puréeing the garlic, ginger, lemon juice and garam masala. Make sure to work the marinade well into the chicken, covering the pieces all over, and refrigerate for about 15–20 minutes in a glass or non-reactive bowl.

Next, make the green olive paste like in the Jaituni Kumbh recipe. Note that it will be without the garlic and ginger, which were used in the garam masala marination step above. Add the dry spices like in the Jaituni Kumbh recipe and combine well. Marinate the already marinating chicken with this green olive paste for 1–2 hours, refrigerated.

When you're ready to serve, remove the boneless chicken pieces, skewer through and either cook in a hot tandoor or over coal in a barbeque or grill, till chicken and olive paste just start to brown and char.

Like the mushrooms, serve with a green olive chutney.

15: THE END OF INDIGO AS WE KNEW IT

INDIGO

protein
greens

SOMETIMES THE END COMES with a big bang, a flash of recognition. At others it ends with the slow drip, drip, drip of Chinese torture. For Indigo, it was a bit of both.

While there has been much speculation and some vague reporting in the press, with some comments by me on what transpired—and how deGustibus went down, at least under the flag of the Akerkars—I would like to set the record straight here, once and for all. While I have withheld some key names in this account, in the interest of not entirely burning bridges, this story is so instructive to anyone in business that I feel it my duty to share it. Plus, it's just too juicy a tale.

The year 2007, when we were ranked Number 75 on San Pellegrino's World's Best Restaurants list, marked the pinnacle of Indigo's golden years. There followed so many restaurant awards, glowing international reviews and world rankings that I lost track. The Indigo Delis were a big hit. I had an amazing team; we were innovating, even as food trends were evolving, always one step ahead. As I got to travel the world more during off seasons, my cooking got further refined.

Many restaurants, often trying to copy us, had come and gone. Some staff that had left us attempting their own version of Indigo also failed in fairly short order. Meanwhile, we were going from success to success; our sales graphs showed upward growth of 15 to 20 per cent year on year for a decade. It defied all common sense.

And then I hit a wall. I had reached a plateau and got complacent. I did not feel challenged and when that happens, I lose interest.

Truth be told—and if this is not the venue, I don't know what is—I have always had a perverse desire to fail. If you look at everything I have done, from my first time in a kitchen while I was at Franklin & Marshall College, to graduate school at Columbia University, to starting a catering business, to Kuteeram, Indigo, our delis right through Neel and Tote, I've thrown myself into situations I had no business getting into. Faced with daunting challenges, I seem to push myself to the brink of failure. Then I sort of wake up at the last minute and say to myself, 'I cannot let myself fail.'

I confess that I tend to bite off more than I can chew. More than I *think* I can chew. Then my competitive instinct kicks in and, rather than choke on my own meal, I rise to every occasion. It may be linked to a fear of success but I truly think I try to tempt failure. I make myself face—and then face down—my insecurities. I acknowledge my abilities, including overcoming self-doubt, and eventually not only master something but excel at it. I set benchmarks, then I put my money where my mouth is.

I push myself into difficult spaces and then manoeuvre—or squirm—my way out, recognizing that serious study will help me. Many times it was studying the ledgers that forced me to success. When the books were telling me that bankruptcy was a real possibility, I pushed myself. Yes, like many Maharashtrians, I'm a good number-crunching clerk. And that definitely has helped me over the years. So has my tendency towards OCD behaviour. If I want to play amateur psychologist, I may posit that this has something to do with my early years of stuttering. I was too shy and embarrassed to participate in social intercourse. So I became an observer, not a partaker. I could not control my speech and I could not control others' reactions—thus my obsessive-compulsive focus on controlling everything else.

With Indigo, we'd passed all those challenges in spades. But now I was witnessing a lack of creativity in my own product: Indigo's plates followed the same pattern of protein, starch and vegetables. Our plates and plating used the same colours. Same, same, same. We were becoming dated. There was no growth. Woody Allen, in the great 1977 film *Annie Hall*, said about relationships—'A relationship, I think, is like a shark, you know? It has to constantly move forward or it dies. And I think what we got on our hands is a dead shark.' I can say restaurants and relationships have a lot in common.

In hindsight, it might have required little more than re-plating, modernizing. Or I could have been clever and rather than be 'the chef', I could have paid more attention to growing the business.

The irony is, given the psychological profile I offer of myself, if Indigo and our other restaurants had fallen behind, I might have stepped up, gotten a second wind.

Around this time, we were experiencing an economic boom in India. This was 2008 and the financial crisis in the US that led to a major international recession was yet to trickle down to countries like ours. Therefore, there was a spate of companies buying and selling restaurants. Why restaurants? Because owning a restaurant was and still is a sign of prestige, something you brag about at cocktail parties, yet know very little about managing—not to mention know very little about what good cuisine is.

The Tote restaurant project was well into construction at this point, and getting expensive to sustain. We were running up a slippery slope trying to keep it and the company moving forward. Had we bitten off more than we could chew? Probably. No, actually I'd say, definitely. It was clearly time to start looking at taking on some serious bucks to fund our quantum expansion. Our board knew this and started hunting around for private equity, or a fund to either buy in or buy us out. The late Homi Aibara—of the hospitality consulting firm Mahajan and Aibara, a member of our board since inception, a dear friend and my business mentor—helped steer us in creating a kickass business plan and a valuation that was gold. We met with several private equity funds and in early 2008 were introduced to (names changed) Harry Sabs of LC Ventures, based in Singapore, who was ready to invest through their Mauritius investment arm, LI Holdings. We received a term sheet from him with an offer to purchase 60 per cent of deGustibus Hospitality for

₹75 crore—which meant a ₹125 crore overall valuation (or $28 million at the time). Not too shabby.

Once that was accepted and executed, the painful but necessary process of due diligence began—on both sides—that detailed vetting of purchaser and buyer to make sure everything's copacetic, with no hidden skeletons. Simultaneously, we also completed a very aggressive business plan and expansion programme. Their due diligence came to an end, as did ours, and the complex buy-in, which involved some of my shareholders exiting in addition to a fresh equity injection into the company, was well into negotiation and finalization. Everything up to this point was moving along swimmingly well, and we even started rolling out our expansion in anticipation of the funds coming in. The Tote construction, which had slowed to a snail's pace, went into overdrive, as did the development of a massive, multi-cuisine catering kitchen in Sewri for Moveable Feast. We were also adding more Indigo Delis. Harry wanted us to continue the rollout, even though Tote was looking like it would become more expensive than we imagined and we hadn't even signed yet.

Big mistake ... and then things started getting really weird.

By the end of June 2008, as we hit the slow season, our revenues started drying up. We were rolling out our expansion on internal accruals rather than fresh capital—never a good idea, I can say, with the wisdom of hindsight. We started having cash flow problems. Harry offered to tide us over with ₹2 crore ICD (inter-corporate deposit), which was to be repaid when our deal would close in the next month or so. That cheque bounced. Then, over the next couple of months, through the middle of August, we had several other infusions of funds from Harry Sabs and his companies that never actually came into our account. We saw numerous bank transfer documents, scans of telegraphic transfer advices, emails from bankers and a ton of other correspondence from Hong Kong, Singapore, New Delhi and Pune, relating to these fund transfers. Nothing. Bupkis. Harry Houdini Sabs had made many, many crores vanish into thin air. Were all the documents he sent us magnificent works of Photoshop art? Maybe. We can't be sure, but it seems incredible that none of the funds ever hit our account. Oh, we did once receive $100 from some unknown silk company in Hong Kong at the same time as we were to have received a transfer of $7,00,000 by way of share application funds. We later discovered the $100 came from (what else?) another Harry company, and when queried, he said he'd sent that as a trace to understand why the $7,00,000 hadn't made it to our account earlier.

We were bleeding. Badly. By mid-August we started borrowing crores of rupees in ICDs from the market at exorbitant rates of interest to keep us afloat. Our dialogue with Harry continued. We wanted to believe. We had to. We were even introduced to his backers from Natixis Bank in Paris and others from Hong Kong on a visit to Mumbai. That gave us confidence. He continued to give us money from his other associate companies, but the cheques continued bouncing or were withheld for one reason or the other. Through all this, we still inched closer and closer to executing the final deal, which gave us still more (false) hope. He was finding it difficult to organize bridge finance but would have no problem closing the deal and making the final investment. That's what he told us and given company law and banking regulations that existed for foreign investment at the time, it was somewhat plausible, though not probable. We continued to give him the benefit of the doubt.

Finally, in mid-September of that year, we were ready to sign the first part of the deal with Harry. Yesssss! Finally we could shout, 'Show me the money!' Our patience had paid off. But then nothing happened. He continued assuring us with one hair-brained scheme after another that he was making arrangements for the money and that he was still keen to raise the funds, but internationally the financial markets were collapsing. We realized his funding had dried up. He was now scrambling to make good, but he didn't come clean. He should have been honest with us, but he never said a thing. We continued to borrow from the market as we bled out.

Then out of the blue, towards the end of October, we suddenly received a random transfer of ₹2.75 crore from Harry without any supporting paperwork. Odd, we thought at the time, but we took it nonetheless. We eventually executed and signed all our agreements with two associate companies of his, LI Holdings Pte Ltd and IH Concepts Pte Ltd, in mid November, once we'd completed all the 'conditions precedent' to close them. Everything went into escrow with the lawyers till such time payment was made. Again, nothing came. We were screwed!

In early December we received a legal notice from the MD of a company in Goa that Harry's LI Holdings had bought into earlier. Apparently, after buying into them, he'd withdrawn close to ₹14 crore from the company and given us the ₹2.75 crore from that. Sorry as I felt for their MD and their company, we'd received the money directly from Harry, so we really had nothing to do with them. 'Money,' Homi Aibara always said, 'is fungible.'

Then Harry made one final bid in an attempt to see our failed transaction go through. His own funds may have dried up and his investment companies unable to raise the money, but he still managed to drop a bombshell on us. He'd just been appointed joint head of the private equity division of a very large blue-chip private equity fund that he'd convinced to buy into deGustibus instead. Wow! The private equity company was a wholly owned subsidiary of a large Indian conglomerate with a stellar reputation, so we were thrilled. To seal the deal, Harry arranged a lunch at Indigo with me, several key execs from the growth fund and himself. Which I dutifully set up.

However, Harry did not show up. Red flag, right? Well into lunch, the conversation was all small talk, about family, food, the state of the economy in general terms. Now I was getting antsy.

'So ladies and gentleman,' I cleared my throat, 'are we here for a social gathering or to talk business?'

They all looked at me, like, 'What are you talking about?'

'I was under the impression that this was an introductory session, considering you are planning to buy into deGustibus.'

'Where did you hear that?' one of them responded.

'From Harry Sabs.'

At the mention of his name, I espied glances amongst them, to the effect of, 'Harry again?'

I relayed Harry's version of reality as he explained it to us. They said none of it was true. That was the moment I realized Harry was a complete fraud, that he had forged all the wire transfers and that he was a master storyteller.

'Well, now that I understand, please do enjoy lunch,' I offered. Quite civilized of me, I must say. After all, they and I had both been duped.

A few days later I got a call from those same men, who asked me to come in to their office. It was their turn to learn more about the machinations of Mr Sabs, to comprehend how deep a hole he had potentially dug for them. It turned out Harry had worked a similar non-existent deal with another F&B company in Delhi after joining the blue-chip company fund. They were looking to hive off a couple of operational divisions of theirs in Gujarat and London; and Harry was keen to acquire them. Without the money in hand, he did what he did best—he forged his bosses' signatures on letters of intent showing that the blue-chip company fund was backing him to take those operations over. As luck would have it, the F&B company's owner knew the MD of the fund and called him when he saw that they were backing the deal. That's how everything blew up in Harry's face. I believe the man is a pathological liar. In fact, so did the courts of law: he did two or three years behind bars for his fraudulent behaviour courtesy the conglomerate, who prosecuted him before he landed in jail.

Meanwhile we needed an investor—and fast. We were truly close to going belly up. The entire senior team hadn't taken salaries for almost six months. It was getting very stressful. We were extremely aware that there were some 500-plus families who depended on us for their livelihoods. These loyal employees held on for dear life while we tried to look on the bright side ... any bright side. But I saw few.

A childhood buddy put me in touch with the owners of one of India's leading companies. (I will be discreet about naming names in this sordid tale.) I'll call it the Power Company. Its owner—Senior—was known as a hardcore businessman; it was his son—Junior—who wanted to buy in and own Indigo, to give him added coolness and social status among the city's foodies.

We did our financial diligence of the Power Company and it all checked out. However, let me just add an aside to wannabe entrepreneurs selling their company: don't ever forget to also do your diligence about your investors as people, as potential partners, because it really is like marrying someone. Get to know your investors as individuals. Deep pockets do not necessarily make for a good marriage. And a prenup can only cover so much.

It turned out that the law firm the Power Owners used was the same one that Harry Sabs had used when we signed with him. So the Power Owners already had a readymade shareholders' agreement for the buy-in. Negotiations went pretty quickly and were quite lopsided in their favour. The Power Owners held a gun to our heads and squeezed the trigger slowly. They knew we were desperate to prevent deGustibus from imploding post the Harry Sabs fiasco, so they offered us a fraction of what we were actually worth. We'd lost a ton of value as a company during our expansion in a time when the Indian financial markets were collapsing, in 2009, and they squeezed us for all they were worth. We had no choice, no alternative buyer, so we had to sell out to the Power Owners and Power Company. Cheap. It was June 2009 when they bought in.

Initially Junior and I saw eye to eye, more or less, as I began the painful process of slowly turning things around. But that changed pretty quickly. We had the funds to finally complete the Tote project, and that went into overdrive. By the end of August it opened to much fanfare and we threw a huge party for almost a thousand people to announce it. It rocked from day one. The Mumbai Lakmé Fashion Week happened a month later in mid-September that year. Its grand finale party, which is held at the end of the week, is a big Mumbai event for the who's who of the city. Junior decided he wanted the company to host the party at Tote. I was against it and explained to him that it would send the wrong message if we burned a ton of money to host a party when people hadn't gotten paid in months. I reasoned the timing was wrong and it would kill the employees' morale. He didn't get it, and was insistent on holding the party regardless, saying he'd fund it in his personal capacity instead. That made no sense and I was against that too, explaining to him that as a new owner, it would be wiser for him to use those funds to pay the employees' salaries instead of throwing it away on a party. We were discussing this at one of our weekly meetings with Junior and the Power Company's CFO, when things got really heated. The CFO turned to me and said, 'If Junior wants the party, you'll have the party … you answer to me.' I told him to fuck off, when suddenly Junior turned around and snapped, 'I own this company, I own you, so you'll do as we say!' That was it. I stormed out of that meeting.

Things started deteriorating; my relationship with Junior became strained. I finally had to have a long private meeting with his dad, who realized that things had gotten quite tense with Junior and me, and suggested I deal only with Senior from then on. That suited me just fine and I thought, *Finally, enter the voice of reason.* But blood, I soon discovered, runs thicker than any other liquid. As time went on, it became clear that Senior was in control of the purse strings and every decision. He was an old-school businessman—cutthroat and ruthless.

Now, there was another character in this almost Shakespearean tragedy. He will go by the fictitious name of Benedict here. Benedict had joined deGustibus many years earlier as a manager and risen through the ranks. I remember when Malini and I first interviewed him, he'd said he saw himself as a director on the deGustibus board in five years. That statement should have set off warning bells, but I'm not sure the full meaning of his ambition really sank in back then. Naively, we eventually made him a senior executive a couple of years after the Power Owners and Power Company bought in, and thereby created our own monster—the Caliban in our own little adaptation of *The Tempest*, good ole Will's play about magic, betrayal, love and forgiveness. I am still working on the forgiveness part.

Benedict saw an opportunity with the Power Owners. He realized pretty early on that a rift was quickly forming between us and them, and jumped ship. Here was his chance. They had deep pockets and, as majority shareholders, controlled the board and the company too. Benedict became the eyes and ears for the Power Owners in deGustibus, and reported everything we did operationally back to them. I was still the managing director but in name only. My MD wings were clipped and any strategic or operational decisions I made that Benedict didn't concur with wound up being vetoed or quashed by the Power Owners. At first I couldn't understand why this was happening on a regular basis, but I soon figured out it was Benedict's way or the highway.

The turning point really came when we opened Indigo Deli in Bandra. We'd been evaluating the Deli's expansion into other parts of Mumbai and were looking at a couple of spaces. Unbeknownst to Malini and me, Benedict had pretty much finalized negotiations on a Bandra space with the blessings of Senior. He waited till the two of us were travelling away from Bombay to sign the lease. We only learned about the Bandra lease signing a day later. I blew up Benedict over a phone call for operating behind our backs. He apparently shed some tears over that and decided that from there on in, his allegiance lay solely with the Power Owners.

One of the demands I'd made when the Power Owners bought in and that Senior had agreed to was for them to release my parents' flat, which my parents had offered as collateral since 1999 when deGustibus took its first bank loans to fund the building of Indigo. The same security was used over and over again for ten years, each time the company needed bank funding or to raise debt for anything. Senior had promised to do this but requested that it not form part of the shareholder's agreement we signed with them. We were all newly-weds back then and I had no reason to distrust or suspect his intentions, so I let it go at that. In 2011 my elderly parents decided they wanted to sell their flat and we realized that the lien had not been removed yet. I raised the matter with Senior at a board meeting and to my horror he denied having ever promised that. Over the better part of that year I continuously pushed to see this through, but to no avail. Finally, a year later and to squeeze us, he said the company would be happy to release the lien on their flat, provided Malini and I came up with the ₹1 crore fixed deposit to give the bank as collateral to securitize the company's outstanding debt. We didn't have the funds and he did, but he forced us to raise them knowing that I had to free up the flat. We eventually did, but with great financial strain on us.

In early 2012 at a board meeting, Malini opposed Senior somewhat vociferously, which didn't sit well with his old-school male chauvinistic side. No one, let alone a woman, had ever stood up to him nor contradicted him in a minuted forum such as a board meeting. It just wasn't done, and in fact Senior always preferred to meet before board meetings to iron out any argument or disagreement that might arise beforehand. Soon thereafter, Senior in his capacity as chairman relieved Malini from her position as director of marketing, branding and communications and cut off her salary too. He offered no reason to her for this decision, which was taken unilaterally, arbitrarily and without justification.

Then Senior took away our house rent allowance that the company had always paid for. He'd orchestrated for it to be a board decision that he could hide behind, so it didn't appear he was doing it in his personal capacity. The bitter irony was that the decision to no longer cover our rent was made by the very directors for whom the company was paying house rent—Benedict and another, whom I shall call Arnold, included. They'd turned another screw, squeezing the life force out of Malini and me. We'd lost her income stream and now had to cover our house rent too. At the same board meeting, Senior also tabled a resolution that put him in charge of all financial and management decisions of the company. In a board controlled seven to two by the Power Owners, it passed without much discussion, other than strong protests from Malini and me that were brushed aside. Our shareholder's agreement prevented them from firing me, but they'd begun neutralizing me (or is that neutering me?) instead.

Something had to change and real quick. We had to get rid of the Power Owners, cut off others' heads and restore some semblance of what the company we'd built actually stood for. We began conversations with Patu Keswani of Lemon Tree Hotels, who was in an acquisition mood, to take over deGustibus, buy out the Power Owners and put us back in the driver's seat. I was put on a very steep 'mergers and acquisitions' learning curve and was being coached on how to speak to and push Senior to sell out, at favourable terms to Lemon Tree to boot. In a nutshell, I said I was fed up with things and was going to leave deGustibus to join the Lemon Tree group unless the Power Owners sold out to them 100 per cent instead. I'd reached the end of my tether, I postured. We could no longer work together and one of us had to leave. I made it very clear to Senior that we'd finally reached that agree-to-disagree point in our relationship and cautioned (threatened?) him that our irreconcilable differences would rapidly drive the company into the ground and kill his investment. His exit to Lemon Tree was actually a good deal for him and would free him up from the disproportionate time he was spending learning the hospitality business at the expense of his many hundred-crore energy and power business. He actually agreed. The price was set, and the paperwork began.

'Shit happens,' it is said. And so too in this case. Just as things were moving along swimmingly, we ran into a problem with the lease of the Indigo Deli at Colaba and it stood to be shut down. The Bombay Port Trust, which owns 90 per cent of property in the Fort and Colaba area, including the building which housed the Deli, suddenly decided to move the courts and serve eviction notices to almost all their tenants over some archaic rent suit that had been stagnant in the courts for decades. Senior said they'd build another Deli across the road on a war footing, and at their cost entirely if the original one was forced to close. They just didn't want Patu's valuation to change, or at least by much, anyway. However, the Colaba Indigo Deli was a cash cow and Patu decided to devalue the company and lower his offer drastically because of its imminent closure. Understandable, but he devalued it way too much and refused to listen to reason. He gambled that Senior was by this point desperate to sell and would fold regardless. Big mistake. For him and, more importantly, for me. The deal fell through and things went back to the way they were before all the posturing started. With one difference. I never lived up to all my threats of leaving and walking away, but ate humble pie instead and stayed on. The Colaba Deli stayed open too.

Senior was now pissed with me and the bloodless coup began. Benedict was made a director on the board—one more in the Power Owner's camp. What transpired over the next few years was a methodical and calculated attack on Malini's and my positions in the company. It got ugly. They came at us on multiple fronts—through boardroom manoeuvring and control, by burdening and stretching us financially on a personal level and by a steady undermining of our ability to run or give the company direction. As frustrating and debilitating as it was for us, in hindsight I have to say it was sheer evil genius. The things you learn.

It started soon after the Lemon Tree deal fell through. The first thing was the creation of a ₹15 crore convertible debenture issue. Senior knew very well that Malini and I wouldn't be able to subscribe to this, so a dilution was on the cards for us. As managing director and promoter, I still had veto powers and objected vehemently to this mechanism. Modifying the shareholding pattern from a fresh equity call was the last and least favourable option available to us, but they'd made it a top priority for obvious reasons. Then something even more onerous and alarming started happening: minutes of board meetings began circulating that were full of holes and inaccuracies, clearly fudged. Objections and oppositions from Malini and me were conveniently being softened, if not ignored totally. I used to edit and sign off on the minutes before sending them out to the board, but that was now being handled by Senior. I caught discussion items that were totally fabricated, and then, on several occasions, even fictitious meetings. I brought all of this to the attention of Senior and the board, but little happened. I developed an aggression at these board meetings, lashing out constantly to protect what few rights Malini and I still had in the company that we'd founded and built. The onslaught was relentless.

The head office was moved from where it was, near the Mahalaxmi Race Course, to a vacant old office space of the Power Owners at Nariman Point. I was against the move, as we'd lose more of what little operational autonomy we had left. 'It's a cost-saving decision because it's our own premises,' I was told. I couldn't argue with that until I found out Senior was, in fact, charging the company rent!

I was going over our annual human resource budgets in early 2013 when I noticed that the entire company organizational hierarchy had been rearranged. The buck now stopped with Benedict rather than me as the MD. I was conveniently sidestepped; the marketing and PR team that I controlled (post Malini) now reported to him and heck, so too did all the senior chefs in the company.

'There's a mistake in your org chart,' I told our HR head. 'You need to fix this before we submit the budgets for approval.' He looked at me kinda sheepishly and said, 'Senior made these changes together with Benedict and has also already passed the budget.'

About the same time, Indigo made it to the Number 28 spot on the San Pellegrino 50 Best Restaurants in Asia for the 2013 Awards List. Pretty amazing for a fourteen-year-old restaurant. The awards are held in Singapore, and are a huge international media and industry event with chef interactions, lunches, dinners, etc. The entire team at Indigo was ecstatic and super proud. I immediately decided to take a few chefs to Singapore to attend the awards, and to meet and interact with fellow chefs from around the world. We were also planning on eating at several restaurants in Singapore to give our chefs an insight into new culinary trends. We have an annual budgeted amount for such 'exposure & R&D trips' for our chefs to keep them abreast of what's happening internationally, and this excursion was within the approved budget. We'd been budgeting for these trips every year, promising our chefs such 'study' excursions, but hadn't undertaken any for several years. The senior chefs were frustrated that the company was doing nothing for their growth, while their peers in other companies were doing these things every year and growing as craftsmen.

So, I made all the bookings and informed the chefs we were going. There was much excitement and anticipation. I went to chat with Senior about several matters and mentioned to him (not asked) that Indigo had made the prestigious list, that it was a huge honour and that I was taking some of our chefs for the awards and to spend a few days in Singapore. He got upset and said no, he wasn't approving the expense. I said that there was nothing to approve as it was already budgeted. I thought he would be happy and proud of the achievement, but instead he just admonished me for increasing costs. I then offered to pay for the entire trip personally to respect his wishes to curtail company expenses, since I had already made all the bookings and informed the chefs about the trip. He got upset and behaved like that was a personal insult to him. Eventually, to keep the peace, I cancelled the trip entirely, to the total disappointment and demotivation of the chefs. I also lost a fair amount of money personally since I'd charged the non-refundable flights and hotel bookings to my credit card.

The company decided to start looking at spaces for setting up Indigo in New Delhi and expand the Indigo Deli footprint in Mumbai too. Benedict was tasked with the job and identified Deli spaces in the Inorbit Mall in Malad, and another one in Andheri. Except for doing a second flagship Indigo in Delhi, I objected to all the others, as the demographic fit was wrong for the Delis. It didn't matter. To circumvent my veto, they simply passed a resolution denying me authority to negotiate or sign the leases for any of these projects. Actually it was more clever than that. Rather than openly deny me the authority to drive these projects, they deviously opted for Benedict and Arnold to helm them instead. Same result, though, and they were covered by plausible deniability too.

In our ongoing development of the Indigo project in Delhi, several of us had taken turns to travel to Delhi in connection with finalizing commercials, overseeing design and to study the market. Benedict went to Delhi one weekend to meet with the landlord. I wasn't aware he was going and when asked, Arnold said it was to finalize some commercials and continue keeping the landlord engaged. When Benedict returned, I asked him how the trip went and he casually said, 'All okay ... and by the way, the landlord is coming to Bombay with his architects on Friday to show them our outlets and restaurant interiors' and would I keep myself free for them? Without any other info, I was called that Friday to join them at the Deli in Colaba for lunch. When I arrived, only the architects were there. The landlord had gone to meet Senior with Benedict and sign the agreement for Indigo New Delhi. I was neither aware that the agreement had been finalized, nor that it was being signed. It was all orchestrated to keep me away from interacting with the landlord while he was in Bombay, before it was signed. The landlord had agreed to Indigo because of the relationship Malini and I had with him from many years earlier. We were the ones who first broached the subject with him and introduced him to the company. To be kept in the dark on this was humiliating. Furthermore, they had even decided on the project architects without consulting me or Malini, who had always driven the design of all our restaurants.

The Indigo Deli project in Delhi went much the same way, with well-orchestrated minimal involvement and minimal inputs from me. Arnold gave me the layout for the space and I began working on the kitchen design with Chef JD, the corporate exec chef of the Indigo Delis. The kitchen area was an oddly shaped, inadequate space, and JD and I attempted several layout iterations to design the kitchen. This took time, yet Arnold decided to ignore my efforts and rush through a design because of the pressure of project timelines from the board. My inputs were no longer asked for and the project was completed.

The kitchen was poorly designed and incapable of supporting the number of anticipated covers and restaurant operations. There was inadequate space to work, hygiene was atrocious and working conditions terrible. Chef JD was extremely frustrated and disillusioned with the way we were approaching all our new projects—banging them out without thinking through operations with a long-term view to sustainability or quality. Once the Deli in New Delhi opened, we had many issues dealing with food production and quality, which could have been avoided had more thought and planning gone into developing the project correctly.

We opened the Delhi outlet without a full contingent of staff. In fact, we had only hired 50 per cent of the required, sanctioned service team when we opened to the public. No training had been undertaken at all. This all took its toll. We received a tremendous amount of adverse publicity and complaints about shoddy service, food quality and poor hygiene from the public at large on various social media sites.

Morale in the company, and especially among the senior management team, was at an all-time low. They were well aware of what was being done to me by the board and the Power Owners and were dismayed and upset by it. In an attempt to protect themselves against a possible exodus of our disgruntled senior team, Senior and the board pushed through an ESOP (employee stock ownership/option plan), thinking that they'd buy loyalty by dangling a carrot to them. Oh, did I mention that I had no idea this was happening, or that it was even finally executed in my absence? The team saw the ESOP for what it really was—a heartless, desperate buyout of their loyalties. During the senior staff appraisals that I conducted that year, everyone had much to say about where they saw us headed as a company. It wasn't pretty. Chef JD wrote me an email voicing the concerns of most of the staff:

> ... I very strongly feel that we as a team have stopped learning from our mistakes. We hire the wrong people, burden them with responsibilities they're not capable of shouldering and then lament when obvious and predictable results begin to show. Our strength today lies no longer in operations but in crisis management ... firefighting or whatever we chose to call it. We have the audacity to venture into a new city and open a restaurant with less than a third of its manpower in place. With its entire crew entirely untrained ... Something has got to give ... We are gradually being riddled by these fissures ... because today these weak structures have become the norm ...

Then, as if the dysfunction and sabotage weren't enough, in January 2014 Benedict sent out an email announcement about doing another branch of Neel with an attached banquet space in the suburbs of Andheri and called for a board meeting to discuss the project. At this meeting, the viability and merits of the project were tabled but it was evident that the decision to undertake it had been pre-discussed and approved (yup, you guessed it) without my knowledge. The meeting was a farce. I raised concerns about our staff's morale and state of mind, especially our Chef Mukhtar who was already extremely disillusioned with the way Neel was being run at Tote. I had had many meetings with him and learned he was tired with the lack of training, attention to detail, inadequate staffing, poor maintenance and general lack of support for the quality-driven restaurant he and I were trying to create at that venue. He mentioned that he had had other offers and was considering leaving. I persuaded him to stay on, with the assurance that we would rectify matters. I also questioned the quality of the physical space in Andheri and suggested that it was probably inadequate and not befitting the style and design of restaurants for which our company was known. My concerns were rudely shot down and brushed away. The project proceeded.

Chef Nitin and I spent many hours working on the kitchen drawings and layout for this project. It was our eventual conclusion that the space was not suited to support or be developed as both an à la carte restaurant and a banqueting facility. The kitchen and back of house designs for these two formats have highly different requirements and the space was inadequate to support both. Nitin was concerned that the operational plan Benedict and Arnold decided on to support this kitchen's production remotely from the Moveable Feast kitchen was extremely risky and not advisable. The MF kitchen was already operating beyond its capability and under extreme pressure during the seasonal months. Since the Andheri kitchen was too small to have the required stores, butchery, prep, bakery and cold room facilities for banqueting (and a restaurant too) it had been envisioned that the majority of these functions would happen at the main MF kitchen and the nearly finished product would be transported to Andheri every day. Nitin was doubtful about being able to handle this additional load and maintaining food quality and hygiene standards.

At a meeting in August, I told the board that, based on what Nitin and I had discerned, it was inadvisable and risky to undertake both operations at the Andheri space. Arnold and Benedict said that they did not believe my assessment was accurate and *they* were confident of getting the kitchen design layouts done to support both operations.

The kitchen's design was eventually loosely based on a layout I had done much earlier, but much of the space allocation for back-of-house functions were clearly forced, inadequate and not thought through. The restaurant and banqueting space opened, never took off, never turned a profit and eventually closed within the year.

During this time, Indigo in Delhi was being built, along with the other restaurants in Mumbai. It was severely delayed and ironically, we opened the Indigo Deli in the Ambience Mall in Vasant Kunj well before we opened the flagship Indigo. A perfect example of what not to do when expanding to a new city. You don't start with a lesser concept when you need to make a grand entry. I had been travelling back and forth between Mumbai and Delhi for many months and raised some serious concerns about the way and the rate at which we were expanding as a company and the impact it was having on our present operations. In an open letter to Senior and the board, I underscored many of these issues.

Building value was paramount for us as a company, but it could not happen at the expense of existing operations, nor in ways that affected our brand and reputation in the industry as a quality-driven, market-leading restaurant company. We'd taken on too many projects simultaneously without adequate project management or project implementation capabilities. Site supervisors and managers were constantly shuttling from location to location between Mumbai and Delhi, leaving sites unattended or unsupervised in their absence. There were instances when either no representatives were present at site, or we'd left the site to be managed by unqualified workers who had neither the capability nor understanding to oversee the project. This resulted in many instances where work was badly, carelessly or wrongly done and had to be undone or redone. The poor management of our Delhi site had also resulted in theft of material because of inadequate security and supervision. Needless to say, it was a waste of money, effort and time.

In all projects, it is important that there be a single point coordinator who interacts with all contracted external agencies. In this case, anyone and everyone seemed to be taking decisions. Equipment was wrongly purchased on occasion. Decisions having a direct impact on the overall design of the space were made by those who had no business doing so. This again resulted in us having to undo or redo certain work. As we developed new projects, we should have been absolutely clear about the roles, functions and responsibilities of various people entrusted to deliver them, and it was equally important that those people focused only on paying attention to their responsibility area. This was not happening.

Important as it was to deliver our projects on time and within budget, the creation of beautifully designed spaces, built with attention to detail and quality, was equally necessary. The motivation to complete a project cannot be driven only by budget and timelines, if to do so means deviating from the basic principle of delivering a well-designed product of quality. We cannot and must not compromise on the design and build quality simply because we find ourselves going over budget or falling behind on deadlines.

Our new project management and implementation team was the same team responsible for the ongoing maintenance and upkeep of all our existing restaurants in Mumbai. Everyone was pressured and occupied by our new projects, and we faltered repeatedly with the maintenance part. We could not afford to have one restaurant suffer at the expense of the other. But it was happening, and much too frequently.

Manpower was also an issue. It was difficult to find skilled and capable staff for all our restaurants. We had been hiring, but I sometimes questioned the quality of those hires—whether many had been selected merely to fill positions, or whether they really had the necessary profile for the job. We were also removing people from our existing restaurant operations to buttress inadequate staff in the new restaurants, leaving manpower holes behind. Indigo in Mumbai, for example, was several people short in the kitchen. Some had been transferred to Delhi; others had left because they were being overworked due to a major staff shortfall. I was concerned about the pressure on and stress levels of the existing staff during the busy and demanding high season, which was to fall upon us pretty soon. We could not afford to have any more people leave.

Our Indigo Delhi opening was probably the most important undertaking for us as a company since we first opened Indigo in Mumbai in 1999. Expectations would be very high, and we would be scrutinized and judged by an eager and highly critical public. It was vital for us to be impeccable, thoroughly prepared and absolutely ready before we opened , without compromise. I was concerned that as we neared the completion of this project, we continued to recall people to Mumbai from Delhi, leaving the construction and finishing unsupervised. There were still many issues that needed correcting. The final finishing, which is the most critical phase of any project, was entirely ignored and instead of having the project team in Delhi finish and deliver what we'd set out to do, they'd all been recalled to Mumbai to attend to our other projects. This was just wrong.

Needless to say, none of this went down very well with the powers that be.

Chef Nitin, the other chefs and I spent a lot of time developing a new, sophisticated, world-class menu for Indigo in Mumbai and New Delhi. We revamped our old, outdated style of food. Between 2012 and 2014, we were repeatedly recognized for this, both nationally and internationally, winning several awards and accolades, including making the San Pellegrino Asia's 50 Best list in 2013. No small feat. Yet I was accused of not having turned Indigo's food around, and of not doing an adequate job on the New Delhi Indigo menu, at least according to the 'expert opinion' of Benedict, et al.

Benedict and Arnold had convinced Senior and the board that the menu we were developing was way too 'advanced and sophisticated' for the average Delhiite and that it would bomb badly.

'The need of the hour,' Benedict said in a board meeting, 'is for us to be safe and minimize risk in Delhi. We should serve the tried-and-tested best-of-Indigo dishes from the last fourteen years.'

Never mind that Delhi, as India's capital, had an enormous expat population with all the embassies and missions located there. Never mind that it probably had the highest transiting international tourist traffic in the country too, not to mention a wealthy, well-travelled, local gourmand cognoscenti. According to Benedict and Arnold, the only thing that would sell in Delhi was kukkad or chicken ... in any shape or form. I fought this tooth and nail relentlessly.

'If you really wanted to be absolutely safe and have minimum risk, why do Western food at all?' I argued. 'Chinese or Indian is better, and certainly safer and risk-free. Indigo has always been about its food, and not about doing what everyone else did. My reputation is at stake, and I'd never let food that wasn't "correct" be served at any of our outlets, especially a new flagship restaurant in New Delhi.'

No dice. I could see they weren't buying it.

It became more and more clear that their leadership had zero to do with food and everything to do with cutting corners, less about hospitality and more about profit. I was reaching my boiling point. Then came the moment—like the *aha* moment I'd had in graduate school when I knew academia was not for me.

I was up in Delhi, overseeing the development, testing and tasting of new dishes when the sous chef asked, 'Why are we doing this? It's not on the menu any more.'

Rather than look caught off guard, I mumbled, 'Oh sure, I forgot.'

I immediately called Nitin. 'WTF?'

'I didn't know how to tell you,' he said, falling silent, like a kid caught with his hand in the cookie jar.

'Tell me *what*?'

'They called me in and told me they have created a new menu based on all the bestselling dishes on earlier Indigo menus. They told me they would fire me if I told you and did not implement their menu. They decided that since you weren't willing to revisit the menu or listen to their opinions about what would work in New Delhi, Benedict would guide me on the food.'

I asked, 'Why didn't you tell me? How could you do this to me after all that we'd built together and achieved this last decade?' Silence.

That was the moment I knew it was over for me. Like that moment at Columbia, my spirit was finally broken in an instant and that took quite a while to accept. I saw through the veil; on the other side was deception, hypocrisy—everything we wanted Indigo and our whole deGustibus brand not to represent. I was ready to relinquish my hold on the baby Malu and I had borne in 1999, rather than have a product go out that did not meet our purposefully high standards.

Now began the drip, drip, drip. But a lot more had to trickle before complete lights out. The last two years of expansion *had* needed funding, and Senior had funded most of it from his own deep pockets as loans to the company. The earlier debenture issue never materialized. Here's the thing, though: except for the main Indigo in New Delhi, I wasn't really up for doing any of the other Indigo Deli projects Benedict, Arnold and the rest wanted to rush into. The fit was totally wrong and I kept opposing them. So, when Senior and the Board suddenly decided to double the authorized capital of the company to ₹10 crore, and approve a compulsorily convertible debenture issue to fund it, I again opposed that. I had to. It would have a critical material impact on our shareholding in the company. There was no way Malini and I had the funds to participate in the rights issue, so a forced dilution was inevitable. The fact was that as a company, we were in this mess because we'd wasted money on failed or poorly thought-out projects. The irony was that, taken out of context, my constant opposition to (their) projects could look like I was attempting to consciously and deliberately stall the company's growth. Never mind that they were bad projects and should not have been developed in the first place. I read that spot-on, as I soon discovered.

At a board meeting—we were having them quite frequently by this time—they sprung a real doozy on me. First, Senior announced that the company was moving banks and that I would no longer have signatory authority on the new accounts. He let that sink in and then continued, 'The board would discuss the report submitted by the *committee of directors on the role and contribution of the managing director in operations and projects of the company.'*

It was actually happening. I had been charged with 'ineptitude' and 'impeding progress' on business development—business development, mind you, that I was opposed to, based on my deeper understanding of restaurants and restaurant trends. Wow! I was stunned. They'd quietly laid the groundwork for building a case to have me removed as MD because of incompetence? They kept me isolated from projects they developed, away from most involvement in day-to-day operations and then, when things went south, they conveniently played their 'But you're the MD and responsible for the company' card. How low could they stoop?

I was given the sole copy to read. I said: 'I want a copy of this report so I can reply to it in detail.'

Senior had the gall to say, 'That will not be possible as it is a very sensitive document and in the interest of protecting the reputation of the company, we cannot give you a copy.'

'How do I reply and refute each of these allegations,' I countered, 'if I don't have them in front of me? You've made very serious accusations and allegations about my ability to continue as the MD in this company, yet you're denying me the opportunity to provide an accurate or fair rebuttal.'

He replied, 'Take as much time as you need here and now and make all the notes you want in order to reply to the report. But it cannot leave this room.'

I looked over at Arnold and Benedict, the authors of the report. There was total and uncomfortable silence in the room. They swallowed hard, refusing to meet my gaze.

Holding back tears now, I said, 'Really? Has it come to this? Look me in the eye and tell me to my face that you believe any of this so-called report you've fabricated?'

Not one of them said a word.

'In that case,' I said as I got up, shaking, 'I want my strong objection to this report and its contents minuted, and also that I reserve the right to reply to it in full.'

I stormed out of the meeting.

My mind was made up now. That was the last straw. I had to go. But first I needed some insurance.

I was up against people who inhabit corporate boardrooms. I was most at home in the kitchen. With all the corporate restructuring and manoeuvring, it was not surprising that I made a few mistakes. So Malini and I engaged some heavy-hitting legal counsel to guide and support us through it. We readied a lawsuit against Senior and the board, and I would have sued them for mismanagement and oppression before the Company Law Board, since my position and rights in the company were being seriously and systematically undermined and destroyed.

I trusted no one except for my personal assistant, who had worked for my father before me. But they'd fired her. They'd already removed our entire PR and marketing team. It was like snipers were picking off my troupe behind me.

It takes a lot for me to give up anything but I finally got to the point—the enough-is-enough point.

The next time I met Senior, I said, 'It's time. I want out.'

I spoke from my heart, not from any coached, manipulative strategizing mindset.

'You either buy me out at the current valuation or I will walk with zero in my pocket.'

He looked up, realizing that I was sincere and serious. I went on.

'I can't sleep at night. I have stress attacks. It's affecting the lives of my family. I need to get on with my life, find my next thing.'

That was it. Thus began a whole new and final chapter of our relationship: the haggle, that time-honoured tradition of negotiating the actual worth of something. In India the ritual has almost religious undertones. For four months or so, we went back and forth. I started at ₹120 crore—what we were actually worth at the time. He started at the figure they'd invested into the company five years earlier. Really?! Get real. We kept inching our way to a confluence, but it took time and a ton of strategic bargaining to get there. The one good thing to come of these 'highly confidential' meetings was as soon as they started, he agreed to stop all the corporate restructuring and game-playing to let me go peacefully. It's just as well because my petition for the Company Law Board was ready and I would have filed it had our negotiations broken down.

But after nearly five months, one day I went to his house and announced, 'I'm tired of this conversation. You're rich and powerful.

I am not. To you this is like a parlour game. But this is my life. I have a family to support, kids to send to college, a life. To you it means nothing. To me there is nothing else.'

I told him I would agree to all his terms, provided he closed the deal within a week. His reaction completely took me aback: he teared up. This tough guy, this unbending man whose heart, I was convinced, was made of the same hard metal as his machinery, broke down and cried. Why, I will never really know. That he realized he had destroyed me and finally felt some sympathy for me? That now, the hours we had spent together, which substituted for a social life for him, would be over and he would be left alone in his lonesomeness?

We shook hands in a warm atmosphere and I left. The next time I saw him, it was like that whole crying scene had never happened. He was the same unfeeling man he had been all along.

My only regret is that I didn't sell out two years earlier. On the other hand, I don't think of it as wasted time. I actually learned a lot in those several months he and I had regular meetings. If it wasn't in his office, it was at his home two to three times a week. I'd go over to his flat in the evenings and we'd shoot the shit for hours on end, over several whiskys—the two of us like buddies, catching up on life. Often, he'd ask me to stay over for dinner.

Those conversations enabled me to get inside the head of a hardcore businessman. He kept saying hospitality should play second fiddle to making money. I said hospitality is what makes you the money. In the beginning, his ridiculous statements would evoke my similarly but opposite ridiculous statements. But over time I found that rather than respond to his sometimes really offensive comments, if I probed deeper into his rationale, I learned a little more about the context that drove his opinions. This alone helped temper my reactive modus operandi. Walking a mile on his side of the street was instructive to me, something I could use in future dealings with this species of businessmen. I can also say it has taught me to take the time to listen first to people, to really 'hear' them.

But it also taught me—or reminded me—that I personally never want to end up like that.

At one point I told him, 'You know, we have spent more time getting to know each other in the last four months than we had in the last five years.' I said I thought that if we had spent more time preventing destruction and creating construction, we would not have ended up where we were.

What made me sad for him—and for people like him whom I have encountered in hospitality businesses and other spaces—was that here was someone so powerful in terms of wealth, yet poverty-stricken in terms we like to associate with being human.

Letting go of deGustibus, Indigo, the delis, our other outlets and everyone involved was the hardest thing I have ever done, or will do. This was my ego on the auction block here. I was inextricably tied to the business. It was my raison d'être for more than a decade and a half. How do you let go of that? It was like divorcing your own children.

Who would I be if not Rahul, chef–owner of Indigo?

Time—time off from being me—would provide the answers. In due time. But first I needed to rediscover the Rahul I had lost.

lemon
ricotta
pickled
goji berries
smoked
eggplant
coriander
scallion salsa

16: LIFE AFTER DEGUSTIBUS: MY ADULT GAP YEARS

'Get back, get back, get back to where you once belonged.'
— From 'Get Back' by John Lennon and Paul McCartney

SOMETIMES LIFE AND TIMING conspire to make one believe there is a Plan, that there are no coincidences and everything falls into place as and when it should. What happened next in my life reconfirmed that belief.

I was certainly burned out and more to the point, felt burned by the way things had deteriorated with deGustibus, leading to my signing a two-year non-compete agreement that essentially tied my hands from continuing to work as a chef ... for the time being, at least. By early March 2015, we'd announced the end of our run with Indigo, the delis and all of deGustibus.

The truth was, I needed a break and was more than willing to paste a neon sign—GONE FISHIN'—on my forehead. Malini was also fried to a crisp. As she put it, 'I was so stressed out—like a wire about to snap with everything.'

This was time to lick my wounds, let them heal and repair. My profession is one of the most demanding. There are a number of studies that show how my line of work takes a toll on body and mind. In one study by Unite, a British and Irish trade union, 44 per cent of chefs reported working between forty-eight and sixty hours a week, with 14 per cent working in excess of sixty hours each week. Asked whether they believe that their work hours impacted their health, 69 per cent answered yes. In addition to the physical demands of working in a kitchen, Unite found that poor mental well-being is common among chefs. As a result of working such long hours, 51 per cent of chefs suffer depression and 78 per cent have had an accident or near miss at work due to fatigue. Many chefs reported taking painkillers (56 per cent), alcohol (27 per cent), and other stimulants (41 per cent) to see them through a shift.[1]

I do not need to read studies to gauge the demands of the job; I was witness to it. On your feet much of the day, if not all, pulling cast-iron skillets from hangers over your head, whipping up creams, endless stirring of pots, all in heat that would melt the devil himself.

I do not take drugs, not for many, many years now, anyway; I'm not an alcoholic or a chain smoker, though I love splitting a great bottle of Spanish Mauro Tempranillo wine, sipping fine eighteen-year-old Aultmore whisky, or nursing the smoke out of a well-rolled Montecristo No. 2 cigar at night. But I have had some physical and mental struggles that add to the challenge ... all of which I seem to have risen above. For one, I have a hereditary medical condition known colloquially as tremors, but professionally as essential or familial tremors. It's a neurological disorder that causes involuntary and rhythmic shaking. It can affect almost any part of your body, but the trembling occurs most often in your hands—which is where I'm affected too. My mother's side of the family has had it. Essential tremor is usually not a dangerous condition and while it is often confused with Parkinson's disease, it is not the same.

For me, it's not terrible. You may notice it when I lift a cup or glass to my mouth. But strangely and miraculously, when I am cutting or prepping food, it does not have an effect. Perhaps my will power is stronger than my nervous system! I went through a battery of tests called nerve conductivity studies; they put electrodes in your arm and increase the strength of a current that passes through. Lovely experience. Akin to torture, I'd imagine. Anyway, they found nothing but my doctor, a wonderful Parsi lady, told me—off the record—that a shot of alcohol helps assuage the trembling, probably because it relaxes the nerves. So I tried it: I'll try any kind of prescription that requires me to imbibe a shot of vodka. Lo and behold, it does work.

Before I do any public speaking, I oftentimes have a nip or two and I am good to go.

Now, mental health is another issue altogether. That is, *my* mental health. I admit to bouts of depression. The World Health Organization estimates that globally, more than 300 million people suffer from depression, equivalent to 4.3 per cent of the world's population. In India, a National Mental Health Survey in 2015 showed one in twenty Indians suffers from this malaise.

This issue struck way too close to home with the death of Anthony Bourdain in 2018, who died by suicide reportedly due to depression. I was a huge (if jealous) fan of his, starting from his book *Kitchen Confidential*, published in 2000, continuing to his Travel Channel series *No Reservations* (2005–12) and then his even more wildly popular CNN series *Parts Unknown* (2013 up until his death), in which regional food traditions became simply a prism through which he showcased places, people and their lives. I could so relate to his work, since he had also started out cooking in New York restaurants about the same time I did. I shared his passion to find out the origin stories of the world's cuisine and, sadly, his fight against the demons in one's mind too.

To be clear, I have never even come close to considering suicide. But such a tragedy does give pause to a person in the same profession. Bourdain thought the profession 'attracts fringe elements, people for whom something in their lives has gone terribly wrong, maybe they didn't make it through high school, maybe they're running away from something'.

It is somewhat consoling to know I am not alone. And you are not alone either, if you wrestle with depression. Where does mine come from? Only the gods know, but I can guess that it has something to do with being a creative person who does not believe he is as good and 'creative' as everyone else says. This discrepancy between other people's perceptions of me and the reality that lives inside my thick head only serves to exacerbate my depression. It's like a psychic disconnect. I am left thinking either they are crazy (they are not) or I am (debatable). This, in turn, robs me of sleep, puts me under unnecessary stress, makes my immune system fight against the sleep deprivation and the downward cycle goes on and on. Self-doubt sucks. And again, since I come off as the bon vivant, the charismatic clown in the crowd, no one is the wiser.

But here I freely confess that sure, I have seen psychotherapists and psychiatrists for many years and continue to do so. These mental health professionals let me grapple out loud with my inner demons, and they do it without the judgement or baggage a close friend or family member would almost necessarily bring to the table. Every now and then they earn their big bucks with a question or comment or insight that completely nails a pattern or habit I am too close to myself to see.

My—ahem—'issues' dominated my landscape and darkened my skies, for the last challenging years of Indigo, followed by the pressures of opening another dining spot after several years' absence. My mental health advisor was there for me, encouraging me to continue swatting away the annoying mental flies of self-doubt, at the same time helping me recognize my enduring strengths.

So as a result of working with a mental health professional, am I a happy-go-lucky, click-my-heels man about town without a cloud of fear, sadness or insecurity in my eternally blue sky? Not exactly. On the other hand, do I feel I have more control over the darker emotions that inevitably bring me (and everyone else) down from time to time? Absolutely.

It took only a few weeks for us to pack up and head for the beaches of Goa. Of course, the media and the rumour mills quickly inferred I might be eyeing my next eatery there. Not true.

You do not have to bend my arm to encourage me to hit the road. I've been travelling abroad most of my life—whether to New York to see my maternal grandparents, to Pennsylvania to attend Franklin & Marshall, to spend summers in Italy and in the years since then to, among others, Singapore, Australia, Spain, France and Thailand. When I was in college, I was a keen amateur photographer, so every time I came back to India on breaks, I used to take off for three weeks with my camera, backpacking without a real plan. I got to see a lot of India that way.

I usually try to fit in one or two diving trips a year. However, I don't travel for work alone: I combine food research with holidays. Eating out reminds me too much of R&D. When I can get to dive as well as dine, though, I consider it a two-fer and well worth any long-haul travel.

I'm not big on sightseeing. If there is something interesting, I'll make the effort. But museums do not move my soul. I prefer experiential physical activity—a safari or trek or hot-air ballooning. Also, I don't like hotels when travelling, though they can be luxurious. A much better way to get to know a culture, its people and even food is staying with locals. I really get the attraction of Airbnbs or homestays when you can interact with the owners. I always stay with locals if I can manage it. I meet people and we exchange addresses and they say, 'Oh, when you come next time, come and stay,' and I say, 'Be careful what you wish for, I will show up.' And I do.

Now, thanks to the little golden parachute my severance package afforded me, I could indulge, along with my wife and kids.

We spent many months just eating out and observing what other people were eating. I noticed no one was taking a step forward. It was the same edamame dumplings and tuna carpaccio everywhere. Oriental

Dinner on board after a day's sailing with Daniela and Antonio in the Aeolian Islands, Italy

Tequila time in the Mediterranean with my floating bar, Antonio

Total decadence... private chopper to a champagne picnic for two at the Whitehaven Beach, Great Barrier Reef, Australia

Malu surfacing in Sipadan, Malaysia

Early morning pre-dive check, Seaventures Dive Rig, Mabul Island, Malaysia

At Darwin's Arch, Galapagos Islands, Ecuador in mid-2019. Sadly the arch collapsed in 2021 from erosion

Yogi Havanagudtime Undadasea somewhere in the Alor Archipelago, Indonesia

Can you spot the mzungu? ... ndugu wakiwa katika pozi! ('brothers in the pose!') Masai Mara, Kenya

was apparently the way to go, and cheap and cheerful appeared to be the order of the day. I thought, 'Is this what I too need to do in order to be successful?' So, I shut myself off for many months and focused hard on what I wanted to do and what I had always done. And that was not to pay attention to what everyone else was saying and doing. Despite my intention to not think about work, I thought about it. Consciously or subconsciously, all of it fed me—fed me ideas for whatever I would do next.

To think way ahead was a luxury. With Indigo, especially towards the end, we were so immersed in the day-to-day drama. We didn't get time to step back and really look at things holistically; we tended to get a little myopic. So part of our travel was for, as they say, *'Dimaag fresh karna'*—step back and live a little bit, taste, enjoy, see, experience and refresh the mind. Also, frankly, just seeing how the world was eating and what people were doing led to interesting learnings.

I observed that hardly anybody wanted to dine, in the old-fashioned sense of the word. People were more interested in tasting a bunch of little things, in the tradition of Spanish tapas or Japanese kaiseki. I was not ready to say the food is secondary to the experience, because it's not, but the experience counts for a lot more than I had thought. It's the ability to hang out with friends and share a convivial atmosphere to eat … that was what people really wanted.

Another inspiration came from seeing the development of open kitchens. It made sense; people wanted to be more participatory in their dining experience. Seeing how things were prepared was believing in them, in the integrity of the product, the cleanliness of the kitchen and the mastery of the chefs. We should have nothing to hide. I held that idea and knew that whatever I would do next would have such a set-up. The open kitchen was part of the wave of full disclosure in dining, in relationships—in everything short of politics and some untrustworthy businesspeople (as we had just experienced with deGustibus).

And then, in one unfortunate instant, our lives changed, our focus shifted, our priorities got re-prioritized and became crystal clear. One of a parent's worst fears came true: our second-born daughter Amalia, fifteen at the time, had a stroke.

And that was when we realized The Plan has its own Plan and that we were just actors in a movie which we had to trust would have a happy ending.

The luckiest part was, given the fact that we were not working, we could devote 100 per cent attention to our sweet daughter. Actually, during the first couple of days while she was in the ICU, we had to take the last couple of trips to meet with lawyers and sign the final papers passing our company over to the Power Owners.

It was an extremely difficult period—emotionally and physically—perhaps the hardest period of our lives, Malini and I agree. A fifteen-year-old having a stroke was quite crazily scary. We were on red alert for two and a half years. We didn't even want to think about work; we didn't care. Family and kids are always more important.

Periods like that, Malu later said to me, 'is when you find out who your friends really are. We stood back from everything else. It was hard on our relationship, hard on our parents and very hard on our older daughter Shaan, who loves her sister very much.'

Amalia recovered slowly but surely. However, we quickly discerned a decline in her cognitive abilities. It took lots of rehab and relearning. As she was finishing her junior year in high school, we put in many hours helping her with her homework. A year later, when she started applying to colleges, we were there again to focus on her, unencumbered by work distractions and obligations. When she moved to New York to attend The New School, Malu went with her and stayed on a few months for her own vacation in the city. That also turned out well, because when Amalia had a serious meltdown after a month in college and dropped out, her mother was there to help her decide what to do next. And that was to follow a long-held passion for food, studying at New York's International Culinary Center (ICC).

Malu was there at a critical turning point for Amalia. Again, I have no idea how we would have gotten through that if we had had to run deGustibus through the toxic muck it had become.

The experience with Amalia, combined with what we'd been through with Indigo, brought our nuclear family closer and made us stronger.

charred pineapple & pickled turmeric salsa
baby mustard greens
clams
coconut broth

17: THE PASSING OF A GREAT MAN

JUST AS I GOT in the groove of writing this book, my father passed away in November 2019. The timing seemed somehow in sync with the universe.

He was just shy of his ninety-sixth birthday, and frail. While our family and his legions of friends mourned his passing, he had done as much as any man could do, so we decided to celebrate the life and times of Anand Akerkar.

On Dad's last birthday in 2019

I have written more about the female influences on my life—my mother and grandmothers, various girlfriends of more or less significance, and the loves of my life: Malini, Shaan and Amalia. But Dad has—excuse me, had—a very profound effect on me.

I am like him in that I can't hide anything. But he was much more diplomatic about it. He had a wicked sense of humour and I think he used that as a diffuser, rather than confront people. He had a mysterious side; he was wry and sarcastic. He could keep a deadpan face while ripping you to shreds. It was something that bothered me when I was younger. He was not confrontational. If he felt he was being shafted, he would rise above it. He said it wasn't worth the fight. He had a great sense of the right and ethical thing to do in any situation.

Shootin' the shit and hangin' with Daddy-o

What he achieved in his career was completely pioneering when he started out. He was what today would be called a thought leader, introducing and innovating public relations strategies, interpreting trends from the West for an Indian market. PR in India? Who had enough budget to allocate funds speculatively on PR in the India of the 1960s and '70s? And who, from the consumer end, had enough disposable income to be tempted to buy some luxury perfume or plop down a chunk of money on real-estate investment opportunities in the Seychelles?

Yet my Dad found a way.

In the process, and almost coincidentally as far as he was concerned, he became financially comfortable and highly admired. Mom, my sister Tiki and I were the direct beneficiaries of this.

He led by example. He never pressured me to join the ranks of the working class. Well, maybe he simply wanted me to secure work—keyword: security—that would also feed my soul and stimulate my mind.

Sundays be like ... father and son bonding, 1979

How much respect he had garnered in his lifetime was evident at his funeral, where I managed to muster the courage to say a few words (without breaking into tears) in front of hundreds of his loved ones.

I recalled the lost period in my life after I'd dropped out of the PhD programme at Columbia University. It was a crucial turning point when I had no idea what I was going to do. I recounted the ridiculous number of things I had tried and left behind. Dad never said a thing all through that year. It must have been tough on him; after all, I was pissing away a serious education. Yet, he just asked how things were, what plans I had—no pressure. He'd casually send me leads to the many friends he had in pharmaceutical or chemical companies across the globe—saying that I should send them my résumé if I was interested. But of course I never did. Again, he said nothing critical.

He was an extraordinary father and I tried to practise that non-pressure patience thing with my daughters, letting them find their own ways while also keeping a watchful eye out that they don't go so close to the edge of the cliff as to ... well, as to become too much like me. I clearly haven't been very successful at that, and I often think I'm nowhere near as capable as I'd like to be—as he was.

He never held my hand, never told me what or how to do things; rather always gently steered me into arriving at a decision or making a choice of my own. And once that happened, he always encouraged and supported my decision, whatever it was, one hundred per cent. He never told me how to live. He lived and let me watch him doing it. That is the definition of a role model.

I spoke about the heydays of Indigo, back in early 2000, when ace cricketer Sachin Tendulkar opened his restaurant in the neighbourhood not too far from it. There was a virtual media blitz about Tendulkar's for several months leading up to its opening. Dad was at a cocktail party one night when a friend came up and asked him, 'Anand, is Rahul worried about Tendulkar's opening?' Dad, deadpan as always, replied, 'Tell me, if Rahul picked up a cricket bat tomorrow, would Sachin be worried?'

My father gave me the greatest gift any parent could give to his offspring: he believed in me. Always, unequivocally and probably even when he might have had doubts, he demonstrated his faith in me.

Was he a perfect father? No. He made mistakes; he was fallible. He was human and taught us that it was okay to be so. But he always provided for us, not necessarily materially, but with amazing life experiences, education, values, morality, correctness, love. And he always made us laugh. His gift of encouraging us to see the lighter side of this crazy world we live in is something both Avantika and I have put to good use, sometimes at the most absurd times, but always with a tip of the hat to dear old Dad. Mom also gets credit for some of that quality.

As a young man, I often thought Dad to be an idealist and somewhat out of sync with the real world. We'd say he was old-fashioned. We often chastised him for the number of times he'd complain bitterly about the degradation in human values, and the deterioration of the city and the environment around us. Little was right, and all of it was getting worse, according to him. It was quite irritating at times—even if or especially since he was often right.

Dad expressing his views on life on his birthday in Jan 2018

The truth is, my father was not just a visionary but also an idealist, oftentimes frustrated and irritated by others' acceptance of mediocrity. In fact, he spent a lot of his life trying to make things perfect and beautiful around him, and we will always be grateful to him for that.

He was also very conscious of his reputation. On many occasions, as I was about to make important decisions, he'd tell me that the only thing anyone had in the end was their name and what it stood for.

I often find myself saying, 'Oh God, I've become my father.' That was something I never wanted to become. But looking across that packed room at his funeral, at the faces of the scores of people whose lives he had touched, I can only hope people remember me with the same respect they had for him.

I didn't spend too much time with him in his last months, and I deeply regret it. But I did grieve in the year or two before when I saw the grim writing on the very short wall as he struggled against various ills and ailments. I'd often felt more of a kinship with my mother; we 'got' each other. With my dad, I'm reminded of and resonate with that great line attributed to the American writer Mark Twain: 'When I was a boy of fourteen, my father was so ignorant I could hardly stand to have the old man around. But when I got to be twenty-one, I was astonished at how much he had learned in seven years.'

Some consider the attribution apocryphal. No matter. It rings true for most men and their sons.

Months after he departed (I loathe saying 'died' as much as I loathe saying 'departed' or 'passed'), it hit me like a sledgehammer: he would not be there for me to talk to and bounce ideas around with, which was our custom. I can't do that now, ironically at a time when I could most benefit from his wisdom.

There's another great thinker's saying about fathers that also struck me hard. Psychiatrist Sigmund Freud wrote that the death of a man's (or boy's) father is the most important psychological event of his life.

I am finding it extremely therapeutic to even write these thoughts now, to realize how much he meant to me, how much he moulded me into the man I am.

Here's a fish preparation we did at Qualia that took inspiration from a Konkan coastal gassi that Aji made so well, and Dad loved so much. A typical fish or prawn gassi is a smooth orangish curry made from several spices and coconut (milk or flesh, depending on its source), balanced by a tanginess that comes from using kokum and/or tamarind as a souring agent. We pickled fresh turmeric root and used that as a souring agent instead, creating a sweet-sour chutney with charred pineapple and sukhat (tiny air-dried prawns or krill) to provide a pop of bright freshness.

RED SNAPPER, CLAMS, BOK CHOY, SUKHAT, PINEAPPLE AND PICKLED TURMERIC SALSA, WITH COCONUT BROTH (From Qualia)

INGREDIENTS FOR 4 PORTIONS

4 red snapper fillets (120–130gm each, skin on)

2 teaspoons olive oil

1 heaped tablesoon cold butter

Coconut Broth

2–2½ dozen large clams

1 cup coconut milk

¼ cup vegetable stock

2 Kashmiri or Byadgi red chillies, cut in two

2 teaspoons coriander stems

1 teaspoon grated ginger

1 tablespoon jaggery

1 teaspoon freshly grated turmeric root

3 tablespoons butter, cut into 1–2-inch cubes and refrigerated

2 teaspoons chopped chives

2 teaspoons freshly squeezed lemon or lime juice

Salt

Braised Bok Choy

12 baby bok choy

1 teaspoon chopped garlic

2 tablespoons dry white wine

Salt and pepper

1 tablespoon olive oil

Pickled Turmeric*

250 gm fresh turmeric root

1 cup white wine vinegar

1 cup water

2 teaspoons salt

3½ tablespoons sugar

Pineapple Salsa

½ cup charred pineapple, diced small

1 tablespoon diced pickle turmeric root

1 teaspoon chopped coriander leaves (cilantro)

2 teaspoons freshly squeezed lemon or lime juice

1 tablespoon honey

Salt and pepper

Garnish

1 tablespoon sukhat (tiny dried shrimp) deep fried, crispy

1 tablespoon roasted coconut shavings

1 tablespoon coriander cress

---

* You need a minimum of four days to pickle the turmeric, and it will keep for several months, refrigerated.

DIRECTIONS

Coconut Broth:

In a saucepan, add all the coconut broth ingredients except the clams, butter, lemon juice and chives, and cook on a low flame till the liquid reduces by half and the broth is nicely flavoured. While the broth is reducing, scrub the outside of the clams with a coarse sponge or wire brush to remove any attached grit or dirt. Strain the sauce into another saucepan, bring it to a slow boil, then lower the heat and add the clams to it. Cover with a lid and cook till the clams open up in the coconut broth. Take off the flame and monté the coconut and clam broth with cold butter, some lemon juice and chopped chives.* Set aside warm to be used immediately.

Braised Bok Choy:

Heat a frying pan with some oil and add the chopped garlic, and then add the cleaned heads of bok choy. Sauté till the garlic turns golden brown and the bok choy just starts charring. Deglaze the pan with white wine, lower the flame, cover the pan and let the bok choy cook in the wine steam. Season with salt and pepper and make sure the bok choy does not discolour but remains tender and cooked.

---

* Beurre monté is an emulsification of butter and water used as a sauce or poaching liquid. Monter au beurre is the process of adding cold butter to a sauce after you've taken it off the heat. Adding the chilled butter produces a similar emulsification effect, adding body and shine to an existing sauce. Sauces can be finished with butter, to luxurious effect, with a technique called mounting: for a rich, glossy, butter-mounted sauce, add pieces of well-chilled butter to the heated sauce and rotate the pan steadily, allowing the butter to emulsify slowly.

Pickled Turmeric:

Scrub and wash all the dirt from the fresh turmeric roots and pat dry. Separately, in a saucepan on medium heat, bring all the pickling ingredients to a boil, and once boiled, pour the hot pickling liquid over the turmeric root, seal the jar and refrigerate when cool.

Pineapple Salsa:

In a mixing bowl, mix all the salsa ingredients and set aside, refrigerated.

Cooking the Snapper:

Rinse the snapper fillets under running water and pat dry with a paper towel. Lightly score the skin of the fillet, trying not to cut too deeply into the flesh. Rub lemon juice and season the flesh side of the fillet with salt, but leave the skin as dry as possible. In a non-stick or seasoned sauté pan, add oil and when hot, place the snapper fillets skin side down and cook over a low flame till the skin turns golden-brown and crisps. At this point, add some butter to the pan and when it melts, use a tablespoon to baste the flesh side of the fillet with it. Take off the flame, flip the fillet and let it sit for a short while in the hot pan, flesh side down.

Assembly:

Divide the coconut broth with clams into four soup plates or shallow bowls, place the bok choy in the centre of the dish and then add a fish fillet skin side up on that. Spoon a teaspoon or two of the pickled turmeric and charred pineapple chutney on the fish and sprinkle some of the crispy fried sukhat over that. Garnish with fresh coriander cress and toasted coconut shavings.

18: WITH QUALIA, A RETURN TO THE ESSENCE OF THE SENSES

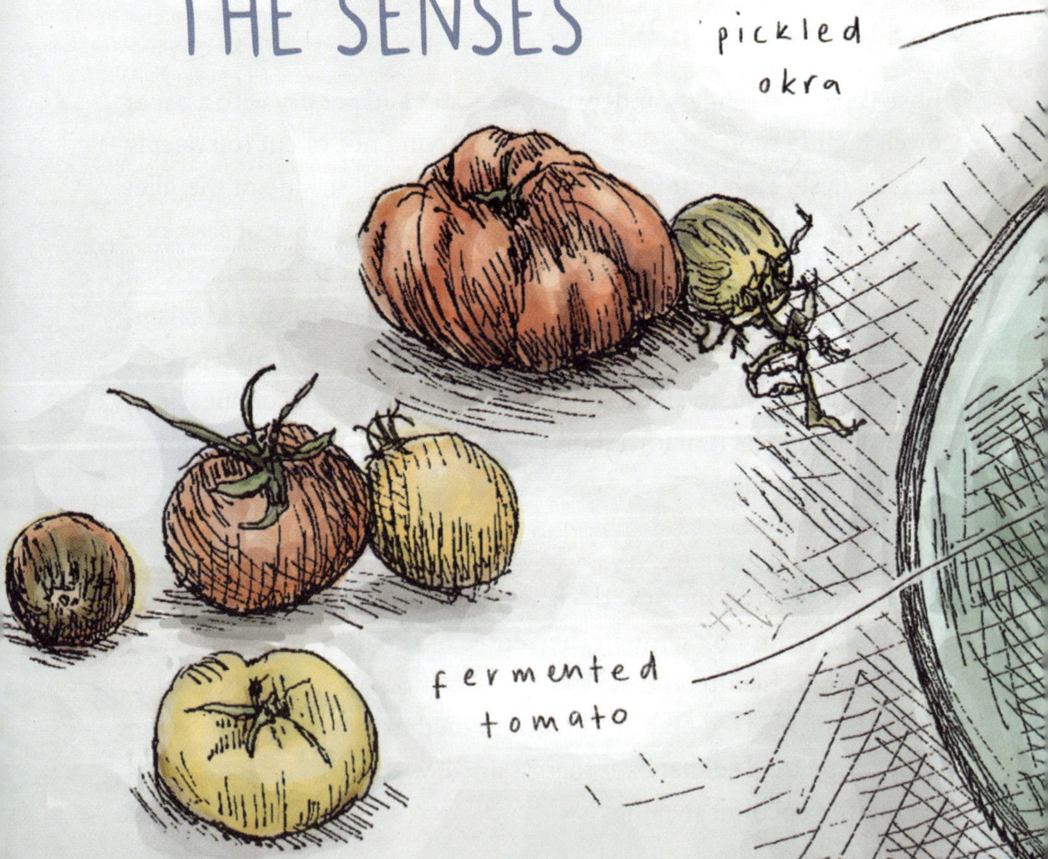

charred octopus
goan chorizo
burrata
pickled celery

'Freedom and happiness are found in the flexibility and ease with which we move through change.'
—Siddhartha Gautama Buddha

IN THE END, ONE'S greatest competition is always oneself, isn't it? In my case Indigo, the Indigo Delis and my other restaurant successes were a very tough act to follow.

Yet, after a three-year hiatus, my itch to create new dishes, to cook and serve hungry mouths, to entertain on the culinary stage was irrepressible. It superseded any self-doubt or insecurity that I could not get it up (so to speak) and reinvent myself—and in the process add some new tastes and dimensions to the dining scene in India and, hopefully, beyond.

But in the twenty years since I had opened Indigo—a hit from day one—the dining landscape in Mumbai had changed dramatically. In 1999 we were the first very successful stand-alone non-Indian restaurant. Even in the Indian category, there weren't many top eateries not based in hotels. With very little competition at the time, the world was ours to take. We could have been mediocre and still would have made some kind of splash. So we exceeded all expectations—perhaps because there were no expectations in this niche dining experience.

By the time we really started putting my new concept together in 2017—with space chosen, investors lined up, two chefs already on board, walls coming down and going up and the beginning thoughts of what I wanted to do next—the number of top-grade stand-alones had skyrocketed to the hundreds, according to the National Restaurant Association of India. Add to that the great influx of quick-service restaurants (known in the industry as QSR) and chain restaurants—from McDonald's, Pizza Hut and Barbeque Nation to casual-dining chains like Mamagoto, Oh! Calcutta and the Socials—and it was clear I would need to do something outstanding to distinguish my new venture from the rest of the dining options.

I was also competing with my younger self—not a fair contest at all in a profession that is highly demanding physically. I was approaching sixty, an age at which most chefs have retired their aprons. Even forty, my age when I opened Indigo, is considered getting up there in today's age of twenty-something cooking phenoms.

But none of this mattered to me. My passion to cook trumped all these odds. Even a flagging economy and increased cost of everything were not going to dispel me.

In fact, when I looked around at who was doing what in India's restaurant world, I was encouraged, because I did not see much that I wanted to emulate. While there were a handful of young chefs and restaurants that were pushing the envelope, serious about what they were doing, I mostly saw gimmicks and poor imitations. I saw disrespect for the natural tastes of ingredients. I saw shortcuts. I still saw wait staff service that did not rise to the international standards I had tried to make part of my hospitality signature along with the food. I therefore saw a great opportunity to still showcase my brand, or rebrand, as it were.

Once the buzz got out that I was going to open a new eating establishment, clichés abounded as to what I would do and why. Was this my second innings? Was it my third act? Was I coming out of retirement? Or, the one that really stung: was I making a comeback? Comeback from what? As far as I was concerned, I'd never left. Sure, I left deGustibus—or it left me. Whatever; I was not dead, man. I travelled, I spent quality time with my family and, more importantly, my mind was quite alive and well. Ideas were rumbling and formulating in there.

The truth was that from the cuisine perspective I sort of knew what I wanted to do. I told people interviewing for kitchen jobs, and anyone else who asked, that I would develop a menu that was 'loosely Mediterranean'. As for ambience, the goal was not a high-end sophisticated scene. Not necessarily fine, but fun. There was a lot to do before we opened, though.

We didn't want to recreate the vibe at Indigo; that was a special time and a special place, but a different time and a different place. One could not recreate it. And anyway, what creative person would want to replicate anything, especially themselves?

But there was one thing I did want to retain: the sense of fun. Fun dining, not fine dining. Unfortunately, that phrase 'fine dining' has become synonymous with expensive and esoteric, a place you go on special occasions and rarely in between.

That said, I would trot out all my past successes to entice investors for my next project. While I went on that dog-and-pony fundraising ride, I was also on scouting missions, following up every real estate tip I heard. At one point I explored taking over the casual dining space in the lobby of the Four Seasons Hotel, Mumbai. That didn't work out but it got me thinking that that area—the Worli–Lower Parel commercial area—would be an excellent base for what I had in mind. Lower Parel had been a centre for cotton mills; by 1915 there were more than eighty mills there. After the Second World War, under strong competition from Japan, they declined. Gradually, government norms that once restricted the redevelopment of mill lands were relaxed. As a result, high-profile builders quickly took possession of these land parcels. Between 1990 and 2010, the majority of the mill lands were acquired and redeveloped. Soon high-rise apartment complexes, high-end hotels like the Four Seasons and Ritz Carlton and other commercial properties sprung up like wildflowers. Around them, like mushrooms, there quickly followed restaurants. At last count there must be 400 or so.

This area appealed to Malu and me, in part because it was so unlike the old neighbourhood of Colaba, where we'd established Indigo. But the other part was that this new development area was afire with creative energy. This would be a good locale to make my stand … again. All we needed was the right venue and the right financial deal.

Meanwhile, I began thinking about building my team, in the kitchen and front of the house.

Building one's team, as I've said before, is crucial to any business. It's all the more important, I feel, in a restaurant, because of the interdependence we have with each other, and with our guests. A plate that comes to your table gets touched, literally, by several hands in its making. Not only that, but we work in very tight quarters, dancing around each other like a ballet troupe doing graceful pirouettes, but executing tasks with sharp knives in our hands, under fire literally and figuratively, each order requiring us to work at utmost speed. Talk about deadlines; we have one every five minutes or less. So chemistry and cooperation are essential; if we don't get along with each other in the kitchen, your order will reflect it.

This holds even more true with the selection and hiring of an executive team. The members are the leaders in each area of restaurant operations. Their styles of work and working together set the attitude and actions of the rest of the staff.

My idea was to bring back a few who had worked with me at Indigo, since I knew they would know my style and help teach the others. The others would be young staffers who would either come from other restaurants or who I felt had the necessary traits—eager, smart, naturally warm and friendly—even if they didn't have relevant work experience. They would be easy to mould and train.

My first hire would be my chef de cuisine, someone to work closely with me to develop recipes, give shape to the cuisine and the menu, drive the entire kitchen operation and then be my right-hand man once we opened—basically a solid second-in-command for all our food services. Not an easy ask.

Tarang Joshi had worked for me for two years at the end of my run with Indigo. Though we had followed different paths to this career, in so many other ways he was perfect and a great complement to me then.

He'd gone to a hotel management school, Rizvi, in Bandra, Mumbai. He then went to work for five-star hotel restaurants, first at the award-winning Oberoi Rajvilas in Jaipur, then the Taj Lands End in Bandra. He also worked for the Six Senses group in the Maldives and even for a Swissôtel in Kolkata. He'd had some solid experience by anyone's measure.

But Tarang has other qualities that appealed to me even more. Firstly, and luckily for him, in several of those hotels his bosses were Europeans, so he learned the slow way of apprenticeship, moving up the kitchen ladder, not cutting corners, learning and mastering good technique, putting quality over quantity. And then, most importantly, he is an independent thinker who puts food first. In other words, he was not really suited for working in a hotel kitchen that has to prep for up to three or more outlets plus banquets and room service and in environments where the cost is much more important than the product.

The truth is, I did not work directly with him that much at Indigo initially. That fell to Nitin. But I kept a corner of my eye on him and apparently he kept both eyes on me. He stayed with Indigo for three years, from 2012 to 2015, rising to chef de cuisine, and eventually played a big part in developing the menu for the second Indigo flagship in Delhi with Nitin and me. But as he saw the writing on the wall and the slow decline of my food-first philosophy and the loss of my control over Indigo, he left our company some time before the proverbial you-know-what hit the fan. He took a position at The Glass House in Bengaluru where he was an instant hit, incorporating local influences mixed with classic dishes.

Our paths crossed a few years later. He contacted me asking about a career move and his interest in doing a particular restaurant. I told him I was preparing to open a new restaurant and wondered if he was interested. I explained that I wanted to return to exploring true and elemental cooking over wood and charcoal, that people had forgotten how to do traditional roasting, braising, pickling and fermenting. I could almost see his mouth watering, though we were on the phone. He was planning to stay in Bengaluru, where he had settled down with his wife and daughter, but the chance to work with me proved too enticing. I sealed it by flying down to see him face to face and describing what I wanted to create. He moved back to Mumbai to join me. I was thrilled.

So I had my chef de cuisine and right-hand man in Tarang. He was the first to join the Qualia team and was instrumental in developing the menu with me, able to totally understand what I wanted to do with the direction for the restaurant. Tarang is a truly gifted and technically skilled cook, blessed with an amazing palate and an uncanny, intuitive feel for culinary creation. He's also a great leader and patient teacher, and I'd be remiss if I didn't acknowledge his massive contribution to Qualia's culinary success. Besides, we work really well together.

Now I needed to put together the rest of the pre-opening team. What I needed most from them was a shared understanding of the food-first hospitality-driven philosophy for which we had become known. Plus I needed to sense their passion to learn and grow.

All of this came together with my next hire, Ash Moghe, who had had seventeen years of experience in Toronto and New York when I brought him on as Number Three in our kitchen. He'd actually volunteered at Indigo in the late 1990s after we'd just opened, while he was still in culinary school. He came in one day, out of the blue, requesting to see the kitchen because he'd never seen a professional restaurant kitchen in India. His interest and curiosity alone were unusual back then. But what impressed me most was that he'd cooked in the traditional French style and had an old-school attitude in the kitchen. He and his family moved back to India around 2015 and he immediately joined Indigo Deli to work with me, not knowing that I was no longer with the company. He only found out I'd left much later. Ash, like Tarang, is a skilled and adventurous cook, forever exploring new avenues to combine ingredients on a plate. He's a taskmaster in the kitchen but makes time to teach those he leads.

Dessert holds a special place for diners, as it does for me personally. All our deGustibus restaurants had become famous for their delicious and inventive sweet endings to dinners. I needed someone excellent to head our bakery and pastry department. Technically Rachelle Andrade was a baker when we hired her. She was completely honest that she had not been a pastry chef and not even worked in a restaurant. She'd been working as head baker at Magazine Street Kitchen. But she agreed to learn more about desserts and being a pâtissière as she started her dessert chef journey, with Tarang's help. Soon she was doing original recipes like adding pickled celery to a charred chocolate cake and pickled berries to a rice pudding with crispy fried rice.

As with the bar scene at Indigo, I wanted to make Qualia's bar a people magnet. For that you need a great mix of original cocktails, the kind a guest orders a second and third time, and someone in charge who understands the chemical compounds of those ingredients, with a gregarious personality to sell them. I'd initially hired someone else for the job, but before he began work, Ranjeet Shirke arrived on our doorstep one day and so impressed me that I hired him on the spot as our beverage manager and sommelier. Like Nitin who'd worked overseas for a while, he exuded that customer-engaging can-do attitude that comes from quality international experience. He'd been working since he was twenty, bouncing through restaurant bars from Mumbai to Singapore to Dubai, winning mixology competitions. He understood that we'd want to use fresh fruit and herbs in our cocktails. As a wine expert, he also helped me refine our list to include 120 different labels, featuring wines from countries, regions and grapes not usually seen on menus in other Indian restaurants.

I was excited. The team was coming together really well, and we started food and cocktail trials at home, much like we did when I started Under the Over almost thirty years earlier. It took a fair amount of trial and error to find just the right culinary expression I was looking for and for Tarang and Ash to really get a handle on it, which allowed them to start creating on their own too. We did several months of trials, in many cases revisiting the same dishes over and over again as the pickles matured and the dish's mouthfeel and flavour profile evolved. What became very clear was that since these were early days in the pickling process, we'd really be able to get a feel for which way a dish was heading and peg down the final recipe and dish construction months down the road, when we were able to move into the restaurant kitchen and work with evolved pickled product. In many cases the flavour and texture differences were quite dramatic, forcing us to entirely rethink a dish before we opened. Also, the restaurant was going to have a wood-burning hearth, grill and oven; food cooked that way on wood and coal could never be recreated or approximated at home with a domestic electric oven and low-pressure gas stove. We'd have to continue with a bunch of food trials once we actually started cooking in the restaurant kitchen. And we did.

The development of our cocktail menu and our wine selection happened concurrently. Ranjeet was present through all the food trials and really understood the flavour profiles we were looking for in the cocktails to work with the food. We drank a lot. Similarly with the wines: we sampled many on the way to building our list. The whole process resulted in a valuable by-product: the team bonded as we ate and drank together over several months, sharing what we came to call 'Our Table of Love'.

Tarang Joshi

Ash Moghe

Rachelle Andrade

Shaan Akerkar

Colin Rodrigues

Ranjeet Shirke

(All photos by Sheena Sippy)

The Qualia bakery and dessert girls in the pose. L to R: Supriya, Jessica, Rachelle, Huma, Amanda, Divya

Months before we'd even located the restaurant space, I already knew I wanted to call the restaurant Qualia.

'Qualia? Really? That's what you want to name a restaurant? In India? A word people won't know how to pronounce, much less translate? They won't even know what language it comes from!'

That, paraphrased, was the reaction we often got when we landed on the name. I didn't care. Like any new concept or phrase, I knew we could explain it and teach people a little in the process. Did anyone even think of putting together the oxymoronic phrase 'the new normal' until the normal became abnormal?

The term qualia—pronounced KWA-lee-ah—derives from the Latin adjective *qualis*, meaning 'of what sort' or 'of what kind' in a specific instance, such as 'what it is like to taste a specific apple, this particular apple now'. The Oxford Reference Dictionary defines it as: 'A philosophical term for sensory experiences that have distinctive subjective qualities but lack any meaning or external reference to the objects or events that cause them, such as the painfulness of pinpricks or the redness of red roses. The term is virtually synonymous with sense data.'

What chef could not love that? And what sense-awake person could not relate?

I encountered the word 'qualia' at the end of 2015. I'd just come off a diving trip around Alor Island in Indonesia after spending a week in Bali. During that holiday I read neuroscientist V.S. Ramachandran's book, *The Tell-Tale Brain: A Neuroscientist's Quest for What Makes Us Human*, in which the word comes up several times. Ramachandran describes it as 'the ineffable subjective quality of conscious experience'. This can apply to experiencing such sensations as looking at a setting sun, or smelling a rose, or sipping wine. And while critics, reviewers, philosophers and others try to put words to those senses, no words can make you 'feel' them.

This is precisely what I wanted guests to feel when they came into Qualia and dined there: a subjective experience beyond words. This word stuck in my mind as my own philosophy of food, and of life.

Once you've had great success with one architect, why wouldn't you return to him for another go at restaurant design? Kapil Gupta and his partner Chris Lee of Serie Architects, the team that had done such a marvellous job for us at Tote, winning a bar design award and turning an old space into something bright and modern, was an obvious choice. We went to Kapil hoping to commission his involvement in Qualia. The problem was that in the intervening years, Serie had become even more successful and much in demand. Further, restaurant design was not their main thing; it's considered niche in that world. Though Serie Architects had done breathtaking designs of huge projects—art centres, courthouses, museums, university buildings, high-rise offices and others around the world—they had only done Tote among restaurants. So, though we had worked excellently together in the past, I was slightly doubtful if he would take us on.

But as soon as he walked into our new space, he said he immediately thought this was something special to work with, that it had, as he put it, 'the DNA of a fabulous restaurant—good bones'. It was a delicious prospect he could not refuse.

The space is about 4,000 square feet in total, a rectangle about 100-feet long and 40-feet deep and 18 feet from ceiling to floor. One 100-foot-long windowed wall faces a sidewalk and a private street that enters the Lodha World Towers, a complex of three high-rise buildings for residential and commercial usage which the Lodha Group describes as 'a powerful symbol of Mumbai's unfettered aspirations and unstoppable drive'. Not sure I completely agree, but we did have drive.

As I explained to Kapil, who was already familiar with my food and my sense of restaurant-as-theatre, my whole vision revolved around the open kitchens that I had so admired elsewhere. I wanted people to see all the magic behind what we do. And I wanted it to be interactive so that folks could speak with chefs even as they were cooking.

Years ago I had decided I was paying way too much to design consultants who basically transcribed my kitchen designs into CAD (computer-aided design) drawings, specced out the equipment for electrical, plumbing and drainage requirements and then charged me an arm and a leg. The engineer in me decided I could do the same thing. I purchased and downloaded CAD software on my Mac, took two weeks off work and taught myself how to create kitchen layout drawings. I'd give my equipment layout drawings to our MEP (mechanical, electrical and plumbing) technical consultant to work out the electrical loads, plumbing and drainage requirements along with the HVAC and exhaust details to support my kitchen design, and in the process save a shitload of fees. I'd been doing this ever since we built the Indigo Deli at the Palladium Mall. Kapil's team simply incorporated my kitchen and back-of-house drawings into their overall design scheme and off we went. Easy peasy. (It actually took a little more than that, but in essence that's what happened.)

There were some givens we had to work with and around, among them three large floor-to-ceiling structural columns in the centre of the space. Kapil suggested we could use them as natural partitions, making separate but intimate dining and drinking areas. To add to the separateness and give the whole restaurant that dramatic staged feel, he designed brass chainmail curtains that gave enough privacy while still letting people peek through to see who else was there and what they were eating.

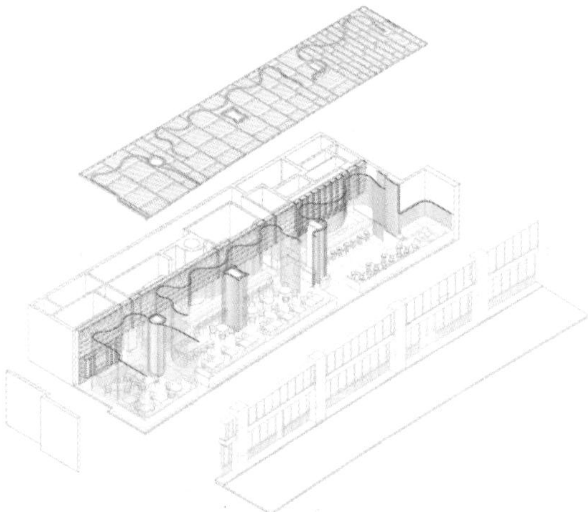

Qualia axiomatic design scheme by Serie Architects

When one stepped into the restaurant, it would give the feel of something big and important and meaningful going on. This was your classic 'grand entrance'. You could be in Manhattan or Singapore or other cities where 'grand' fits.

The kitchen was configured as a linear arrangement of three distinct activity zones: the bar, the bakery and the cooking stations. Above each of these sections dangled a bronze chainmail screen. The screens gently undulated, much like heavy velvet theatre curtains. Behind and above the stations were high shelves showcasing all the pickled and fermenting items in large glass jars—almost 500 of them. The shelves acted as a proscenium—an arched or square structure erected on a theatre stage to frame the action of the play. The idea, as Kapil explained it, was that the curtains would represent 'the unveiling of Rahul 2.0, with the curtains going up on a new culinary adventure with Chef'. Malini and I loved it.

We also were very concerned about lighting and acoustics. It annoys me when you can't hear the people you're dining with due to boisterous conversations at other tables bouncing off the walls and ceilings. Kapil took care of that with a ceiling designed as an array of timber frames, within which rows of timber louvers absorbed and directed sound to a thick layer of sound insulation foam above.

Lighting is so much more important in restaurants than many people understand. I abhor walking into a restaurant that is either lit so brightly that you almost need sunglasses; or that is so dimly lit you need a miner's lamp to see your food, let alone your dinner date's face. It kills all possibilities of an atmospheric and intimate dining experience. Those who care about such things take notice of carefully placed lighting overhead, which focuses light directly on the diner's place setting so that when their next dish is served, it feels like the star it should be.

We wanted the sense of warmth and intimacy lighting has the ability to achieve, so we commissioned lighting designer Kanchan Puri, who manifested this vision brilliantly. Of course we had a running start with floor-to-ceiling windows, so we let Kapil know we wanted seating to be as close to them as possible to benefit lunch and early dinner guests. Long, rich maroon-cum-burgundy leather banquettes ran down the front side of the restaurant. Each table was illuminated with dish-shaped copper pendant lights suspended overhead.

One other observation about the design before I go on to the food, which I know you are already salivating to read about. Kapil masterfully mixed textures and used a palate of complementary colours. He balances the polish of some green marble tables with the warm red mahogany of other tables with the sparkly specks sprinkled on black terrazzo floor tiles and wall finish with more browns in the timber ceilings with the bronze and gold chain curtains. It's a lot to take in but it all harmonizes so well.

While we loved every little touch and how it all came together, there was a slight disconnect between our idea of elevated casual food and the grandness of the environment. Some people said they felt overwhelmed upon walking in—like 'Have I dressed properly?' or worse, 'Can I afford this?' These feelings were quickly assuaged, however, once people were seated and saw the reasonable prices, were greeted by warm and enthusiastic wait staff and tasted the food.

'A restaurant featuring pickled and fermented foods? Really?'

That was the reaction we often got (before they tasted from our menu).

Implicit in their earnest queries was befuddlement: what new spin could I possibly bring to a cooking tradition that goes back in India to the Tigris Valley in 2030 BCE, when that civilization learned how to soak local cucumbers in salt, vinegar, sugar, chillies and various spices until they morphed into pickles?

Every Indian kid can recall their mother's or grandmother's kitchen shelves, sunny windowsills and pantries chock-a-block with big sealed glass or ceramic jars, offering the promise of tangy spiciness. No meal, at home (of course) and in almost any Indian restaurant serving local cuisine, can be complete without a small plate of pickled vegetables. Just to make it clear, though, Qualia did *not* serve pickled relishes at tables automatically.

The Hindi word for pickle or relish is achaar. According to *Hobson-Jobson: A Glossary of Colloquial Anglo-Indian Words and Phrases,* compiled in 1886 by two British Indophiles, the word āchār was mentioned in 1563 in works by Garcia da Orta, a Portuguese physician who happened to be Jewish.

To me, the erstwhile biochemical engineer eternally fascinated by the reactions and interactions between substances, there is something magical about the alchemy that takes place when all these ingredients are combined and left to sit for a while.

There's also something metaphorical about pickling for me. Just as pickling changes the taste and character of ingredients, time has changed the direction and intention of my culinary journey over the years. Qualia was an example of my alchemy. More pickling will surely alter my chemical components, and it will be reflected in what I serve to those adventurous palates willing to follow my changes. And if pickling helps preserve and extend the shelf life of ingredients, please put me in a glass jar, soak me in brine and pull me out in a few years.

Dr Orta would jump out of his grave with joy if he saw what we did with pickling and fermenting all kinds of vegetables, fruits and other produce. Tarang and Ash constantly worked out multiple methodologies to pickle and ferment anything and everything we could lay our hands on, experimenting with the process and balance of sugar and salt and acid. Beets, corn, elderberry flowers, chamomile, chillies of all kinds, mustard seeds, radishes, okra, quail eggs, mackerel and other seafood—nothing was out of bounds for us to play with. The brines were complex; typically, we were brining green tomatoes with celery, garlic, fennel, peppercorns, sugar, vinegar and water; small purple brinjals in honey, vinegar, peppercorns, yellow mustard and kalonji (black Nigella seed); beets in red wine, dill, star anise and honey—to name a few.

We took what's best in season, decided (guessed, actually) on a pickling mix we thought would achieve a particular end product that we could use in a dish several months down the road. We put away 20 to 30 kilos of the stuff in pickling jars on shelves to visit later. Managing the pickle jars was a job in itself; we would move them down from the higher to the lower shelves, closer and within reach as passing time matured them.

The alchemical magic to me is that each dish evolves in taste as the pickle matures. Besides being very healthy, pickling makes dishes pop with a wonderful freshness that comes from the beautiful, bright acidity rendered by the preservation process. Not all our food had this taste, but a lot did.

We'd planned to open in April 2018, if not earlier. We were being optimistic, considering the predictable delays inherent in any construction project. But then, with disaster after disaster, I began to wonder if the Lord had singled me out to endure plagues of Biblical proportions. Were the Hindu gods messing with our minds when the monsoons were so bad in 2018, especially in Lower Parel, that we were forced to wait again? Those rains were followed by leaking and waterproofing issues that took yonks to resolve. In December of that year, when a spate of fatal restaurant fires in the city finally forced the fire department and the municipal corporation to enact strict, enforceable fire-safety rules for restaurants, my open-plan kitchen, wood-burning hearth and pizza oven now required us to install multiple firefighting and fire-containing systems that we hadn't originally planned for or budgeted. That meant more delays and more cost overruns.

As if that wasn't enough, the government in its infinite wisdom decided to punish the restaurant industry by taking away the input tax credit available under the newly instituted GST (goods and services tax) regime a year earlier. The bottom line: our project cost now increased by an unbudgeted ₹1.5 crore.

The hits just kept on coming. Major problems with our own air conditioning and ventilation systems gave us pause. In hindsight, we realized that our MEP consultant didn't really understand how an open, wood-burning hearth functioned and just how much radiant heat it really produced. His flub cost us more time and money.

Finally the skies cleared, literally and figuratively, and Qualia opened on 18 April 2019, two weeks after my sixtieth birthday.

Tarang and Ash plating up at the Qualia pass

Actually doing some work at Qualia for a change!

The Qualia team after we won Best New Restaurant and Best New Wine Destination, and I won Restaurateur of the Year in 2019!

Condé Nast Traveller *Top Restaurant Awards 2019 winners. L to R: Sameer Seth, Gauri Devidayal, Heena Punwani, Divia Thani Daswani, Prateek Sadhu, Floyd Cardoz, me, Thomas Zacharius, Rahul Gomes, Yash Bhanage and Hussain Shahzad*

Upon opening, and as we had predicted and hoped, we got a lot of media attention, based on my track record. 'Perhaps the most anticipated opening of the year,' crowed *The Times of India*. *Architectural Digest India* and *Travel & Leisure India* echoed the sentiment. That led to great business … for a while. We assumed that that publicity would sustain us for quite some time. But we missed a beat on the PR and marketing side. We were living in the past, resting on the laurels of Indigo's great success with PR. But these days, with such a flattened media world—so many genre-specific websites, so many food bloggers, so much 'noise' from so many outlets, too many options for internet surfers with the attention span of a fruit fly—one needs to keep plugging away to stay in the limelight. Perhaps we did not focus enough on the immense influence the digital world's social media platforms and apps have on almost everything. By the time Malini and I realized we needed to ramp up our announcements of special events, offers and other news on a regular basis, we had to play some catch-up.

It would be an understatement to say that, still struggling with my own lifelong self-doubts and insecurities, I found great vindication when Qualia won Best New Wine Destination at the India Wine Awards 2019; and both Condé Nast Traveller's and Zomato's Best New Restaurant Award for 2019. Our entire team, front and back of the house, was flattered and elated, as well they should have been, inasmuch as these awards are pan-Indian and the accolades reflect the whole restaurant experience, not just the food. Personally, I earned the Restaurateur of the Year recognition at the Indian Food Awards 2019, truly the icing on the cake.

The recognition was great, but what we really needed were footfalls and cash flows. We opened without an alcohol licence and things were slow(ish) at first. But once we got the licence a month later, Qualia really took off and we had rapid and encouraging growth for the first six months. Sure, we had a few teething problems as was to be expected, but I was pretty happy with the way we were doing overall. I was happy working again with my handpicked team, even happier standing at the pass as the last from the kitchen to see the plate before it goes to the table. From there I would chat with our diners, keep a hawkish eye on the food that passed and watch our very capable service team soigner (a French restaurant term for 'take good care of') our guests. I loved the energy the open kitchen generated. And it went both ways; guests could watch us and we could watch our diners, and witness their joy when they ate.

Qualia had a vibe; it buzzed. We had a super music mix (thank you, daughter Shaan), innovative and delicious cocktails, an impressive wine list, friendly attentive service and, dare I say, food that rivalled the great restaurants of the world. So satisfied were we with the process and growth that we dared to begin thinking about how to keep growing the business as we approached the tail end of 2019.

But things changed. For the worse. Pretty rapidly. Somewhere in an animal market in Wuhan, China, a bunch of SARS-CoV-2 viruses decided to jump species from whatever animals they originally infected to become pathogenic to humans. It was early January 2020 and the contagion soon took on pandemic proportions worldwide.

Here's a small sampling of menu items that incorporate pickled things that will surprise and reward your palate.

YELLOWFIN TUNA LOIN, CURRY LEAF AND SESAME RUB, AVOCADO PACHADI, PICKLED BEETS (From Qualia)

The beets need to pickle for a minimum of four days, so you need to start this dish well in advance!

INGREDIENTS FOR 4 PORTIONS

4 fresh yellowfin tuna loins, ~ 100–120 gm each

Pickled Beetroot

4 medium red beets

¾ cup white wine vinegar

¾ cup water

2 teaspoons rock salt

3 tablespoons sugar

1 medium cinnamon stick

8–10 whole black peppercorns

1 tablespoon fresh dill leaves with their stems

Curry Leaf and Sesame Rub

2½ cups ~175gm dry curry leaves

2 tablespoons roasted split chickpea lentils (chana dal)

2 tablespoons roasted split black gram lentils (urad dal)

2 teaspoons roasted whole black peppercorn

1 teaspoon roasted cumin seeds

2 tablespoons white sesame seeds

2 teaspoons roasted coriander seeds

½ teaspoon roasted fenugreek seeds

2 tablespoons desiccated coconut

3 roasted dry red chillies (Kashmiri or Byadgi)

1 teaspoon citric acid

Avocado Pachadi

1 ripe avocado

½ cup hung curd (yoghurt, hung in a muslin cloth for several hours)

2 teaspoons chopped fresh coriander (cilantro)

1 large fresh green chilli, chopped

2 teaspoons freshly squeezed lemon juice

Rock salt to season

2 tablespoons vegetable oil

1 teaspoon black mustard seeds

1 teaspoon roasted split black gram lentils (urad dal)

10–12 fresh green curry leaves

½ teaspoon asafoetida (hing)

Scallion Oil

1 cup freshly cut scallion greens

2–3 large spinach leaves

⅔ cup olive oil

Garnish

2 tablespoons scallion oil

1 tablespoon beetroot pickling liquid

1 tablespoon micro mustard greens

DIRECTIONS

Pickled Beets:

Wash, peel and cut the beets into wedges and place in a sanitized pickling jar. Wash the dill leaves and chopped dill stems, and place in the jar along with the beetroot wedges. In a saucepan, heat all the remaining pickling ingredients and bring to boil. Once boiled, take off the heat and pour the hot pickling liquid and spices over the beets and seal the jar. Make sure the beets are completely immersed in pickling liquid. When cool, refrigerate for at least four days before using ... longer is better!

Curry Leaf and Sesame Rub:

In a dry mixer-grinder, combine all the ingredients except the sesame seeds and process to a fine powder. Transfer to a bowl, mix in the sesame seeds and store refrigerated in an airtight jar.

Avocado Pachadi:

Cut the avocado around its seed and split into two halves. Remove the seed and scoop out the pulp into a blender jar. Process the avocado along with chilli, coriander, hung curd, lemon juice and salt to a fine thick purée and transfer to a bowl. Heat the oil in a small pan till very hot and cook the mustard seeds till they splutter and pop. Remove from the flame and while still hot, add the urad dal to the hot oil. Once it browns (fairly quickly), add the curry leaves and asafoetida to the hot oil and fry till crisp. Add most of the hot oil tempering to the avocado purée, mix it well, and transfer to a piping bag with a wide nozzle, making sure to reserve some of the mustard seed and crispy curry leaves to be used as a garnish when plating. Store refrigerated till ready to use.

Scallion Oil:

Bring a pot of water to boil and blanch the scallion greens and spinach for a minute. Immediately remove and transfer to an iced water bath to stop further cooking. When cooled, squeeze out as much water from the leaves as possible. Blend the blanched leaves and olive oil in a blender till well emulsified, and using a muslin cloth, strain and discard the solids from the green scallion oil into a plastic squeeze bottle.

Tuna Loin:

Season the tuna loins with a sprinkling of salt and lemon juice. Pour out the curry leaf and sesame rub on to a plate and roll the loins in the rub, coating them all over. Heat oil in a non-stick pan and sear the spice-rubbed tuna loins all over till cooked medium rare with just-warm, pink insides.

To Serve:

Pipe some avocado pachadi on to a plate, cut the tuna loin in two, on the diagonal, and place them next to the pachadi, on the plate. Add 2–3 wedges of pickled beets to the dish and separately whisk a teaspoon of the beet pickling liquid with the scallion oil and drizzle the purple green emulsion over the plate. Garnish with micro greens and spoon some mustard seed and crispy curry leaves on to the pachadi.

FERMENTED TOMATO, BURRATA, PICKLED CELERY, AVOCADO SOUP, ALMOND (From Qualia)

The tomatoes need to ferment for a minimum of four days, so you need to start this dish well in advance!

INGREDIENTS FOR 4 PORTIONS

Fermented Tomatoes

8–10 ripe, red tomatoes (~½ kg)

2 celery stalks

4–5 cloves of garlic, peeled

10–12 whole black peppercorns

2 bay leaves

1 litre water

2 tablespoons salt

Avocado Soup

1 large, very ripe avocado

½ cup chilled vegetable stock

1 green chilli

¼ cup sour cream

1 teaspoon chopped fresh coriander (cilantro)

2 teaspoons chopped, blanched spinach leaves

2 teaspoons freshly squeezed lemon juice

2 teaspoons honey

Salt and pepper

Pickled Celery

4 celery stalks

4 tablespoons white wine vinegar

4 tablespoons sugar

1 teaspoon salt

Heirloom Tomato Salad

¼ kg ripe heirloom tomatoes (assorted—yellow, green, red)

¼ kg fermented tomatoes

1½ tablespoons white balsamic vinegar

¼ cup extra- virgin olive oil

2 teaspoons chopped parsley

2 teaspoons chopped chives

2 teaspoons honey

Salt and pepper

Garnish

2 tablespoons micro greens

4 small burrata

½ cup chopped pickled celery

2 tablespoons roasted almond flakes

1½ tablespoons extra- virgin olive oil

DIRECTIONS

Fermented Tomatoes:

Wash the tomatoes and prick the tops and bottoms a couple of times with a fork to puncture the skin. Place the tomatoes, celery stalks, garlic and spices in a sterilized mason jar. Separately, in a pot, bring the water to a boil, add salt and pour the hot liquid over the tomatoes in the jar leaving an inch of free space on top. Seal the jar and let it sit at room temperature for several days. After 3 to 4 days you will notice the liquid in the jar turns cloudy. This is good. It's supposed to. After the second day, you will need to 'burp' your jar by opening and resealing the lids to allow the fermentation gas build-up to escape. You'll see bubbles rising up like crazy through the liquid and popping at the surface around the fourth day. The tomatoes are ready to eat at this point, but you may choose to let them keep fermenting. They'll get funkier as time goes on. Whenever you decide to stop the fermentation transfer the jar to the refrigerator to slow down the fermentation if not totally stop it. Just remember to 'burp' the jar every 3–4 days even while refrigerated.

Avocado Soup:

Cut the avocado in half around the seed and scoop out the pulp. Discard the seed and skin. Combine the avocado pulp with the other ingredients in a blender and process to a thick soup or purée consistency. Refrigerate, well covered to prevent it from discoloring, till you are ready to use.

Pickled Celery:

Pry and snap off the celery stalks from the head and wash them well under cold running water to remove any dirt. Trim and discard the white broader base of the stalk. Using a vegetable peeler, lightly peel the celery down the stalk, along the convex side, to remove the fibrous, thread-like outer layer. Discard the fibres. Continue using the peeler and with a little more pressure, shave off long ribbons of celery peels. Alternatively cut thin, half-moon slices of the peeled celery stalk. Marinate the celery ribbons (or half-moon slices) in a dressing of the vinegar, salt and sugar and store in a non-reactive container, refrigerated for 2–3 hours before use.

Heirloom Tomato Salad:

Wash and cut the heirloom tomatoes in different shapes (wedges, rounds, halves, slices) depending upon their size and colour. Using a pair of kitchen tongs, remove a few fermented tomatoes from their brine, peel off the skin and cut them into wedges. Combine all the tomatoes together and dress them with a vinaigrette made from the vinegar, oil, honey and herbs. Adjust the seasoning.

Assembly:

In a shallow bowl or coupe plate, place the marinated tomatoes along one edge of the plate and pour some of the avocado 'soup' beside them in the center. Garnish the tomato salad with pickled celery, micro greens and roasted almonds flakes. Place a cut-open burrata on the tomato salad and drizzle some extra-virgin olive oil over it and the tomatoes. Season with crushed black pepper and a little salt.

SMOKED EGGPLANT, LEMON RICOTTA, PICKLED GOJI BERRY, CORIANDER SCALLION SALSA (From Qualia)

The goji berries need to pickle for a minimum of 2 days.

INGREDIENTS FOR 4 PORTIONS

Smoked Eggplant

4 medium eggplants ~200 gm each (bharta baingan)

1 tablespoon roasted pine nuts for garnish

Marinade

1 tablespoon chopped garlic

¾ cup olive oil

½ cup white wine vinegar or sherry vinegar

2 teaspoons roasted and ground cumin seeds

1 tablespoon chopped parsley

1 teaspoon chopped rosemary

1 teaspoon chopped thyme

Salt and pepper

Lemon Ricotta

⅔ cup ricotta

1 tablespoon mascarpone

1 tablespoon roasted garlic paste

2 tablespoons freshly squeezed lemon juice

Zest of 1 lemon

Salt and pepper

Coriander Scallion Salsa

1½ cups chopped coriander (cilantro)

1½ cups chopped parsley

1½ cups chopped scallion greens

1 tablespoon freshly squeezed lemon juice

2 teaspoons honey

1 green chilli deseeded and chopped fine

¼ cup olive oil

Salt and pepper

Pickled Goji Berry

½ cup goji berries

¼ cup white wine vinegar

2 tablespoons sugar

1 small cinnamon stick

1 teaspoon whole coriander seeds

8–10 whole black peppercorns

1 teaspoon salt

⅔ cup water

DIRECTIONS

Smoked Eggplant:

Roast the eggplants by turning them over an open flame till they soften and their skins char and blister. Peel off the skins while the eggplant is still warm but be careful to leave the stalk intact and attached to the pulp. In a non-reactive bowl, whisk all the marinade ingredients together and marinate the warm eggplant for about 4 hours. When you are ready to serve them, heat them slowly in an oven at about 180 C.

Lemon Ricotta:

Combine all the ingredients together in a blender and process till smooth. Empty the ricotta into a wire mesh strainer and using the back of a spoon, rub and force the ricotta through the sieve into a bowl to ensure that the paste is free of any lumps.

Coriander Scallion Salsa:

In a stainless steel or non-reactive bowl, combine all the salsa ingredients together and mix well. Set aside covered till ready to use.

Pickled Goji Berry:

Put the goji berries into a sterilized mason jar. Separately, in a sauce pan on medium heat, bring all the pickling ingredients to a boil, and once boiled, pour the hot pickling liquid over the goji berries, seal the jar and refrigerate. The goji berries are ready to use after a minimum of two days pickling and will keep for up to a month refrigerated.

Assembly:

Divide the lemon ricotta equally in four plates, and spread it out with the back of a spoon. Lay a hot, smoked eggplant on the ricotta and garnish it with a generous helping of coriander scallion salsa, roasted pine nuts and pickled goji berries.

GRILLED OCTOPUS, GOAN CHORIZO, BLACK-EYED BEANS, PICKLED OKRA (From Qualia)

The okra needs to pickle for a minimum of 4 days so you need to plan accordingly.

INGREDIENTS FOR 4 PORTIONS

Octopus

2 medium octopus (~½ kg each)

2 medium onions

2 medium carrots

3 celery stalks

2 trimmed, cleaned leeks (mainly white bulb)

1–2 teaspoons freshly squeezed lemon or lime juice

1 cup dry white wine

10–12 whole black peppercorns

2 bay leaves

1 tablespoon of thyme

1 cup olive oil

Juice of 2 lemons

Salt and pepper to taste

Black-Eyed Beans

200 gm cooked black-eyed beans (boiled till tender but still firm when pressed between thumb and finger)

1 tablespoon chopped garlic

2 tablespoons chopped onions

2 teaspoons chopped tarragon

2 teaspoons chopped parsley

2 teaspoons pommery mustard (grainy)

2 teaspoons white balsamic vinegar

1½ tablespoon honey

2 tablespoons olive oil

1 cup chicken stock

¼ cup butter cut into one-inch cubes and cold

Salt and pepper

Pickled Okra

100 gm okra

⅔ cup white wine vinegar

⅔ cup water

2 teaspoons salt

¼ cup sugar

1 teaspoon coriander seeds

12–15 fresh curry leaves

8–10 whole black peppercorns

Goan Chorizo

150 gm Goan Chorizo

2 teaspoons chopped garlic

1½ tablespoons chopped onions

DIRECTIONS

Octopus:

Cut the vegetables into large pieces and add them to a large pot of water along with the spices, herbs and wine and bring to a boil. Once boiled, lower the flame and let it simmer for about 30 minutes before adding the octopuses to it and cooking them on very low flame for about an hour till tender. Remove from the liquid, cut off and discard the head and bony beak and divide the tentacles into equal portions by weight and size and then marinate while still warm in olive oil, salt and pepper, and a squeeze of lemon or lime.

Black-Eyed Beans:

Heat the oil in a pan and cook the chopped onion and garlic till tender. Add the boiled black-eyed beans and chicken stock to the pan and cook till 80 per cent of the stock is evaporated before adding all the other ingredients except the butter, and cook for another 4–5 minutes. Take the pan off the flame and monte the contents with butter—i.e., add the cold butter a cube or two at a time and incorporate into the beans, mixing constantly with a spoon as the butter melts.

Pickled Okra:

Wash the okra in cold running water and pat dry. Slit open the okra, length-wise, with a paring knife, to allow pickling liquid to penetrate inside, and put in a sterilized mason jar. Separately, in a sauce pan on medium heat, bring all the pickling ingredients to a boil, and once boiled, pour the hot pickling liquid over the okra, seal the jar and refrigerate when cool. You need a minimum of 4 days to pickle the okra, and it will keep for up to a month or so refrigerated.

Goan Chorizo:

Remove the chorizo filling from its casing and in a sauté pan on low heat, cook the meat, onion and garlic till well cooked and integrated. NOTE: there's enough fat in the chorizo to cook everything without the need to add any additional oil to the pan. So don't! Remove and transfer to a bowl along with its fat.

Grilling the Octopus:

Cook the marinated octopus tentacles either over a charcoal or gas grill or in the oven at 180°C till tender and lightly charred. I prefer charcoal or wood.

Assembly:

Divide the black-eyed beans among four plates. Top with a tablespoon of cooked chorizo in some of its fat and finally add the grilled tentacles and garnish with pickled okra sliced in two.

ghavane
tondli
masale bhaat
batata ani
tilachi bhaji
kharvas

EPILOGUE: THE YEAR THE WORLD GOT ROYALLY 2020'D

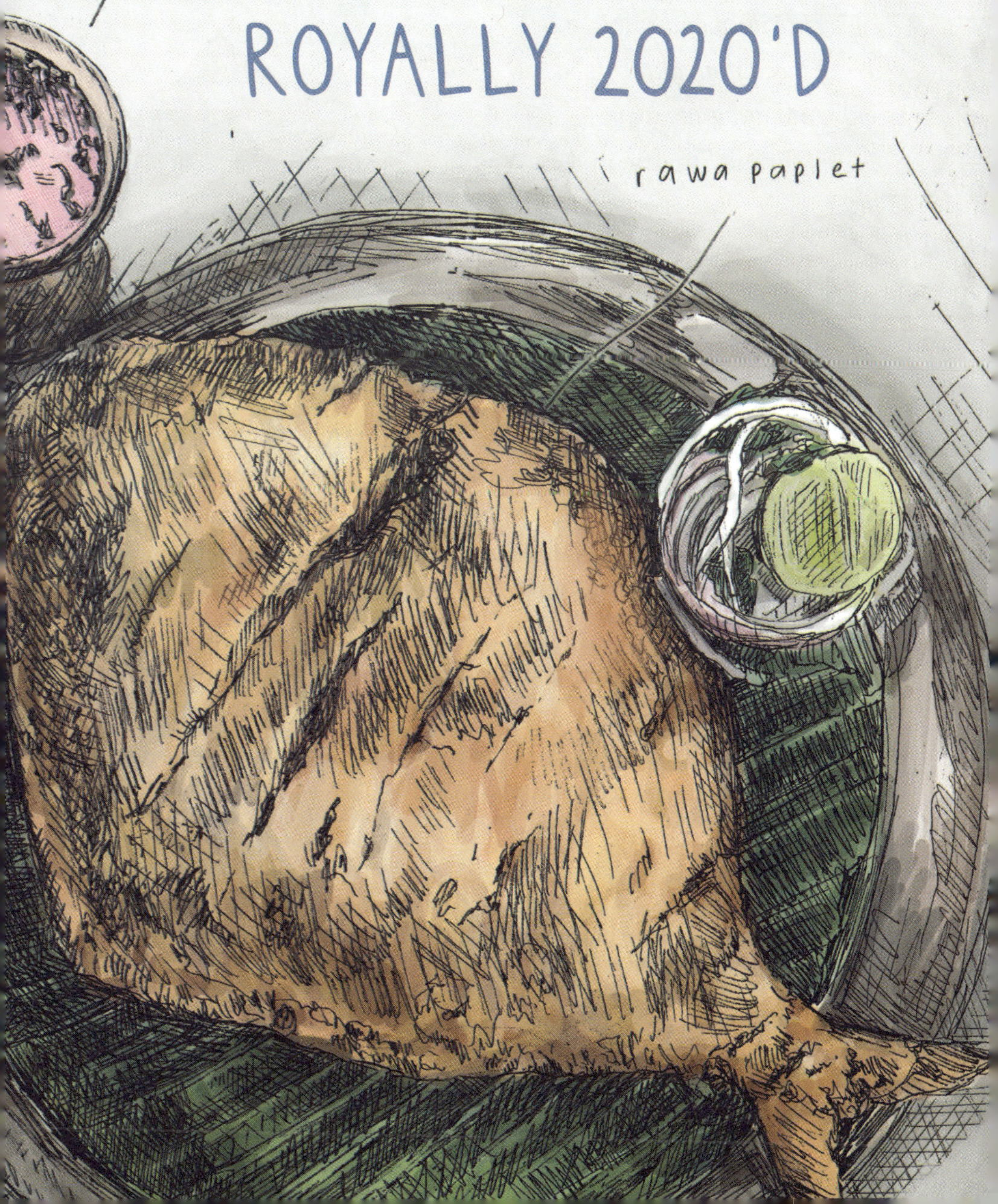

'Yes, there were times, I'm sure you knew
When I bit off more than I could chew
But through it all, when there was doubt
I ate it up and spit it out
I faced it all and I stood tall
And did it my way ...'
—Frank Sinatra, in 'My Way'.

BARELY TEN MONTHS AFTER Qualia opened and was slowly getting its legs, India and the world shut down due to the global viral pandemic known as COVID-19. With our own backgrounds in the sciences, even as early as January 2020, Malini and I recognized the potential severity of the situation. Sales at Qualia started dropping drastically during what should have been our busy months. Yet, we had absolutely no idea it would become even worse than our projections, leaving such a devastating impact on so many lives and livelihoods.

By the first quarter of 2020, the entire world was trying to learn to pivot in 'these challenging times', a phrase that quickly became an abhorred cliché during the COVID-19 pandemic. The worldwide lockdown, which lasted so much longer than anyone thought at first, created an economic tsunami for most businesses. Those suffering the most were brick-and-mortar companies in public places, which were forced to close to protect the community. Particularly hit were restaurants and bars.

These are locations where people congregate closely together, most often inside, and masks are not an option when you are eating and drinking.

Crises like these test one's mettle on almost every human level—emotionally, psychologically, physically and importantly, economically. These situations make us all pivot on a dime (or a rupee). Mumbai, like so many cities around the world, went into total lockdown from the end of March in an attempt to control and prevent the spread of the contagion and, as many infectious disease pundits liked to say, 'to flatten the curve'. For the first few months, when we thought the pandemic would not last too long, we closed Qualia completely until we could figure out our next steps. No one really had a sense of when it would let up and each uncertain day dissolved into the next. By the middle of May we were getting antsy. Our income and cash flows had totally dried up, vendors to whom we owed money were screaming and the crisis was fast becoming an existential one. We had to do something, and quickly, if we were to stay alive. Several restaurants and so-called dark delivery-only kitchens had restarted food deliveries—something that was deemed an 'essential service' and permitted by the government under the lockdown. Qualia's cuisine and menu was always designed to be cooked and eaten à la minute—French for made to order—as all good restaurants' food is, and we had to make some major changes if we were to jump on the delivery bandwagon. So, we created a totally new and very limited menu of simple, wholesome, hearty comfort food that appealed to a much larger demographic.

But first we had to put together a team to produce it. Most of our staff had left the city to go back home to less-populated rural towns and villages when the lockdown started. Fortunately, a handful of the original team—sixteen in all—were still in Mumbai. We called them in and sequestered them for a couple of weeks in our premises. We bought mattresses, and they camped at Qualia, dormitory-style, for the two-week quarantine period. When none of them showed any symptoms, we tested them for COVID-19, and when found free of infection, they formed a safe bubble in residence at Qualia. The senior staff travelled to and from their homes with their own transport in isolation. Then we began the business of delivery in earnest with that well-isolated team.

Rogues' gallery of the sequestered Qualia food delivery team during COVID

Orders trickled in. But not enough. The delivery model—a kitchen-only operation—is not sustainable for a restaurant designed for a dine-in format. It cannot be. Two-thirds of our space are the front of house and the dining room, fitted out with sexy interiors and air conditioning—all aspects that are useless and an expensive waste of resources and square footage when all you're doing is making and packaging food for takeaway and delivery. All the while, mind you, we had basic upkeep expenses. Costs would not change, unless we made dramatic changes. We'd already cut back our staff to a skeletal team doing deliveries and even they were not paid their pre-COVID wages; we couldn't afford to. Everyone took a salary cut to help the company stay afloat. Malini and I were beyond grateful and very proud of the team for their combined sacrifice in trying to keep Qualia alive. We hadn't taken a salary in six months and were living off our small savings.

It soon became apparent that merely selling burgers, pizza and simple pastas wasn't going to cut it. We needed something more to offer, which was when Qualia's Weekend Family Meal took form. Other restaurants and chefs ventured into tailgating—dining in the parking lot outside the restaurant in your car—or produced do-it-yourself meal kits in an attempt to keep consumer interest ticking. Tarang, Ash and I researched different international and regional Indian cuisines each week. We put together a five- to seven-item 'feast-for-the-family', including dessert, and an 'almost cocktail' that only needed the addition of a spirit, and offered the whole thing as a dining experience for four to six people. With offerings from Latin, European and the Levantine countries to South America, North Africa, and Kerala, as well as Maharashtrian and Gujarati dishes, our reheat-and-serve spreads were very successful and generated quite the buzz.

Malini took over the bakery and, with Amalia's help, converted some of our managers into bakers. Ma-Baker, as Malini came to be known, was relentless in her self-taught baking avatar. Mother and daughter produced the most amazing gluten-free, grain-free and sourdough breads, along with brioche loaves and New York-style bagels (that Amalia had mastered at the ICC), and even began supplying hamburger buns and other breads wholesale to other restaurants. I made desserts for a while and did several Instagram Live and Zoom cooking master classes. Shaan did all our social media and marketing blasts. Servers learned to cook. We were all multitasking. Music blared, we cooked, we packaged, we delivered and we had a ton of fun.

We were convinced that keeping going during the first lockdown would only benefit us once things returned to some semblance of normalcy in a vaccinated world as people pushed on through into the 'post-COVID era'. Those eateries that were able to survive the carnage that befell the restaurant industry would surely kill it once things recovered. They had to, right? It was obvious, wasn't it? People had been stuck at home, devoid of dining and socializing outdoors. We just had to hold on.

Yet, whatever we earned from all these efforts barely covered the salaries of our team or kept the restaurant functioning and operational or, most importantly, kept the brand alive. In the larger picture, it really wasn't sustainable at all. Something had to give, but the not knowing and uncertainty were killing us. There just wasn't a way to project or predict anything to model and manage our cash flows. We were living hand to mouth. Barely.

The lockdown kept extending throughout the country. Everyone was in dialogue, negotiating hard to restructure their rents with their landlords. There was hardly any stimulus to support the restaurant and hospitality industry during this extended period of shutdown. As a result, many restaurants and food businesses folded. We were treading water, barely keeping our heads above, and only managed to keep afloat because of the sporadic fund influx from our generous and very patient investors. But even that was beginning to be questioned. 'How much longer,' they wondered, 'would we put good money after bad?'

Our payables were mounting by the day; we didn't pay rent for six months. Meanwhile, after several months of discussions, we renegotiated our lease agreement with our landlord. We even decided to rejig the interior, shaving off 1,000 square feet of the restaurant and returning it to the landlord to cut down our rental overheads by 25 per cent. We'd have to move the bar to the other end of the restaurant and dial it down to a mere service bar function, but hey, anything to cut costs!

At the same time, we explored other options. The worst would be to throw in the towel and shut down Qualia entirely. That would be like cutting off the blood flow to my brain.

And then, in October 2020, the lockdown was lifted. Dine-in was again allowed, albeit at much reduced numbers. We took advantage of Qualia's stunning frontage—the wide beautifully paved private sidewalk—and set up about thirty seats for kerbside outdoor dining, which we called Qualia Qurbside. That was the prescribed socially distanced dining format internationally, and for once the local authorities, in a moment of rapid action and clarity, allowed us to serve outdoors.

Amalia destroyed after hand-crafting pasta all day for a Qualia dinner at the ITC Royal Bengal, Kolkata

It's amazing how quickly people overcame their cabin fever and isolation and started entertaining again, albeit with severe restrictions. Birthdays, anniversaries, engagements, graduation, you name it; any reason to gather, socialize and celebrate was okay. They needed to get out and party hearty. Costs weren't a consideration. This worked well for several chefs and restaurants as they went on road trips, invited to cater private events all over the country and abroad. The Qualia team did several. From taking over restaurants from Goa to Nairobi (before the lockdown was announced), and catering dinners in Delhi, Hyderabad, Chennai and Kolkata, to name a few, we were cooking food and popping up all over. For one dinner for 300 people, we even rolled, cut and stuffed, 45 kilos of five different types of hand-made pasta.

As I struggled with the finances, Tarang and Ash created a new, spot-on, finger-licking-good menu. They simplified our dishes without losing that Qualia spin and appealed to a wider demographic with simpler, delicious, familiar comfort food. Ranjeet reworked the bar to stimulate sales. It clicked and we were thronged—only on weekends at first, but it was a start.

It would be a while before things returned to some facsimile of earlier normalcy. Then again, there might never be a return to normalcy. In the beginning I recoiled from the increasingly popular phrase 'new normal', but slowly I had come to accept the truth. The science doesn't lie and from what I could read and see, the world would have to adapt to the idea that new, potentially lethal viruses would be part of human existence. New plans would have to be made.

Plans? What were 'plans' in a time rife with such clichés as 'uncertain', 'unprecedented' and 'challenging'?

Sic transit gloria mundi (Thus passes the glory of the world).

As this book was being completed, COVID claimed another victim. It was with a heavy heart and much sadness that we announced that Qualia would end its brief but glorious run. We tried hard to keep things going but it was unsustainable. The all-clear to start a restricted dine-in service, which took effect in the spring of 2021, enabled a dramatic turnaround, but for us it was too little too late, considering we had been open only ten months before the pandemic, not enough time to establish a loyal and repeat customer base.

This 'death' was not as devastatingly sad as the conservatively estimated 5,00,000 lives lost in India during the first two waves, nor the 4.5 million worldwide. And we are not alone among restaurants and bars forced to close. By summer 2021, the Federation of Hotel & Restaurant Associations of India predicted that some 50 per cent of restaurants in India would permanently close.

Things looked up when the first lockdown ended in late 2020, and we were able to dine-in again, albeit with restrictions of hours of service and numbers of guests at the same time. There was hope we'd survive after all.

Unfortunately, that phase was short-lived. Mumbai was locked down again when the second COVID wave hit in the first quarter of 2021. This time it knocked us way back, basically unrecoverable as it turned out. All that momentum and positivity we'd generated came crashing down overnight. Business came to a virtual standstill and our cash flows all but dried up. Our investors, hit in their own businesses, lost their appetite to keep funding our operations. Debt and liabilities mounted. We tried again to renegotiate and restructure our rent. We couldn't afford to pay our employees any more, and morale understandably dropped to an all-time low. Despite these setbacks and disappointments, our team plodded on, working tirelessly, hoping we'd find the funds and they'd get paid ... eventually. We hoped for a miracle, but none came.

Even in its short life, Qualia had won numerous accolades. We received our last recognition with great gratitude, but also with some bittersweet irony. As we were on the verge of shutting down for good (really for bad), Qualia was selected by the prestigious World's 50 Best Restaurants for 2021 in the brand's category of 50 Best Discovery.

Those chosen in this category, launched in 2019, receive votes from 50 Best's international experts, featuring more than 1,600 reviews of venues in seventy-five countries, combining destinations from several other World's 50 categories. It was a major honour coming from a 1,700-strong academy of the world's leading food and drink writers, chefs, restaurateurs and bar owners, global gastronomes and regional cuisine specialists. I especially appreciated that the voters 'got' what we were doing, as this comment in the 50 Best Discovery listing put it:

> Shelves of pickles hint at the fermented nature and sweet-and-sour flavor of many of the dishes, though the Mediterranean inspiration of the kitchen keeps the cooking approachable, even when pasta comes turbocharged by pickled black garlic or pizza topped with Brussels sprouts (this is a kitchen that knows how to bake—the breads at Qualia are excellent).[1]

All that aside, the numbers just did not add up. We were haemorrhaging. One could attribute our demise to bad luck and worse timing. In the end, the reality was that it became economically unsustainable during the pandemic. We drew some solace from knowing that our cuisine and our service was world class and had nothing to do with our closure.

In the weeks that followed, while we wrapped up, clearing out refrigerators and shelves full of pickled product, I made sure to give credit and heartfelt thanks where it was due: to each and every passionate member of our team. I was proud of their perseverance and devotion through 2020 and 2021.

History will determine the culinary legacy Qualia leaves behind. But it remains for me to acknowledge and salute the tireless efforts of a super dedicated and creative group of young men and women—the entire Qualia family—who never stopped believing. In themselves. In our food. In our hospitality. In being the best.

Living through those times had an upside: we were forced to rethink everything we did, to examine what's 'essential' and what's 'non-essential'. It made us re-prioritize the very important from the marginally important from the unimportant. It taught us patience, a really hard one for me personally.

Those of us weathering this viral storm also learned to be flexible, to roll with the proverbial punches, to have not only a Plan B but a C, D ... and, if necessary, all the way to Z.

I cannot predict what I'll be doing by the time you read this book. 'Predict' may well join the number of words that have lost their meaning or value. In this new unpredictable world, though, what I can predict is that eventually this time shall pass. In the words of Kevin Costner, in the film *Field of Dreams*, 'If you build it, [they] will come.' So we keep building and, if necessary, rebuilding.

These are the words and philosophy I've always lived by. No virus or flood or any other adversity is going to deter me from striving to always outdo myself. Rest—and dine—assured I will continue to bite off more than I can chew so that you can chew on whatever comes out of my kitchen, wherever and whenever that is.

CHAPTER ZERO

The Postscript to the Epilogue: Coming Full Circle

Birds flying high, you know how I feel
Sun in the sky, you know how I feel
Breeze driftin' on by, you know how I feel

It's a new dawn
It's a new day
It's a new life
For me ...
And I'm feeling good.

—From 'Feeling Good' by Nina Simone (1965)

I THOUGHT THIS BOOK was completed. That I'd laid to rest the last chapter in the story of Rahul Akerkar: chef, entrepreneur, father, husband and occasionally reckless idealist. I'd walked away from the kitchen, the chaos, the compromises, the endless pursuit of perfection—and not quietly either. Qualia's failure had taken a toll, emotionally, financially and existentially. I'd told myself: enough. Let someone else light the stove.

But as Jeff Goldblum's character in *Jurassic Park* wisely mutters, 'Life ... finds a way.'

And it did. It found me.

In truth, it found us—Malini and me—though I suspect, as always, that she saw the writing on the wall before I did. The loss of Qualia left us more than just bereft of a restaurant; it marked the end of an era. Mumbai had changed, too—louder, more crowded, gasping for breath under the weight of its own ambition. And then came the pandemic, pressing pause on everything. We, like so many others, began to question what next. What we owed ourselves. What we owed our children.

And so, with the same instinct that led her to the bungalow that became Indigo over two decades earlier, Malini did what she does best: she took action. Quietly, swiftly, decisively. She made a few scouting trips to Goa, connected with a real-estate broker and found what can only be described as a dream—the kind of house that asks nothing of you except to breathe. A 100-year-old Portuguese bungalow nestled in the village of Socorro, complete with wide verandas, an expansive garden and the whisper of a slower, saner life.

And, as though the universe wanted to drive home the déjà vu, she simultaneously stumbled upon a defunct restaurant space in nearby Arpora. It was charming, full of potential and available for a song. We had no immediate plans for it, but we knew that we'd found the next chapter. Not a restaurant just yet—but the seed of one.

Before we could overthink it, the decision had been made. We packed up our lives in Mumbai and moved. In that single move, we weren't just changing cities—we were changing pace, changing mindsets. Letting go. Or so I thought.

Because even as we tried to hit reset in Goa, part of me couldn't let go of Qualia entirely. The restaurant had been a labour of love and artistry, and I couldn't bear for its story to end with a whimper. So I began looking for ways to revive it—partners who might help absorb the debts, carry the legacy forward and give it another lease on life.

One of those conversations led me to an unexpected door: the Aditya Birla Group.

We had known the Birlas casually for years—our daughters had attended school together—but what opened that door wasn't our personal history. It was Qualia. They had dined there and remembered what they had experienced—not just the food but the feeling. I was soon introduced to Aryaman Birla, the young scion of the empire, and over a series of conversations I began to see an opportunity to save Qualia and furthermore to build something entirely new.

Aryaman wasn't what you might expect of a fourth-generation industrialist. He was thoughtful, sharp and surprisingly grounded. He spoke more like an entrepreneur than an heir, and I quickly learned why. Before stepping into the family business, he'd seriously pursued a career in professional cricket—playing for Madhya Pradesh in the Ranji Trophy, even signing with the Rajasthan Royals in the IPL. But injuries and mental-health struggles led him to step away, recalibrate and return to the business world with a fresh perspective.

In him, I saw a younger version of myself—someone willing to take the unbeaten path, someone who didn't see convention as a ceiling. Under his leadership, the group had launched Aditya Birla New Age Hospitality (ABNAH), with ambitions to create premium hospitality and dining experiences. Our alignment seemed almost karmic.

I joined ABNAH as director of cuisine and creative director, and suddenly I was back where I belonged—sort of.

The transition was not without growing pains. Since the 1990s, I'd been my own boss, answerable only to my own standards and instincts. I micromanaged, not out of control-freakery, but because every detail mattered—to the food, to the guest, to the bottom line. In the corporate world I found a system that relied on delegation, working in silos and on PowerPoint decks. At first I kept my distance, watching, trying to understand how decisions were made, why they moved so slowly and who actually took accountability seriously. What I realized was both unsettling and liberating: the people in the room didn't always know the answers. But I did.

Years of being on the floor, in the fire and in the red had taught me more than I'd given myself credit for. Slowly I began speaking up. Offering alternatives. Proposing methods honed not in boardrooms but in restaurant kitchens and dining rooms. To their credit, Aryaman and the team listened. What began as my discomfort soon turned into confidence. I wasn't here to assimilate; I was here to contribute and eventually to be accountable.

We found a location for our first restaurant—a raw shell in a newly constructed office complex in Worli, Mumbai. It wasn't perfect but it had potential. And it gave us something to build. I called back my old team—Chefs Tarang and Ash, with Sonam behind the bar—and together we got to work. There was a hunger in us, a kind of creative urgency. After years of lockdown and loss, this wasn't just about food, it was about rebirth.

The result was Ode, our first premium casual-dining restaurant under ABNAH. The name reflected more than homage to ingredients, to technique, to memory. It was a love letter to everything I'd learned along the way.

And people got it.

The reviews were better than we could have hoped. *Condé Nast Traveller India* called it 'approachable, accessible and also astonishing'[1]. *The Infatuation* described it as 'sophisticated, comforting, and straight-up irreverent'[2]. The flavours were speaking for themselves. From smoky burnt cucumber with kiwi salsa and peanut thecha to apricot-glazed pork ribs in a Khandeshi-kala-masala-inspired mole, to fusilli with chicken livers and grappa—the menu wasn't just about fusion or novelty. It was about storytelling. And I was incredibly honoured to be named among the Top 10 Standalone Restaurant Chefs by India's Hospitality Horizon Top Chefs Awards of 2025. In the accolade, they wrote: 'From perfecting every plate to boldly pushing the boundaries of flavour, his dedication speaks through every dish served at Ode. This award is a proud moment for all of us—and a delicious reminder that something truly special is cooking here.[3]'

That praise could not have come at a better time for me and my team.

Following Ode, Chef Mukhtar rejoined me and we launched Waarsa, a refined take on Awadhi cuisine, and Bay21, an event and banqueting space at Mumbai's iconic National Centre for the Performing Arts (NCPA). Each concept brought its own challenges ... and joys.

And me? I've changed too. Maybe not completely. I'm still stubborn (Aries, remember?), still exacting. But I've learned to bend a little. To accept that sometimes achieving 80 per cent is good enough if the spirit is intact. I've learned to trust the process, even when it doesn't look like mine. And I've learned that reinvention isn't betrayal—it's growth.

So yes, this is the postscript. But only to this chapter of my life. The stove's back on. The knives are sharp. The team is humming. And there's still so much left to cook.

Until next time,

Bon appétit.

ACKNOWLEDGEMENTS

THIS BOOK WOULDN'T EXIST without a whole lot of people who nudged, pushed, carried and occasionally dragged me to the finish line. It's also been a reminder that nothing worthwhile is ever done alone. So here goes ...

First up, Perry Garfinkel, my scribe, mind reader, and verbal sous-chef—thank you for turning my verbal spaghetti into actual sentences. You somehow managed to capture my voice better than I ever could, and then shaped the chaos of my life into something resembling a coherent narrative. Thank you for your craft, your calm and your stubborn insistence that I actually finish this.

To Camila Giraldo—your beautiful food illustrations brought each chapter to life. Somehow, your art captured not just the dishes, but the memories and emotions they carried. Thank you for painting flavour into every page.

To HarperCollins Publishers India for patiently believing in this story and giving it a home.

To my sister, Avantika, for always watching my back and being a voice of reason and counterfoil to all my hairbrained ideas—thanks for helping to keep things kosher. And to my parents, Jinx and Anand, thanks for raising me with just the right mix of encouragement and benign neglect. And for not blinking (too much) when I told you I was tossing three degrees and a perfectly reasonable career in biochemical engineering down the drain to become ... a cook. Most parents would've suggested therapy. You said, 'Go for it.' That took guts. Or maybe you just gave up. Either way, it worked.

To Amalia and Shaan, my brilliant, brave, endlessly forgiving daughters. You came along for the ride without ever asking for a seatbelt, and somehow made me feel like I was always doing something right. Thank you for the pride, the perspective, the occasional reality checks and for your patience and love. You're the best things I've ever made.

To Malini, my partner, my person, my sharpest critic and fiercest supporter. You've been beside me through every burnt dish, missed dinner and mad idea. You pushed me when I dragged my feet, questioned me when I got cocky and celebrated me when I got it right. You held my hand and occasionally raised your voice but you never let go. This book, like everything I'm proud of, has your fingerprints all over it and there's no version of this story, or of me, without you.

To chefs Nitin Kulkarni, Jaydeep Mukherjee, Mukhtar Qureshi, Tarang Joshi, Ash Moghe, Irfan Pabaney, and the many others—friends, mentors and teammates who stood beside me in hot kitchens and during high-stakes moments. Thank you for showing up, lifting me up and keeping the food (and occasionally the chaos) under control. Whatever success I've had is as much yours as mine.

And lastly, to Aji, my grandmother, the original food whisperer. It was in your kitchen, surrounded by the smells of roasted spices and stories told over simmering pots, that I fell in love with food. You taught me that cooking was more than a skill—that food could be love, story, memory, and identity all at once. I carry your lessons in every dish I make.

To all of you—thank you for making this life possible, and for sticking around while I learned to chew.

NOTES

Chapter 3: In a New York State of Mind

1. Page 75, *The New York Times* food section article—'Diner's Journal', *The New York Times,* 6 June 1986.
2. Page 76, 'Mise en place is the religion of all good line cooks.'—Anthony Bourdain, *Kitchen Confidential: Adventures in the Culinary Underbelly* (Ecco, 2007).

Chapter 4: A Career as a Chef? Fuggeddaboudit!

1. Page 101, Colleen Taylor-Sen on dining out—Colleen Taylor-Sen, *Food Culture in India (Food Culture around the World)* (Greenwood Press, 2024).

Chapter 5: An Italian Intermezzo

1. Page 118, 'The perfect meal . . . '—Anthony Bourdain, *Kitchen Confidential: Adventures in the Culinary Underbelly* (Ecco, 2007).
2. Page 119, Kazu Katoh on umami and Umami Burger founder on umami—Hannah Goldfield, 'You Think You Know Umami', *The New Yorker,* 19 March 2015. https://www.newyorker.com/culture/culture-desk/youthink-you-know-umami

Chapter 8: How I Met My Partner in Culinary Crime

1. Page 165, definition of homeostasis—'Homeostasis', Encyclopedia Britannica, https://www.britannica.com/science/homeostasis

Chapter 11: Indigo Raises the Bar

1. Page 226, definition of 'foodie'—Paul Levy and Ann Barr, *The Official Foodie Handbook* (Olympic Marketing Corp, 1985).
2. Page 229, Escoffier's definition of chefs—https://www.escoffier.edu/blog/culinary-pastry-careers/what-makes-agood-sous-chef/#:~:text=These%20skills%20go%20hand%2Din,of%20the%20hands%2Don%20management
3. Page 235, Natrajan and Jacob on vegetarianism—Balmurli Natrajan and Suraj Jacob, '"Provincialising" Vegetarianism: Putting Indian Food Habits in Their Place', Azim Premji Foundation. http://publications.azimpremjifoundation.org/372/1/Putting%20Indian%20Food%20Habits%20in%20Their%20Place.pdf

Chapter 12: Making Waves with Food and Wine

1. Page 286, survey by Havas Worldwide—Jenna Amatulli, 'A Surprising Amount of Millennials Want Dinner More than Sex, Study Says', HuffPost, 27 July 2016. https://www.huffpost.com/entry/a-surprising-amount-of-millennials-want-dinner-morethan-sex-study-says_n_57990143e4b0d3568f85996b#:~:text=The%20report%2C%20from%20ad%20agency,a.k.a%20a%20lot%20of%20the

Chapter 14: Tote and Neel: Flipping the Script on Failure

1. Page 320, Shakti Salgaokar review—Shakti Salgaokar, 'Food review: Neel takes over Tote on Turf, one kebab at a time', *DNA*, 21 November 2013.

https://www.dnaindia.com/lifestyle/review-food-review-neel-takes-over-tote-on-turf-onekebab-at-a-time-1592074

2. Page 320, Vir Sanghvi on Chef Mukhtar Qureshi—Vir Sanghvi, 'Eazydiner Foodie Awards Best North Indian (Standalone): Neel'. https://www.virsanghvi.com/Article-Details.aspx?key=1294

Chapter 16: Life after deGustibus: My Adult Gap Years

1. Page 361, Study by Unite on chefs—Daisy Meager, 'New Study Reveals Just How Unhealthy It Is to Be a Chef,' *Vice*, 4 May 2017. https://www.vice.com/en/article/ypagxv/new-studyreveals-just-how-unhealthy-it-is-to-be-a-chef

Epilogue: The Year the World Got Royally 2020'd

1. Page 428, Comment in the 50 Best Discovery listing—https://www.theworlds50best.com/discovery/Establishments/India/Mumbai/Qualia.html

The Postscript to the Epilogue: Coming Full Circle

1. Page 434, Review of Ode in *Condé Nast Traveller India*—Roshni Bajaj Sanghvi, 'From Tarte Tartin to Thechas, Rahul Akerkar's New Restaurant in Mumbai Is an Ode to a Life in Food', 19 December 2023. https://www.cntraveller.in/story/rahul-akerkar-new-restaurant-worli-mumbai-cocktails-food/
2. Page 434, *Infatuation* review of Ode, 24 April 2024—https://www.theinfatuation.com/mumbai/reviews/ode
3. Page 434, accolade for Rahul after winning award—https://www.instagram.com/p/DLZWO4QIs1d/

ABOUT THE AUTHOR

RAHUL AKERKAR is a chef and restaurateur who has helped change the way modern India eats. Abandoning a PhD in biochemical engineering, he trained in New York kitchens and returned to Mumbai to open restaurants that ignored rules, embraced ingredients and trusted diners to keep up. After founding the trailblazing Indigo, recognized as one of the world's top restaurants, he went on to open other globally renowned eateries, including several Indigo Delicatessens, Neel, Qualia, Ode and Waarsa.

Akerkar is known for doing things early, doing them differently and occasionally walking away at the wrong—or exactly right—moment. He lives between Mumbai and Goa, where he continues to cook, write, and ask uncomfortable questions about food, hospitality and success.

HarperCollins *Publishers* India

At HarperCollins India, we believe in telling the best stories and finding the widest readership for our books in every format possible. We started publishing in 1992; a great deal has changed since then, but what has remained constant is the passion with which our authors write their books, the love with which readers receive them, and the sheer joy and excitement that we as publishers feel in being a part of the publishing process.

Over the years, we've had the pleasure of publishing some of the finest writing from the subcontinent and around the world, including several award-winning titles and some of the biggest bestsellers in India's publishing history. But nothing has meant more to us than the fact that millions of people have read the books we published, and that somewhere, a book of ours might have made a difference.

As we look to the future, we go back to that one word—a word which has been a driving force for us all these years.

Read.

Harper Collins · Harper Sport · HARPER FICTION · HARPER NON-FICTION · हार्पर हिन्दी

HARPER LEARNING · HARPER VANTAGE · HCCB HARPERCOLLINS CHILDREN'S BOOKS · 4th · HARPER PERENNIAL

HARPER DESIGN · BOOKTOPUS · HARPER BUSINESS